Contents

Postcolonizing the
Commonwealth

This book has been published with the help of grants from the Canadian Association of Commonwealth Literature and Language Studies (CACLALS) and the Office of Research, Wilfrid Laurier University. We acknowledge the financial support of the Government of Canada through the Book Publishing Industry Development Program and the Canada Council for the Arts for our publishing activities.

Canadian Cataloguing in Publication Data

Main entry under title:

Postcolonizing the Commonwealth : studies in literature and culture

Includes bibliographical references and index.
ISBN 0-88920-358-X (pbk.)

1. Commonwealth literature (English)—History and criticism.
2. Commonwealth literature (English)—Study and teaching (Higher).
3. Postcolonialism. 4. Postcolonialism—Study and teaching (Higher).
I. Smith, Rowland, 1938- .

PR9080.P575 2000   820.9′9171241   C00-930511-4

© 2000 Wilfrid Laurier University Press
   Waterloo, Ontario N2L 3C5

Stephen Slemon's article "Climbing Mount Everest: Postcolonialism in the Culture of Ascent" has been published in *Canadian Literature* (58 [Autumn 1998], 15-41).

Cover design by Leslie M

Printed in Canada

Contributors

Jacqueline Bardolph, the former Dean of Arts at the University of Nice, died in 1999.

Edward Baugh is a member of the Department of Literatures in English at the University of the West Indies (Mona) and (frequently) its Chair.

J. Edward Chamberlin is a member of the English Department at the University of Toronto.

Cherry Clayton has taught at the Rand Afrikaans University in Johannesburg and at the University of Guelph.

Margaret Daymond is a member of the English Department at the University of Natal, Durban.

Mac Fenwick is a graduate student of English at Queen's University.

Johan U. Jacobs is Head of the School of Graduate Studies in the Faculty of Human Sciences at the University of Natal, Durban.

Alan Lawson is Deputy Director of the Graduate School and Dean of Postgraduate Students at the University of Queensland in Brisbane.

Laura Moss is a member of the English Department at the University of Manitoba.

Nima Naghibi is a graduate student of English at the University of Alberta.

Sheila Roberts is a member of the English Department at the University of Wisconsin, Milwaukee.

Stephen Slemon is a member of the English Department at the University of Alberta.

Rowland Smith is the Vice-President: Academic at Wilfrid Laurier University.

Susan Spearey is a member of the English Department at Brock University.

Cheryl Suzack is a graduate student of English at the University of Alberta.

Acknowledgments

Gary Boire and Roza Cunningham were tireless organizers of the Commonwealth in Canada conference at which most of these essays were first presented. Roza continued to work tirelessly as preparations for the volume progressed. Doreen Armbruster was extraordinarily helpful in preparing the manuscript for the Press. At the Press, Carroll Klein was an ideally collegial and effective editor. Ann Smith was a charmingly exacting indexer. I am deeply grateful to them all.

Introduction

Rowland Smith

All but one of these essays originated as papers delivered in November 1997 at the "Commonwealth in Canada" conference held at Wilfrid Laurier University in Waterloo, Ontario—one of the triennial conferences organized by the Canadian Association for Commonwealth Literature and Language Studies (CACLALS). The only exception, the essay on recent Afrikaans writing by Sheila Roberts, was delivered at the regular, annual conference of CACLALS, held the following spring in Ottawa as part of the Canadian Congress of the Social Sciences and the Humanities. Its obvious linkage to themes and issues raised by the other authors in this volume led to its inclusion.

It is saddening to report that one of the contributors, Jacqueline Bardolph of the University of Nice, a plenary speaker at the triennial conference, and one of the pioneers in the promotion and study of "new literatures" in France, died in 1999 while this volume was in press.

One of the original aims of the "Commonwealth in Canada" conference (the title is the traditional one for CACLALS triennials) was to use plenary sessions to discuss varying approaches to what used to be called "Commonwealth Literature" in various countries. "Commonwealth in a Postcolonial World" was one subtitle thought of to describe this intention. What did in fact emerge, however, was a series of papers, not all of which are included in this volume, that varied significantly in the ways authors conceived of the topic.

While there was no consistency of approach in the plenary sessions on how the field was studied in France/Europe, in Jamaica/the Caribbean, in South Africa, in Australia and in Canada, there emerged

1

during the conference itself a surprisingly insistent set of images, descriptive phrases and topics of investigation in both the plenary sessions and in the sessions devoted to discrete issues, texts and authors. The essays in this volume illustrate that set of implicitly shared concerns. Although written from varying perspectives, they return constantly to issues of difference and similarity, the re-examination of categories that appear to many to be too rigidly defined in current postcolonial practices and to concepts of sharing: experience, ideas of home and even the use of land.

The authors in this collection choose varied topics. To those unaccustomed to debate in "cultural studies" this range may seem arbitrary. What do cowboy songs, Iranian feminists, fetal alcohol syndrome, the ascent of Everest, Natal women settlers and Afrikaans exile-poets have in common with discussions of the development of syllabus and teaching practice in French or Caribbean universities? The answer is that all these topics concern the representation of attitude, value and belief in fiction, "life-writing" such as journals, teaching and public events (including the public reaction to public events).

Commonwealth literature of necessity dealt with the writing of areas colonized by a major European power. Postcolonial theory attempts to explain the common elements in writing from the margins of a world colonized physically and imaginatively from a metropolitan centre. This collection discusses the development of academic practice in dealing with this kind of writing and uses current events to illustrate ways in which the habits of a basically Western academic practice such as "postcolonial studies" can inform political events at "home" and abroad. And in the representation of Empire and colonization, the abiding myths (Cowboys and Indians, the "Conquest" of Everest, Islamic fundamentalists, drunken natives) have their own status and uses. The authors in this volume range freely over all these topics.

Senior scholars such as the late Jacqueline Bardolph of Nice and Edward Baugh of the University of the West Indies at Mona describe the history of their involvement with the teaching and promotion of the "new" literatures in university systems with strongly conservative, or at least normative, concepts of syllabus and canon at the time when they began to introduce the new authors and texts. Established scholars from "settler" cultures, such as Alan Lawson of the University of Queensland and Stephen Slemon of the University of Alberta, use their essays as starting points to discuss the future of a scholarly area in which they have played leading, pioneering roles.

There is an age difference between these two groups of scholars. Edward Baugh and Jacqueline Bardolph were among the first to teach writing known as Commonwealth literature in their respective countries. It was the work of devotees of their generation that led to the acceptance of "new" literatures as respected fields of study both at the undergraduate and the graduate, research level. Once there was a recognized core of scholarly activity in the field, the next generation of scholars developed a theoretical perspective from which to approach that body of literature, and Alan Lawson and Stephen Slemon are leaders in the development of theoretical positions, particularly on the ethos of writing in "settler" cultures such as those in Canada, Australia and New Zealand. In those societies, white colonial settlers struggled with a need to establish the authenticity of their daily experience and cultural milieu in opposition to the implicit claims of "authenticity" from both the metropolitan centres of the colonizing power and the indigenous cultures of the autochthonous inhabitants.

Bardolph and Baugh describe a history of academic development, and the values that underlie the now-recognized field which they helped to establish. Lawson and Slemon use current incidents in the world outside letters to speculate on the future of postcolonial studies and the directions in which their theoretical interests are likely to take a discussion in which there is a strong link between literature, theory and the moral ethos of the world engaged by both.

Neither Bardolph nor Baugh is at ease with the current ascendancy of postcolonialist theory. Edward Baugh suggests, ironically, that the current predominance of postcolonial theory could have led to him titling his paper "The Postcolonizing of Caribbean Literature" (13). As a self-confessed humanist, he argues that the "the basic postcolonializing manoeuvre" of displacing the literature of England from the "centre of literary studies in one former outpost of empire" (12) may not have "resulted, for the student especially, in a structured, centred, truly coherent body of knowledge, skills and approaches. If it has not," he continues, "perhaps we might reassure ourselves that the new positive is the acquisition, however disorienting, of the ability to be suspicious of all 'centres' and to live happily in a decentred world" (12).

Both Lawson and Slemon suggest the need for a new direction. Lawson jokes about his midlife crisis and the "unfinished business" entailed in the midlife crisis of postcolonial studies. Slemon thinks of new attitudes or emphases in the study of the colonial enterprise of the past and the manifestations of that legacy in the commodified present.

Underlying their ironic unease is a sense that the clear-cut distinctions of postcolonial theorists of the last ten years are becoming less useful as markers to further discussion about writing and power and value in a world in which empires of one kind are superseded by empires of another but in which there is a continuing need to understand and rectify the errors of every kind.

At the heart of this mood change is an instinct to understand similarity in situations which suggest difference. Classic postcolonial theory posits an opposition between the centre and the margin, between those with accumulated power and those without, between the settler and the indigene, between the colonist and the colonial official. Fascinating in this volume is the repeated use of metaphors, rhetorical terms and phrases from psychoanalytical theory, all related to the understanding of similarity-in-difference; the uncanny, the recognition of home in the unhomely; the rhetorical device of zeugma to produce a grammatical relation between distinct concepts that are linked grammatically without being equal, or even linked rhetorically in order to highlight difference by use of the linkage. Lawson calls zeugma a trope of collocation indicating "family trouble" (29). Another rhetorical device, that of chiasmus, is cited by Johan Jacobs as a way of understanding the arrangement of opposing and yet intersecting "signs" in the predicament of an Afrikaner who is "in Africa" and yet "not African" (79). Typical of this investigation of new kinds of side-by-sidedness (as contrasted with the kind of opposition posited in a classical postcolonial term like "writing back") is Lawson's use of the 1996 decision by the Australian High Court to recognize both Aboriginal land claims and the settler rights entailed in pastoral leases granted in the colonial days. The possibility of shared or simultaneous use of land in such a legal decision—one which Lawson describes as involving propinquity and proximity (23)—leads to the possibility of sharing cultural experience rather than "resisting" the imposition of alien forms of culture. And at the heart of surprising glimpses of sharing in colonial and neo-colonial contexts usually associated with strife and contest is the idea of the "uncanny"—the unexpected and weird sense of being at home in unfamiliar environments, or of familiar environments appearing unhomely.

These issues are raised in Lawson's essay. The use of chiasmus to explain a literary relation in Johan Jacobs's study of the Afrikaans writer Breyten Breytenbach reveals a similar dynamic. Breytenbach's personal crises in coming to terms with his Afrikaans heritage (which he accepts as inevitable and opposes insofar as it aligns him with the prejudices and injustices of apartheid), his sense of being an African, and his outsider's perspective on the native land to which he returns from European exile, are all related to the problem of home, the familiar and homeliness. In Breytenbach's listing of place names with historical significance which Jacobs points to as an element in the Afrikaner's attempt to create his own mythologized, "native" background, the listing of the sites of battles between Afrikaner migrant-settlers and black locals as well as between Boer and Briton—all with varying victors and varying defeats—suggests an imagistic side-by-sidedness similar to that which Lawson investigates. In imaginative representation of his Africanness, Breytenbach is attempting to capture a simultaneity of historical experience in the hybrid, merged identity of his own return to "home." Breytenbach is not—as Jacobs points out—writing from either the centre or the margin.

Sheila Roberts investigates the use of magic realism and the uncanny in recent Afrikaans fiction as she too focuses on what is an acceptable representation of "home" for a cultural group faced with massive change, a past that must be acknowledged but not celebrated, and a new existence living side-by-side with previous enemies and victims who share most of the history of the other although experienced from the opposing perspective. As in so many of the literary experiences under investigation in this volume, the representation of home and past thus becomes an all-important element in the way writers come to terms with an increasingly hybrid situation, or at least with a situation that is losing its distinctive and identifying markers. Writing of moments of reconciliation, Roberts comments on Etienne van Heerden's *Toorberg* in this way: "that moment demonstrates how powerful and generationally established Afrikaner landowners may begin restoring South Africa to its ancient indigenous peoples through a repatterning of their common history" (88).

Still in the South African context, Margaret Daymond writes of early colonial encounters in Natal between settlers and indigenes, and in particular of the relations between women and "natives." As homemakers, women on the frontier of a raw, new colony are burdened with the obligation to create homeliness in the unfamiliar as well as to cultivate relations with the locals that will ensure survival and a minimum of comfort. In this regard, the class differences between the two women writers studied produce profound differences of attitude and tone even though the proximity of white and black in the nascent colony, as well as the relative independence of the indigenous people, reveal a surprising degree of shared experience in those early days. That background of early shared experience, one is bound to speculate, forms the basis of many suggestions of the uncannily familiar in fictional glimpses of newly shared experience in the rainbow-nation, contemporary South Africa.

What the women settlers in Natal also shared was the experience of womanhood. Their relations with the essentially male ethos of a frontier society are shown to be slightly ambiguous, and their attitudes towards their indigenous female "helpers" or servants illustrate some of that ambiguity. This intermediate status of women in the power hierarchy of settler societies at the moment of settlement is analyzed by Margaret Daymond to "show how their writing both represents and rejects the authority of Empire and both desires and repudiates the authenticity of the indigene" (101).

Cherry Clayton pursues another aspect of the South African literary obsession with the representation of common ground in a nation that has endured years of entrenched separateness at both practical and theoretical levels, together with a long history of sexual interaction and exploitation across all boundaries of colour. The familiarity of those sexual relationships in a world officially divided upon grounds of race is an uncanny marker of shared experience amid separation. Once again, the shared experience of womanhood is a focus of interest. Clayton points to the predicament of African women who lived in a society governed by ideologies of male authority shared by both settlers and indigenes. She investigates this double jeopardy of indigenous women as illustrated in Lauretta Ngcobo's *And They Didn't Die*. For all the specificity of local problems analyzed in the text, the essay is a further example of the surprisingly insistent return to a discussion of elements of sameness and shared experiences (even if from opposing positions) in the literature of colonial cultures examined in this volume.

In his essay, Stephen Slemon writes of the "complicity/resistance dialectic" (63). He sees the history of narratives about the climbing of Mount Everest (usually described as its "conquest") as embodying much of the mystique of classic colonial or imperialistic ideology in its earlier, gentlemanly stage, and much of the exploitative ethos of contemporary "commodification" (62) in its current manifestation. Is it possible, he wonders, to criticize one of these positions without endorsing the other. In this predicament he sees the predicament of current postcolonial practice in the academy. Just as the "native guide" is a stock figure in both colonialist travel writing and in classic Everest-climbing mythology, so the "triumphs" of postcolonialism in university institutions have produced "the 'non-native' *academic* professional, whose job it is to client students up the slopes of cultural otherness, breathing theory as they reach for the top" (64). And he quotes Spivak as arguing that "it is marginality itself . . . that postcolonialism has commodified" (64).

Much of the discussion in this volume concerns the reduction of the "complicity/resistance" model into more complex analyses of similarities in difference and of literary strategies to capture that puzzling element of what is shared even in experiences formerly classified as confrontational. In this regard the collection itself implicitly addresses the midlife crisis in postcolonial theory alluded to in very different (but similar) ways by Slemon and Lawson.

And then there is difference in situations which, on the surface, appear similar. In her essay, Nima Naghibi discusses the situation of Iranian feminists, whose cause has been both anti-imperialist and anti-fundamentalist. She illustrates how the adoption of the feminist cause in Iran by Western feminists soon after the fall of the Shah was problematic for Iranian feminists, who could then be represented as pro-imperialist by fundamentalist revolutionaries. Not only does her essay illustrate the colonizing propensity of Western theoretical models but it also illuminates how influential is the depiction of power relations— the way they are represented—in both cultural and political arenas. The Iranian feminist cause could be seen to be appropriated by Western theorists, who misinterpreted and misrepresented the anti-imperialist ethos of middle-class, educated women in the Shah's Iran. The presence and actions of Western feminists could be represented as anti-revolutionary by fundamentalists who oppose the Iranian feminist cause. Naghibi analyzes a chilling contemporary manifestation of the inappropriateness of metropolitan culture imposing its style on a complex situation beyond its risk-free centre. "By turning Iranian feminist concerns into an international women's concern, Western women elided the particularity and the specificity of an anti-imperialist Iranian feminism. Second, by taking advantage of the Western (imperial) vs. Iranian (nationalist) binary, the conservative clerics successfully defused the radical potential of the Iranian feminist movement" (136).

Representation is again at the heart of Cheryl Suzak's essay on the depiction of the problem of fetal alcohol syndrome and North American native women. Like Naghibi and Slemon and Lawson, she takes a historical event as a starting point to discuss the way cultural and social stereotypes are represented.

Laura Moss, on the other hand, discusses the realist mode of Rohinton Mistry in the context of the expectations of a certain kind of postcolonial orthodoxy. At issue is, again, the possibility of representing multiplicity. Arguing that in postcolonial criticism "'resistance' has been fetishized" (158), she points to "a profusion of studies linking, and sometimes suggesting the interdependence of, political or social resistance and non-realist fiction. If a text does not fit the profile of postcolonial resistance, as realist texts seldom do, it is generally considered incapable of subversion" (158). In challenging this position, Moss argues against critics who "place too tight an ideological hold on realism and are not inclined to recognize the varieties of its possibilities or its capacity for multiplicity" (158).

Although her thesis is to challenge what she sees as postcolonial orthodoxy, Moss is pursuing a recurring concern in this collection: the avoidance of too straightforward (or simple-minded) an imposition of theoretical verity, and the capacity to recognize difference. She is implicitly taking up Slemon's challenge to avoid the straitjacket of too insistent a dialectic between collaboration and resistance. The impetus to explore a theoretical realm beyond such absolutes is implicit throughout this volume, in studies that vary in manner and approach, yet keep returning to the gnawing concern of a too-dogmatic and "centred" element embedded in current postcolonial practice triumphant. What one resists and—as Edward Baugh suggests—what centre one writes back against are not concepts fixed for eternity.

From her opening epigraph, Susan Spearey takes up a concern that others in the volume share. She quotes Sigmund Freud on the uncanny (*unheimlich*), and uses the concepts of "unhousing" and the "unhomely" to discuss identity and the ways in which identity, both personal and cultural, can be tilted and disarranged or rearranged: "Rushdie's (plural) 'imaginary homelands' speak of the multiple affiliations and identifications that come into play in any formulation of subjectivity, of the manifold repressions implicit in each and of the need for a new and revisionary model of charting their shifting interrelations" (169). Describing Rushdie's *Shame* as a novel "which takes as its focus a nation of migrants" (170), she investigates the "connection between the unhomely haunting and the unhousing of the migrant subject" (170). Her concern with the uncanny is of a piece not only with the recurring use of that concept in other essays in this volume, but also of the recurring concern with similarities in difference. By focusing on "shifting interrelations" she is also avoiding the dialectic that worries Slemon. Her margins are everywhere, and the solid centre elusive. She frequently uses the word "suture"—as do other writers in this volume—and this interest in an image of surgical joining is revealing. Alan Lawson's interest in propinquity and proximity as new metaphors for relations between settlers and native populations points to the same kind of side-by-side imagining rather than a conventional colonial concept of conquest, occupation and displacement.

What is "home" is a question linked to what is the "homely," and what is "unhomely." Mac Fenwick discusses the issue of "authenticity" or cultural distinctiveness in an increasingly "globalized" world. The word "globalization" can itself be seen as a manifestation of the problem of unifying sameness in an increasingly commercialized world, one in which the concepts of commerce and commodities produce an imprecise business-speak. Mac Fenwick does not argue this point, but the very term he uses—in its blurring blandness—illustrates the *reductio ad commercium* of a world dominated by the corporate boardroom. (Does any group really use "globalized" in a precise or meaningful way?)

It is in opposition to such equalizing pressures that the writers whom Fenwick studies attempt to come to terms with what is distinctive, local, and therefore that with which they are at home. And what is distinctive about the cultures within which these writers write and feel "at home" is their hybridity:

> Just as Brathwaite writes from within an authentically West Indian nation language, Ngugi writes from within an authentically African novel genre, both of which are the result of a cross-cultural process that rejects iconoclastic notions of cultural purity in favour of a vision of cultural forms as inherently partial, relational and processional. The claim of authenticity in both cases is predicated upon the existence of cultural hybridity. Authenticity can thus be defined in these cases as the raising to consciousness of the processes of cross-cultural exchange. (184)

Fenwick distinguishes the "cross-cultural exchange," elucidated here, from Rushdie's "formulation of migrancy" (184). Whereas Rushdie, Ngugi and Brathwaite "make similar appeals to the processes of cross-cultural negotiation as the source of authenticity" (185), Rushdie's attempt to "universalize" the concept of migration and the migrant's perspective robs it of specific significance: "By saying that the migrant's perspective is universal because everyone is, 'in a sense,' a migrant, Rushdie empties the word of meaning" (185).

Not only does Fenwick's essay offer a gloss on Susan Spearey's treatment of Rushdie, but also it encapsulates the insistent concern in this volume with the possibility of common access, from diverging starting points, to shared experience—or even shared land, as in the Australian High Court Wik decision.

This concept is investigated in the most original and engaging way in J. Edward Chamberlin's exploration of "Cowboy Songs, Indian Speeches and the Language of Poetry." While the two groups can easily be placed into conventional postcolonial categories (indigenous people and invading colonizer), the reality of the cultures that Chamberlin investigates through our imaginative engagement with their songs and speeches has many shared features—and a shared presence on land. Both groups were migrants and both depended on their horses and their culture of horses. And in the end, Chamberlin sees both societies destroyed by the same homogenizing features. Not only does he depict them as sharing cultural values, he also sees them as jointly marginalized: "At the end of the day, cowboys and Indians alike were denounced as barbarians, beyond the pale of the settler society. Indeed, in their apparent acceptance of uncertainty and insecurity, they seemed beyond the pale of civilization. Period. . . . Fences and farmers would ultimately do them both in" (202).

Within this context of similarity in difference he uses the resonance of Indian speeches and cowboy songs to analyze and capture the haunting quality of what made for home and homeliness in the imagination of groups constantly on the move in all weathers and over all terrain. What renders the investigation so evocative is the overriding sense of a doomed way of life in the imaginative representations and in the rhetoric of both cultures.

It is extraordinary how insistently variations on the same concerns surface in the essays in this volume—particularly in the light of the widely differing approaches adopted by the authors. Their tone does not suggest crisis, but the constant movement towards reassessment of too rigid an acceptance of established categories and assumptions is in keeping with Alan Lawson's sardonic linking of his own midlife crisis to the crisis in postcolonial studies. The confidence with which postcolonial studies occupy desirable ground in university literature departments offers a timely context for investigating possible doubts—even if "crisis" is too strong a word to characterize this reassessment. In any case, the volume does reveal how consistently certain attitudes and emphases recur in a sustained examination of the discipline—be it called Commonwealth Literature or postcolonial studies—from a variety of perspectives, national cultures and ages.

1

Postcolonial/Commonwealth Studies in the Caribbean: Points of Difference

Edward Baugh

In this paper the Caribbean will be, for all practical purposes, the University of the West Indies. This is just a report, but a personal one, on the development and condition of Postcolonial/Commonwealth Studies in the University, and more particularly, given the limitations of my knowledge, at the Mona (Jamaica) campus where I work. The phrase "points of difference" was intended to indicate differences between Postcolonial/Commonwealth Studies in the Caribbean and in other postcolonial/Commonwealth locations and academies. Again, because of the limitations of my knowledge, conclusions or suggestions as to those differences will have to be left largely to the perception of readers from the vantage point of their familiarity with the situation in other postcolonial/Commonwealth locations. In addition, it occurred to me latterly that "differences" may also usefully be taken to indicate differences within the Caribbean, since it could be misguided to think in terms of a homogeneous, undifferentiated Caribbean postcolonialism.

I should explain, for those who do not know, that the University of the West Indies has three campuses—in Barbados, Jamaica and Trinidad and Tobago. Consequently, there are three English Departments, to use the convenient, traditional, shorthand label, but a label which is no longer used officially for any of them, although it used to be the name of all three. The Department in Jamaica is officially the Department of Literatures in English. The others would also now have the same name, but for the fact that, apparently for cost-rationalization reasons, they have been repackaged with other disciplines such as Linguistics and Creative Arts. However, as subdisciplines within conglomerates, they *do* consider themselves to be about the business of "literatures in English," rather than just the old, conventional "EngLit." Although there are some similarities in their overall syllabus structure, and in individual courses, and although new program and course proposals by any one must be seen and commented on by the other two, the three departments do their own thing, and there are some appreciable variations in syllabus, which, to my mind, are all to the good and reflect variations in their circumstances.

The name change, from Department of English to Department of Literatures in English, is perhaps the overarching and summary event in the story I am telling. It is itself the basic postcolonializing manoeuvre, indicating a displacement of the history of the literature of England from the centre of literary studies in one former outpost of the Empire. The idea was that West Indian (Caribbean) literature should be the new centre of the discipline. In quantitative terms that is no doubt the case. However, it is unclear in my mind whether that change has resulted, for the student especially, in a structured, centred, truly coherent body of knowledge, skills and approaches. If it has not, perhaps we might reassure ourselves that the new positive is the acquisition, however disorienting, of the ability to be suspicious of all "centres" and to live happily in a decentred world.

In the story of the name change and the reality of which it is only a nominal expression, special mention must be made of Kenneth Ramchand. His pioneering work, *The West Indian Novel and Its Background*, appeared just about then. He quickly agitated for, and got West Indian literature introduced as a full course on the curriculum, initially as an alternative to one of the mandatory EngLit period courses. But what is more immediately to the point here is that, on the nameplate on his office door he identified himself as "Kenneth Ramchand, Literatures in English." It was to take some twenty-five years for that designation to become official; but what it signified had become a reality long before that.

Anyway, very recently I received an e-mail message from a colleague at the Cave Hill (Barbados) campus, Evelyn O'Callaghan. She also happens to be a candidate for the PhD degree, and I happen to be her supervisor. She is working on women's writing about the Caribbean from the beginnings up to the early part of the twentieth century. This project, like most of her recent work, has been determined very much by a feminist perspective. The main purpose of the e-mail message was to let me know that she had managed to finish a fourth chapter: "I finished chapter 4 on Saturday evening. Another 50 page effort, I'm afraid, and boringly predictably postcolonial, but applied to stuff no-one's dealt with." "Boringly predictably postcolonial" is mischievously self-deflating and self-protective at the same time. It is also, I think, a masked way of recording a healthy awareness that theories may be as much traps as enabling mechanisms. The statement is also an amused acknowledgment of how much postcolonial theory now holds sway. There is, of course, a dynamic interfacing between feminist and post-colonial theories, nowhere more so, at least potentially, than in the Caribbean.

Another anecdote is apposite. I was recently an examiner for another PhD thesis, this one by Richard Clarke, also produced at the Cave Hill campus. It is a fine piece of work. The title is "Phallacies: Androgyny, Miscegenation and the Masculine Imaginary." The body of it is a rereading of three classics of the traditional canon: Euripides' *Ion* and Shakespeare's *King Lear* and *The Winter's Tale*. One can see where it is coming from. It draws together, reasonably, a wide variety of theoretical agendas: from Althusser to Freud and Lacan, from Bhabha to Derrida, from Fanon to Saussure. It is concerned with "the postmodern decentering of the Cartesian subject" and it has a deconstructive impetus, investing in the idea of "the radical indeterminacy" of language and of texts. It acknowledges and draws on postcolonial theory to some degree; but, for present purposes, it seemed particularly significant that one of the examiners found a major part of its achievement to lie in the way in which it extends the idea of postcoloniality. Although not about postcolonial texts, the thesis involves the engagement of postcolonial theory with "colonial" texts and even suggests that there may be something of the postcolonial in them.

These two anecdotes are signs of the times, signs of what has, shall I say, befallen us, and of things to come. I might well have entitled this report "The Postcolonizing of Caribbean Literature." The more I think about it, the more the ironic possibilities of that formulation increase.

To put the two anecdotes into historical perspective, it is convenient to go back nearly thirty years, to 1969-70. At the beginning of that academic year I was appointed, for the first time, Head of the Department of English, as it then was, at Mona. I was consequently invited by the local branch of PEN International to give a public lecture. The title was "English Studies in the University of the West Indies: Retrospect and Prospect." The very term "English Studies" now dates the lecture, and is an indication of the limitations on my vision at that time. But I projected myself as being on the side of change, on the side of an effort to break out of the colonial stranglehold on the construction of English Studies as exercised from the "centre," namely, England. "English Studies" was a colonizing project, even though I had a limited realization of this at the time.

I myself had been a product of the department that I was now heading, product of a college, the University College of the West Indies, that had been established in filial relationship to the University of London. The English Studies that I studied was the history of the literature of England, from Beowulf to Conrad (an alien who had sufficiently anglicized himself). It was the syllabus of the University of London. My teachers, all four of them, were expatriate, white, three British and one Canadian. That one was Canadian is a nicely complicating fact. Looking back now through my new-found postcolonial lens, it should have put her on the same side as mine, postcolonial. But she was a Coleridge scholar, and the syllabus did not provide for me to hear anything about Canadian literature from her, assuming that such a thing existed and that she would have been interested in talking about it. The Head of the Department was a Leavisite Englishman. In retrospect I was to realize how thoroughly I was raised on a diet of Leavis and New Criticism, and how much of a dirty young liberal humanist I was, and still am, though old now.

In retrospect, too, one realizes that one did chafe at the limitations, at the unrecognized colonialism of the syllabus. That chafing was one expression of the general will to cultural and national self-determination in that time of the short-lived West Indian Federation and, following that, the beginning of the Independence period for the larger countries. We were beginning to live through and act out the nationalistic stage in the evolution of postcolonial consciousness.

And there was beginning to be a major breakthrough, as I have already indicated in my reference to Kenneth Ramchand. The year in which I gave the lecture to the PEN Club was the same calendar year in which a full course in West Indian literature was taught for the first time. We were also offering for the first time, after nineteen years of the Department's existence, a full course (also optional) in American literature. It was also announced that in the following year we would be offering a Commonwealth literature course based largely on West African literature. We did proceed to offer a course called African Literature, but never one called Commonwealth Literature. One did come into being for a time in the MA course-work program at the St. Augustine (Trinidad and Tobago) campus when the taught MA was started there in the 1980s, but is soon fell into abeyance. That African literature became fairly entrenched at Mona and Cave Hill, and Indian (i.e., of India) literature likewise at St. Augustine, reflects the differing cultural and socio-historical realities and imperatives of the various countries.

In my 1970 lecture I presented the new offerings in West Indian, African and American literature as the start of a liberation from the stranglehold of the English canon:

> I believe that we will have to change the orientation and scope of English Studies. I believe that what it should be for us here in the West Indies now is not the study of the history of the literature of England, but the study of literature in English. . . . We have a world to choose from—Canada, the USA, Africa, Asia, Australia, the West Indies, and, of course, Great Britain. We shall go to it freely and openly, with no bias except that which . . . is natural and necessary to any people in this kind of situation. . . . And in this programme, the study of West Indian literature . . . should have a central and increasingly important place. (Baugh 1970: 58-59)

There was a bit of innocence in that, even naivety, which I can see in hindsight and after all the theoretical water that has flowed under the bridge. But perhaps it was reasonably bold in its time. One local newspaper devoted an editorial to the lecture and particularly cautioned against the danger of such outlandish and questionable ideas as that of introducing African literature. As for the innocence, the proposal carried no suggestion of any reorientation of critical approach, or any methodological strategy which might be necessary for the teaching of these "new" literatures in English. The statement of intent was driven by a nationalistic argument. Although I said that I held no brief for nationalism, and that I knew how dangerous it could be, ultimately I took it that nationalism was natural, and that the important thing was to follow "good" nationalism and eschew "bad" nationalism. Besides, there was an unwitting irony in the fact that I was simply taking over wholesale the same nationalistic principle which, as I tried to show in the earlier part of the lecture, had fuelled the rise of English Studies in England.

Beyond all that though, it was to remain a kind of secret sore on me that the widening of the horizons that I foretold did not really happen, and has still not happened, to the extent that I had imagined. Commonwealth literature as such never came into its own, nor so far has postcolonial literature. West Indian, yes, and African and Indian, which now has even greater purchase with the rise of Indo-Caribbean. But where was the Australian or the Canadian, especially when, irony of ironies, it was mainly Australians and Canadians who were pushing Commonwealth and, later, postcolonial literature? I used to feel a Judas twinge during my long ACLALS years at not having become a great comparativist in the Commonwealth/postcolonial field, and at not being able to speak of our having developed in the Caribbean a variety of courses in Commonwealth literature in its global dimension. Why, for instance, although we eventually reconfigured our program on a genre basis, did we not find it easy to slip in an Australian novelist here or a Canadian poet there? Is it that Caribbean professors and critics are too narrow-minded?

But is any of this really a problem? Are not some biases and priorities, some localized cultural imperatives, perfectly sensible and defensible? Is not every theory biassed in some direction, and determined by time and place and circumstance? At the Mona campus, say, the focus on African, African-American, African-Diaspora and, embryonically but increasingly, Comparative Caribbean, makes an obvious kind of sense and is itself a version of postcolonialism, without investing in a more global postcolonialism. Who knows but that the very fact that Australians and Canadians may be perceived as the main "pushers" of the postcolonial "fix" has itself militated against enthusiasm for a more all-inclusive postcolonial focus. The curiosity of Caribbean critics about, for example, the situation of the literature of the Aborigine within Australia might not seem to be adequately catered to in a book like *The Empire Writes Back*. Besides, postcolonialism was apparently alive and well long before the term was invented, and postcolonial theory has drawn significantly on West Indian writer-theorists such as Kamau Brathwaite, Wilson Harris, Derek Walcott and Denis Williams.

Still, postcolonial theory is gradually catching on, thanks in part to a new generation of lecturers, West Indians, who have had significant exposure to Postcolonial Studies in the Canadian Academy. Most graduate theses are on Caribbean literature and bring, increasingly, some kind of postcolonialist approach to the literature. A recent MA research paper presented at Mona is on "Postcolonial Theory and the Teaching of West Indian Literature in Schools." The MA program at Cave Hill features courses in postcolonial literature, and the undergraduate courses in West Indian and African literature are given a strong postcolonial colouring. At the time of writing, a restructured program in Postcolonial Literature and Theory is being developed. This should go a far way towards improving the circumstances for the teaching of postcolonial theory, since the students will be at the same time widening their familiarity with postcolonial literature. When I taught postcolonial theory as one module of an MA course, "Theory of Literature," one difficulty stemmed from the fact that the students had read virtually none of the creative texts mentioned in *The Empire Writes Back* except a few of the West Indian ones.

Ironically, the debate within Postcolonial Studies about the general applicability of its premises, about the necessity to acknowledge and teach crucial differences within the territory, may prove to be a cause of the continuing viability of Postcolonial Studies. This will depend on the capacity, so far evident, of postcolonial theory to accommodate this debate and not close it off, as well as on its ability to shade into and interact productively with other contemporary theories, its ability to construct itself not as a closed system, but as an open field of different, coincident, conflicting, endlessly dynamic energies. In any event, postcolonialism is doing for the literatures of the Commonwealth, in the Caribbean as elsewhere, what Commonwealth Studies was never able to do.

One final point of difference. I have noticed that in some universities where postcolonial literature is given a special place and taken seriously (for example, Flinders, Macquarie, Wollongong), it is by the same token shunted off on to a sidetrack of the English Department. English Studies remains intact and allows, down the corridor, Postcolonial Studies. This is in contrast to the University of the West Indies experiment.

Reference

Baugh, Edward
    1970   "English Studies in the University of the West Indies: Retrospect and Prospect." *Caribbean Quarterly* 16, 1 (December):48-60.

2

Proximities: From Asymptote to Zeugma

Alan Lawson

I have had some time off from teaching recently. I thought it might be a good moment to think about my midlife crisis. It seems that one of the characteristics of a good midlife crisis is learning how to deal productively with unfinished business. As a distraction from my own midlife crisis and unfinished business, I started thinking about unfinished business in other domains. The field of postcolonial studies might be having its midlife crisis: but I am hardly the first to notice that! What might be more interesting to think about, though, is the way our particular sort of cultures—the ones we have got used to calling "settler" cultures—deal with their unfinished business.

In particular, I have been trying to think of a useful way to talk about how certain kinds of business, narrative business, textual business, remains *un*finished. How certain kinds of stories keep being recirculated, just how readily they can be reactivated, recognized and read.

As a way of concretizing my discussion of the return of the repressed, let me offer you something my friends and I wish had stayed repressed—something that if it circulates too widely might lead to Australia being repressed by the international community. Since the 1996 election in Australia, an extraordinarily ignorant but highly opinionated populist politician called Pauline Hanson has been drawing appar-

---

Notes to chapter 2 are on p. 36.

ently substantial popular support for some very ugly racist views. In April 1997 she established a new political party, called Pauline Hanson One Nation; to mark the launch, her support movement published an oddly anonymous book called *The Truth* ([Hanson] 1997:). Since the book is difficult to get in Australia, let alone here, I will quote some choice bits.

> There are many documented examples of horrific acts committed by blacks against blacks. A former chairman of the Northern Lands Council described his ancestors to me as "murderous nomads." A famous singer proudly described how his grandfather led raids to massacre men from a neighbouring tribe. So why are out schoolchildren now taught a false history that depicts Aborigines as a peaceful, non-violent people living in harmony with nature until the arrival of the brutal Europeans?
>
> Why are schoolchildren not taught some aboriginal tribes killed mixed-race babies by placing them on ant's nests? Why are they not taught about contemporary racism resulting in extreme violence between the various tribes? ([Hanson] 1997:131)

The book then presents a number of "sources, some of which include eyewitness accounts of Aboriginal cannibalism" ([Hanson] 1997:132); it concentrates especially on tales of Aborigines eating their own children. As one of our MA students, Paul Newman, has noticed, this really is the ultimate disappearing race narrative. Then, the Hanson book says, these sources "refute the view of the Aborigines held by the new class. . . . [T]hey weren't romantic liberals" (1997: 137). And, it goes on,

> Another example of [real] genocide is the Maori occupation of NZ. The Maoris arrived in NZ around 1000 AD. The land was occupied by a people closely related to the Australian Aborigines. The Maori exterminated them. . . . The ancestors of the Amerindians, celebrated by liberals in films such as *Dances with Wolves* and *Pocahontas* genocided [*sic*] the original inhabitants to dominate their land. (1997:138)

Not unexpectedly, the next step is to cite the now-discredited view that there were several waves of Aboriginal immigration into Australia and that in this process the ancestors of contemporary indigenous people had—violently, indeed genocidally—displaced an earlier, truly original first peoples. Three narratives are dependent upon this bad history: the revisionist-racist claim that our violent dispossession is a minor part of a longer history of violent dispossession founded by indigenous peoples themselves; the second is the liberal-nationalist view that the Aborigines are really like us (since they are said to be descended from Dravidians expelled from India); and, thirdly, the assimilationist-nationalist view that the Aborigines are Australia's first immigrants ([Hanson] 1997:139).

It intrigues me that we *know* how to read this stuff. At crucial moments we can predict what the next narrative element will be. We recognize some of these elements as belonging to the form of urban myths—just as in the cannibalism story in Catherine Parr Traill's *Canadian Crusoes* we recognize the familiar scandalous tale of children baked in a pie and served to their father because we have read it in *Titus Andronicus*; others we recognize as reiterations of colonialist tropes, familiar from texts of the colonial period. But *how* do they function; how, more importantly, do we explain their persistence?[1]

Even when discursive tropes do not "make sense" empirically—in relation to contemporary knowledge—or in terms of new ideological understandings, they do have a tendency to endure. Their irruption into newer discursive frameworks probably signals a moment of cultural crisis.

What Provoked *This* Moment of Cultural Crisis?

Most obviously it was two native land claim cases in the High Court of Australia (the equivalent of the Supreme Court of Canada).

In 1992, in the now-famous Mabo case, the High Court of Australia established (in fact, *re*-established after about 100 years) a limited legal form of "native title" and thereby seemed to open up the possibility of a vastly increased number of Aboriginal land claims. Most spectacularly, the Mabo decision demolished the doctrine of *Terra Nullius*, which had been thought to apply to the entire land mass of Australia from the moment of first "settlement" in 1788. *Terra Nullius* means either "Empty Land"—or, more precisely, "Nobody's Land." It had the *discursive* effect of "evaluating" the country of its indigenous inhabitants. We *know* that Australia was neither Empty nor Nobody's in 1788 and the first settlers knew it quite well too. So the doctrine of *Terra Nullius* represents—inter alia—a cognitive dissonance, a gap between knowledge and belief—or, to put it another way, a kind of repressed knowledge. It is also "bad history."

In the December 1996 Wik case, the High Court ruled that pastoral leases might not fully extinguish native title since they do not confer absolute title. This reopened the interesting possibility of co-existence. It also was the occasion for mass anxiety about boundaries; from my point of view, it provoked a major crisis in the nation's inability to *read* co-existence, to have an understanding of the grammar of proximity.

Mabo to Wik: A Paradigm Shift in Four Years

Mabo and Wik are absolutely different. The Mabo case allowed for the separate existence of European and Aboriginal titles to land in quite separate locations and it firmly asserted two principles: (1) that Aborigines had historical precedence, and (2) that Europeans had legal precedence. These were principles that most Whitefella Australians could fairly readily comprehend. It can be seen as a conservative judgment in that it asserted a notion of separateness, apartness. There was some land that, because Europeans had not yet done anything to it, might still have some residual Aboriginal claim as long as the appropriate Aborigines had persisted in maintaining contact with it. This land might be said to have been "reserved." No ontological disputation here, just a slightly inconvenient rearrangement of the real estate: there was European land and there was, somewhere else and mostly in undesirable spots, Aboriginal land. Missions, reserves, reservations, locations, homelands—the colonized world is familiar with this sort of arrangement.

But Wik is a different matter altogether. It reinserts a notion of incomplete European occupation—specifically on pastoral leases. Intriguingly, as Henry Reynolds has pointed out, native title was accepted by many pioneer settlers and by the Colonial Office in Britain during the 1830s and 1840s (1996:7). He cites several negotiations between pastoralists and traditional owners throughout the nineteenth century which "led to highly successful resolutions of the problem of providing for the mutual use of the same country" (Reynolds 1996:8). The question of Aboriginal rights became crucial after squatters (large landholders who gained title to land in certain areas merely by occupying it) gained security of tenure as a result of legislation in 1846. Earl Grey, the British Secretary of State, promptly instructed the Governor in Sydney "to take care they are not driven off all that country which is divided into grazing [stations]" (Colonial Office, C.O. 201/382, cited in Reynolds 1996:9). Grey reiterated that pastoral leases granted merely rights to pasturage, and "that these leases are not intended to deprive the natives of their former right to hunt over these Districts, or to wander over them in search of subsistence, in the manner to which they have been heretofore accustomed, from the spontaneous produce of the soil" (*Historical Records of Australia* 1, v. 26.225, cited in Reynolds 1996:9). Grey stipulated that Aboriginal access and use be "reserved" in every pastoral lease: by 1850, all leases in all of the Australian colonies contained such a reservation.

In effect, then, the High Court in 1996 rediscovered this ethical and legal notion of co-existence by finding that native title did survive *alongside* pastoral title, although European title still has precedence over native title when the two are in *direct* conflict. Wik, then, requires quite a shift. It requires not a notion of separateness but a notion of simultaneity, of propinquity, or of—and this is the term I want to return to—proximity; it asserts that two laws—or, even more scandalously, two different systems of law—may apply to the one piece of land.

That two laws might operate on the same site is not a concept unknown in British law—the curiously complicated British land laws even now retain all sorts of residual natural entitlements to right-of-way, fishing, hunting, etc. And in China, during the period of British comprador activity before the annexation of Hong Kong, the British imposed the now well-established doctrine of extra-territoriality which effectively meant that Western citizens acting *in China* were to be judged by Western law; much the same is argued from time to time about Westerners "caught" in the clutches of Sharia Law, such as the two British nurses recently tried for murder in Saudi Arabia.

What we have after Wik, then, is a sign of the historical relationality from which neither the settler nor the indigene can be separated: the indigene cannot be relegated to something that is merely chronologically prior; the settler cannot merely come at the end of history, "the winning post." This might be a way of using "overlap without equivalence," a phrase Bhabha (1998:35) adapts from Derrida.

In this new conception of colonized space, the space of the colonizer and the colonized are *not* mutually exclusive: each moves in the other's direction. Indeed, the Wik case is more or less contemporaneous with talk of reconciliation—which describes that sort of movement. It differs from the 1970s discourse of a treaty—which would have textualized, as in New Zealand, *a* settlement. It requires a grammar of unequal proximity.

A Theory of Affect

You will have noticed that the appeal of the Hanson book is not so much logical as affective. If we are to explain the persistence of certain narrative patterns in our cultures I think we need a Theory of Affect *and* a Theory of Effect in order to explain the joint appeals to what Aristotle called pathos and logos.

If we want to think about the affective functioning of repressed knowledge, a useful place to start is Freud's essay "The Uncanny." "The 'uncanny,'" Freud writes, "is that class of the terrifying which leads back to something long known to us, once very familiar" (1919:369-70). And he goes on to a crucial conclusion:

> [I]f this is indeed the secret nature of the uncanny, we can understand why . . . speech has extended *das Heimliche* into its opposite *das Unheimliche*; for this uncanny is in reality nothing new or foreign, but something familiar and old-established in the mind that has been estranged only by the process of repression. (1919:394)

He then shows us how to draw this from a personal and psychoanalytical into a cultural frame in the following way:

> We—or our primitive forefathers—once believed in the possibility of these things. . . .
>   Nowadays we no longer believe in them, we have *surmounted* such ways of thought; but we do not feel quite sure of our new set of beliefs, and the old ones still exist within us ready to seize upon any confirmation. As soon as anything actually happens in our lives which seems to support the old, discarded beliefs we get a feeling of the "uncanny." (1919:401-402)

These are not new ideas in the postcolonial field but, in the spirit of re-examining old knowledge, and revisiting unfinished business, I want to turn to how this might help us think about "settler" cultures.

The Postcolonial Uncanny

The Australian critic Ken Gelder and his colleague, the social geographer Jane M. Jacobs, have written most helpfully about this in an Australian context, which resonates pretty readily for other settler cultures. Their reading of the postcolonial, post-Mabo, post-Wik, politics and pragmatics of land ownership in Australia is similar to—but more highly developed than—the one I began to outline a few minutes ago. They describe a "postcolonial Australia, where, at the present moment, certain anxieties have arisen which have to do with how the nation seems suddenly to have become unfamiliar to itself. Are postcolonialism and anxiety always tied together?" they ask. Freud would reassure them that it probably is. "There is no doubt," they go on to say, "that [Mabo] gave this coupling a certain intensification. . . . The rejection of *terra nullius* was certainly read by some as the moment when *all* (or at least, *too much*) of Australia might become available for Aboriginal reclamation." Now *I* think this is how Freud, after all this time, can be useful: what is crucial about Freud's uncanny is that it is

not the unfamiliar which is the source of the anxiety: it is what Gelder
and Jacobs call the sense

> of being in place and "out of place" *simultaneously*. . . . [I]n this moment
> of decolonisation, what is "ours" is also potentially, or even always
> already, "theirs": the one may also be the other. And because [*as in
> Canada*] many land claims are either in the process of being dealt with
> or are yet to be made, a certain kind of un-settlement arises which is
> given expression by non-Aborigines and Aborigines alike—at the very
> moment when Modern Australia happens to be talking about "recon-
> ciliation."
>   . . . [W]hat is "ours" may also be "theirs," and vice versa . . . differ-
> ence and "reconciliation" coexist uneasily together. In uncanny Australia,
> one place is always already another place because the issue of possession
> is never complete, never entirely settled. (Gelder and Jacobs 1995:151)

In this new—but also very old—conception of colonial relations we,
that is, settlers and Aborigines, thus "inhabit the same place, yet [as
Gelder and Jacobs say] we seem to inhabit places which are *not*
the same" (Gelder and Jacobs 1995:162). But that is not the end of
the uncanny or of the cognitive dissonance which we have settled
upon the land; Gelder and Jacobs make the valuable postcolonial
point that

> One of the problems . . . with aboriginal land claims in modern Australia
> is, precisely, that the claimant must establish familiarity with the land;
> one must behave, in other words, as if dispossession had never hap-
> pened. There is no room in land claims for the articulation of what we
> might call an uncanny relationship to place, which would draw attention
> to the simultaneous experience of familiarity and unfamiliarity with the
> land. (1995:165)

We can identify now some of the anxious tropes of proximity: of being
consumed by indigeneity; of being lost in the space of the other; of the
Unheimlichkeit of home. They are not unfamiliar to those of us who
have read the public and fictional discourses that have circulated in
(and about) settler cultures. But I want to try to come at this question
of how the tropes *work* in another way.

It's My Midlife Crisis and I'll Revisit My Past if I Want To

Another bit of good advice you get from the Midlife Crisis
Handbook is "work out where you've been." So I want to historicize
how I got here.

In Commonwealth or postcolonial or national literatures we must—at some fundamental level—be interested in the relationship of text and culture—that is, how we "set up" our field and our objects of enquiry.

So, among our foundational methodological questions are:

How does culture get into texts?
How do texts get into culture?
Over the years we have had different ways of talking about this.

Once, when most of you were very young, we talked about themes; now we talk of tropes.

Once, when even I was very young, we talked of identity; now we talk of subjectivities or bodies.

Once, when we were fairly young, we talked of metaphysics; now we talk of ethics or politics or—if we still crave texts—we talk of history.

These, at their best, are more than just changes of vocabulary. They might also be ways of finding new protocols to talk about what we so badly want to talk about, new ways of identifying the objects of our not-entirely-scholarly desire. Maybe they are ways, not of changing the *analytical* frame, but the *heuristic* one, ways of explaining. And I would suggest that the heuristic is one of the modes of postcolonial narrative mediation.

Let me now historicize the line of enquiry that this paper takes.

When I began working in settler cultures in about 1986, one of the things that struck me was a sense of doubleness, duplicity, ambivalence. At the time I called settler cultures "the Second World." It was, I said at the time, meant to be a reading strategy rather than a cultural denominator. That there was a problem with this numerical designation became obvious when I got around to reading Fredric Jameson who had already used Second World to describe the old Eastern Bloc and had installed the ex-colonial or developing world as a Third in what, in his formulation, was clearly a hierarchy. Jameson's infamous article, "Third World Literature in an Era of Multinational Capitalism" (1986), is my nomination for the "Silliest Article by a Major Critic Award." After reading it I blocked out what else of Jameson I had read. Bad move; Jameson became my repressed.

Anyway, I was more interested in that notion of doubleness—and, like many other critics, I had no trouble doing a smart little job on Jameson's incredibly *us*-centric "ordering" of worlds. I noticed that some of those "second-world" formations of doubleness were rhetorical: puns were pretty common and so was my old favourite, zeugma. Of course, a lot of the other manifestations of that doubleness were what we, in our last unreconstructed moments, called "thematic."

Bhabha (out of Lacan) then showed how we could read subjects as "doubled," and so I talked for a while about settler subjectivity as a peculiarly doubled subjectivity, defined by its endless secondariness to *two* primaries: the First World of the cultural origin (Europe) and the geo-legal-temporal First World of Aboriginal peoples. Carrie Dawson (one of the many extraordinarily bright Canadian students who have come to Queensland to do graduate work) has done some terrific work showing the cul-de-sac of endless belatedness that this might lead us into. This is in her work on "imposture" in settler cultures. Recently, in response to her work, I have been thinking about that secondariness to two primaries in a couple of new ways: to think of it not as a dead-end but as a double bind; to think of it as being in relation to *two* objects of (be)longing and thus to think of it not as signifying belatedness but as a strong manifestation of the anxiety of proximity. Not as imposture, as weak mimesis, but needing to be read through one of the tropes of proximity as expressing a desire and an anxiety for a difficult relationality—perhaps impossible, certainly unequal and incomplete.

An obvious move from even that early work on settler subjectivity was the inevitable recognition that the term "settler" itself was, and *always* had been, tendentious, polemic. The word "settler" was itself part of the process of invasion; it was literally a textual imposition on history. This became clearer than ever when, in 1994, the relatively progressive Queensland premier and former Aboriginal Legal Service lawyer, Wayne Goss, objected strenuously to the use of the word "invasion" instead of settlement to describe postcontact Australian history in grade 5 in Queensland schools.[2] And "settler" is tendentious, too; it appears in its "claim" to be part of postcolonialism. Indira Karamcheti (1995) talked of the "Pat Boone, blue-eyed postcolonialism that is going on in Canada and Australia." So, if "settler" is a tendentious, or polemical, term, what efficacious forms does it take?

The settler, it increasingly seems to me, is above all a teller of tales. It is in narrative that settler subjectivity calls itself into being and it is in narratives that it can be located and its symptomatic utterances analyzed. The settler, I began to think, is "essentially" a narrating subject. That is to say, I am drawn to an analysis that is not so much located in "culture" and almost certainly not located in consciousness, but one located in texts or, more precisely, in various forms of narrative (history, fiction, politics, public discourses by and large). I argue that settlers narrate themselves into subjectivity in the act of making particular narratives. And so conflict in settler colonies is frequently a conflict over narrative or representation.

From my point of view, then, the settler is probably a later phase of what Memmi called the colonizer: settlers are colonizers in an ineluctable relationality to indigenes (and indigeneity) while inventing a legitimizing narrative to naturalize their place, to resolve the double bind (or what we used to call ambivalence?), to explain (or explain away) their relation to indigeneity. But whatever the desire for disavowal, there is no disidentificatory gesture available to the settler. The settler seeks to establish a nation, and therefore needs to become native and to write the epic of the nation's origin. The "Origin" is that which has no antecedent, so the presence of Ab-origines is an impediment.

My line of enquiry then becomes: What kinds of stories does the settler tell? In my paper at the Sri Lanka ACLALS Conference in 1995, I tried to isolate two different grand narratives of imperial settlement that could be represented prototypically by *The Tempest* and *Robinson Crusoe*.

> *The Tempest*, I argued, was the colonist as the hero of the colonial romance: a hero whose goal was to return to reclaim home.
>
> Robinson Crusoe's task was to establish himself, to claim the colony as home, and that entailed disestablishing the indigene's priority.

Is it possible to think of a cultural narratology? A cultural rhetoric? How do we find a way of talking about the mode or manner in which these settler stories function? If we see these narratives as *strategies*, we can see them as having material effects, not simply as systemic textual effects requiring explication. They constitute an invitation to notice the particular ways in which these settler narrative tropes *rearrange* the circumstances of our history and of our social relations, and how they foreclose on certain possibilities for social relations.

What gave particular impetus to this set of questions was an apparently fortuitous synchronicity in 1997. In the week that the federal Cabinet gathered in Brisbane to finalize a ten-point plan to disarm the High Court's Wik decision, I was trying out my argument about the profound paradigmatic differences between Mabo and Wik with a group of students. It was clear that the conservative Cabinet had an atavistic need to obliterate the basic assumption of Wik—that is, that two laws, two systems of ownership, could co-exist. I speculated that the prime minister and the pastoralists would need to re-establish something like *Terra Nullius* in order to delegitimize the growing forces that were conspiring to bring about Aboriginal-settler co-existence. This reminded me of those historical moments when the doctrine of *Terra Nullius* actually "gained ground" in Australia. It was not invented, as is often thought, at the beginning of European settlement in Australia but some thirty to fifty years later when an actual conflict over land use began. Then I suggested to my students that there was some urgent cultural revision to be done and I reckoned that in the near future we would see the reinvocation of some of the old settler tropes—maybe miscegenation, cannibalism, maybe the dying race. Tropes that viscerally registered the anxiety, the horror of proximity. Two days later, Pauline Hanson launched her infamous *The Truth*, the book from which I quoted earlier, and it invoked the trope of Aboriginal cannibalism with obvious and explicit intent. And one *could* have predicted that the ultimate trope of the settler being swallowed would be the one.

But de-legitimization (or its apparently benign cousin, exoticization) of the other as a strategy of identity-formation—we are not like them—is not the only function of the settler tropes. We know how to read that way. I am interested in how those tropes register what Gelder and Jacobs briefly referred to as anxiety. The anxiety is to do with desire and identification on the one hand and projection and othering as cultural boundary-marking on the other.

So, how do we rethink the settler paradigm as a mediatory relationship? My suggestion is zeugma. Zeugma, for those of you who cannot quite remember, is the figure of speech in which one word is placed in the same grammatical relation (i.e., it modifies or governs) to two words but in quite different senses—as in Alexander Pope, "Or stain her honour, or her new brocade." Usually the doubled object contains one that is abstract and one that is concrete, or one that is literal and one that is metaphorical.

Some classical rhetoricians distinguish between *syllepsis* in which the "yoking" is fully grammatical and *zeugma* in which it is not, or not quite (e.g., Corbett, 1971). That is fine by me. Indeed, the lack of fit is quite useful. Zeugma, syllepsis, puns are tropes of collocation, of awkward proximity: *they are about family trouble*, as Ross Chambers has observed. They are about things that are relatable but not commensurable. That might be a way of rethinking the new postcolonial relations of land ownership I mentioned earlier: this might be a way to *read* the co-existence of two incommensurable, politically unequal laws or epistemologies. And I think it is helpful to note that zeugma differs crucially from the old model of the simple sentence—subject-verb-object—which has seductively offered a grammar for the outmoded transitive model of imperialism: A does X to B.

And is zeugma not also the paradigm of our continuing problem as postcolonial intellectuals? How to be theorized and grounded at the same time. How to maintain *that* not-quite-grammatical relation?

Rereading Zeugmatically

There are then, I think, some big cultural reading lessons on offer—exemplary textual moments which may be read zeugmatically.

Wik lets us know that one place may be two places at once.

The New Zealand Treaty of Waitangi—which is in both Maori and English—lets us know that a text may be two texts at once.

And I may be one of the few people who thinks Sovereignty Association might be an interesting reading lesson even if it may not be much of a political solution.

Recently in Australia, progressive historians and Aborigines have begun talking of a notion of a "shared history of this place."[3] Zeugma might well be the figure we need to be able to comprehend that history.

What Is a Trope?

This all started when I began to worry about the unreflective looseness with which so many of us were using the word "trope" when we might mean "topos." In rhetoric, a trope is one of the figures of speech—metonymy or, say, zeugma. In Aristotle's *Rhetoric* a topos is one of the "topics" of invention—that is, one of the suitable subjects for the orator. They are what is speakable. On one hand, it might be easy enough to explain how *tropes* work discursively—and synchronically— in any given textual moment. On the other hand, we might be able to explain how *topoi* work *in narrative* (and perhaps more broadly across culture). Whatever these things are, they hover uneasily between tropes and topoi, between rhetoric and narrative.

But I think we prefer to call them tropes, and to treat them as rhetorical figures, because they *function* rhetorically—that is, they *turn* a history, a narrative; they function to persuade; they are strategic, polemical and tendentious. They naturalize particular kinds of relationships. But they are also *persistent*: they can be reinvoked long past what might be thought to be their use-by date. How?

Affectively, I have tried to deal with this in terms of the "uncanny." Effectively, I think my best bet is to allow the repressed Fred Jameson to return—this time the Jameson of *The Political Unconscious* (1981). There, Jameson talks of the "ideologeme, . . . a historically determinate conceptual or semic complex which can project itself variously in the form of a 'value system' or 'philosophical concept,' or in the form of *a protonarrative, a private or collective narrative fantasy*" (1981:115; my italics), and he goes on importantly to insist that "the ideologeme itself [must be grasped] as a form of social praxis, that is, as a symbolic resolution to a concrete historical situation" (1981:117).

Now here is how we might regain our groundedness, our ability to see what we have been calling tropes as *symbolic resolutions to concrete historical situations*; or, as I called it earlier, rearrangements of actual social and historical relations such as the genuinely difficult relation of races and places in the colonial situation; in this sense they may be, or be part of, mediatory codes.

Later in that brilliant book, Jameson offers a model he calls "sedimentation" to explain how "the ideology of the form itself, thus sedimented, persists into later, more complex structures as a generic message which coexists—either as a contradiction, or, on the other hand, as a mediatory or harmonizing mechanism—with elements from later stages" (1981:141). "A specific narrative paradigm continues to emit its ideological signals long after its original content has become historically obsolete: . . . the most archaic layer of content continues to supply vitality and ideological legitimation to its later and quite different symbolic function" (1981:186). (This is intriguingly similar to a point Margaret Atwood makes in her unfinished Harvard PhD thesis.[4])

So what persists into contemporary narrative is sedimented ideologized narrative form. Predictably, Jameson also has an explanation of what it is we see when that sedimented narrative causes tension or fails. I do not have the time to go into it all, but the essential fact is that such a failure or deviation

directs our attention to some of those determinate changes in the historical situation which block a full manifestation or replication of the structure on the discursive level. On the other hand, the failure of a particular generic structure, such as epic, to reproduce itself not only encourages a search for those substitute textual formations that appear in its wake, but more particularly alerts us to the historical ground, now no longer exist-ent, in which the original structure was meaningful. (1981:146)

Perhaps this allows us to think productively about the significance to us of Pauline Hanson's narrative of baby-eating Aborigines. Her narrative is a kind of failure in the sense that most of us can no longer read it, so it directs us to reread the historical ground on which it was once mean-ingful and strategic.

Jameson's final lesson for me comes from his noting that the "ideo-logeme . . . exists nowhere as such: . . . it vanishes into the past . . . leaving only its traces—material signifiers, lexemes, enigmatic words and phrases—behind it" (1981:201). "[I]deologemes [are] free-floating narrative objects . . . which are never given directly in primary verbal form, but must always be re-constructed after the fact, as work-ing hypothesis and subtext" (1981:185). Recurrent themes, then—what we have got used to calling tropes—such as the "lost child," the "half-breed," cannibalism, can only be understood as "so many allu-sions to *a more basic ideological 'sign'* which would have been grasped instinctively by any contemporary reader but from which we are cul-turally and historically distanced" (Jameson 1981:200).

What Are the Settler Narrative Tropes and What Are Their Ideologemes?

Just a brief catalogue for now:

Going Native

This might mean any of:

1. indigenization—that is, a tendentious "settler" identity claim
2. cultural loss/contamination for the "settler"
3. solidarity or affiliation with the other

One of the principal functions of the indigenizing narrative is to legitimize the settler—to put the settler in the cultural and discursive place of the indigene whose physical space has already been invaded. The indigenized settler is the figure who is ready to step in when the native "dies out." The native must *make way* for the settler because there was a legal and moral prohibition against "invasion."

Dying Race

If the natives did not die out quickly enough, their actual dying could be replaced by stories of their dying, by "the last of the tribe" poems and photographs. Discursive space was in need of clearing as much as physical space.

And there is a temporality to all this too.

1. And there is the end of time: the last of his tribe—the dying race.
2. There is the moment *before* time starts, the frozen moment *just before* settlement/pacification—the pre-contact time—figured as prehistory, golden age, essentialist past. In its more negative formation, this manifests as the "bad history" of *Terra Nullius* or as the persistent myth in *all* the settler colonies of "the pre-aboriginal peoples who were here before the first nations." This one is the corollary of the dying race: the indigenes were not here at the beginning; they will not be here at the end.

These are all proximal, asymptotic moments.

Incorporation

This is going native gone badly wrong. There are several complexly related versions of this trope: there is the lost child (who may be captive or foundling or just vanished). The "lost child" trope is a story of incorporation in which the land is a metaphor for native. And, like the captivity narrative, it functions as a cautionary tale for women and children who might think of straying "out of place." Of course, incorporation also includes cannibalism and miscegenation.

Gananath Obeyesekere (1997) notes that what is usually present in the familiar delegitimizing narratives is:

(a) headhunting
(b) cannibalism
(c) infanticide
(d) sodomy

But *cannibalism* is not simply like the other three. Much of the modern literature on cannibalism is directed towards rehabilitating the accused from the taint of cannibalism because modern anthropologists seem to share with their ancestors the notion that cannibalism is the ultimate character flaw. Certainly, it is the final boundary marker of civilized behaviour, the line that no civilized white person would ever cross. Cannibalism is a very particular trope, though—it is about proximity and it is about consumption.

The other trope that functions like this is *miscegenation*. It too contains the tension between anxiety and desire: for absorption, consumption, sameness. Each defines the moment when the desire for indigenization, the desire to stand in place of the native, has *gone too far*; they are then the metaphoric limit-cases for the going-native trope. They are sins of proximity. They might be described as Falling Over the Asymptote.

Asymptosis

This is getting close, but never becoming the same. The "settler's" desire to "stand in" for the native produces ultimately and perhaps inevitably the unspeakable desire for miscegenation[5]— what in South Africa was once called the "taint." The insertion of the settler into the (physical and discursive) space of the indigene is simultaneously characterized by desire and disavowal. The movement into indigenous space must be asymptotic: indigeneity must be approached, even appropriated, certainly photographed, but never touched. This produces in the settler subject an anxiety of proximity. The self-indigenizing settler has to stop just short of going completely native and is, therefore, often represented as sexless.[6] The settler must stand just in front of, in the place of, but never in the body of the indigene. The need, then, is to *dis*place rather than *re*place the other. But the other must remain to signify the boundary of the self, to confirm the subjectivity of the settler. The "other," as a consequence of this "almost but not quite" move, is therefore always in some sense present, always "uncannily" ready for its return.

I think that *authenticity* might turn out to be one of the settler tropes too. It is certainly a device used by settlers to limit and regulate the speaking position of indigenes. Disciplining the authentically native was a form of regulation in apartheid South Africa, in treaty-negotiating Canada, in Australian social welfare arrangements that produced what is now known as "The Stolen Generation." It is a way of determining hierarchies of value and power. But authenticity has a tricky tendency to become *authority*: hence the anxiety in contemporary settler societies about indigenous authenticity.[7] Now that the connection between native authenticity and authority has been firmly, but not uncomplicatedly, established, it seems necessary to regulate who may have access to it.

A Tropology

Having got from contemporary bad politics to classical rhetoric, I would like to conclude with a suggestion that we borrow an idea from some Renaissance and later rhetoricians who had schemes for classifying the tropes. For instance, in the nineteenth century, Theodore Hunt argued that figurative language followed laws of association that could be analyzed in three broad groups (in D'Angelo 1984:63):

Figures of Resemblance

Figures of Contrast

Figures of Contiguity

Figures of Resemblance (or what *we* might call the tropes of Mimesis) include simile, metaphor, allegory;

Figures of Contrast (we might think of them as tropes of binarism) include antithesis, epigram, irony;

Figures of Contiguity are the figures of association, or in my terms tropes of proximity. They include metonymy, synecdoche, paronomasis and antanaclasis, syllepsis and zeugma.

We might then have a way of rereading, of remediating the narrative tropes we encounter. I am suggesting that one could analyze the narrative tropes as expressing particular figures of speech and then read them into a classification of the tropes like the one I just borrowed from Theodore Hunt. To see the tropes functioning in this way as abstracted (re)iterations of ideologically determined, historically contingent narratives might—just—enable us to *re*read them. As Ross Chambers has so usefully said, "What has been mediated can be remediated" (1994:1). The tropes have been used to make colonial history/experience readable; they can therefore be made to make it rereadable. As the Australian historian Alan Atkinson said recently: "European Australians have studiously forgotten not only the ghastly bloodshed involved in race relations but also the careful work of conscience. As a result the past has lost the authority it ought to have" (1997:23). This is what rereading tropically might mean. We have got awfully good at reading the past for its moral and ethical blindnesses: to do that is no longer a theoretical or a methodological challenge. What we need to be able to do next is to find a theorized methodology for rereading the past productively, *not* celebratively, *not* unreflectively, but with an eye to the contradictions that might enable us to learn our difficult place better.

Notes

1 As Sara Mills asks in her 1995 article in *ARIEL*: How do we get past Foucault's argument in *The Order of Discourse* that there are breaks between discursive domains and moments? How to deal with the permeability of discursive domains? While, as Mills says, discursive histories are not at all simply continuous, neither are they marked by the kind of breaks that Foucault suggests.

2 The extended controversy over the curriculum is documented in Land 1994.

3 Henry Reynolds, Alan Atkinson et al. (1997).

4 "[I]t would appear to be a rule that a given literary convention changes more slowly than the use to which it is put" (Margaret E. Atwood Papers, Box 47, quoted in Godard 1987:28).

5 I am grateful to J.M. Coetzee for some suggestive personal discussions on this point.

6 Like Natty Bumppo and other of Cooper's heroes.

7 There are a number of contentious contemporary Australian examples: Koolmatrie, Burrup, Weller, Mudrooroo and Demidenko.

References

Atkinson, Alan
    1997   "The Unelected Conscience." *Quadrant* 41, 6 (June):17-23.

Bhabha, Homi
    1998   "On the Irremovable Strangeness of Being Different." *PMLA* 113: 34-39.

Chambers, Ross
    1994   "Fables of the Go-between." In Chris Worth, Pauline Nestor and Marko Pavlyshyn, eds., *Literature and Opposition*, 1-28. Clayton, Vic.: Centre for Comparative Literature and Cultural Studies, Monash University.
    1997   Personal conversation, Brisbane, 30 May.

Corbett, Edward P.J.
    1971   *Classical Rhetoric for the Modern Student.* 2nd ed. New York: Oxford University Press.

D'Angelo, Frank
    1984   "The Evolution of the Analytic *Topoi*: A Speculative Enquiry." In Robert J. Connors, Lisa S. Ede and Andrea A. Lunsford, eds., *Essays on Classical Rhetoric and Modern Discourse*, 50-68. Carbondale, IL: Southern Illinois University Press.

Freud, Sigmund
    1925 [1919]   "The Uncanny." In *Collected Papers*. Vol. 4, 368-407. Translated by Alex Strachey. London: International Psycho-Analytical Press.

Gelder, Ken, and Jane M. Jacobs
    1995   "Uncanny Australia." *UTS Review* 1, 2:150-69.

Godard, Barbara
  1987   "Telling It Over Again: Atwood's Art of Parody." *Canadian Poetry* 21
          (Fall-Winter):1-30.
[Hanson, Pauline]
  1997   "Surrendering Australia: Mabo, Wik and the Betrayal of Australia." In
          [Pauline Hanson Support Movement], *The Truth: On Asian Immigration,
          the Aboriginal Question, the Gun Debate and the Future of Australia,*
          109-55. Ipswich: [Pauline Hanson Support Movement].
Jameson, Fredric
  1981   *The Political Unconscious: Narrative as a Socially Symbolic Act.* Ithaca,
          NY: Cornell University Press.
  1986   "Third World Literature in an Era of Multinational Capitalism." *Social
          Text* 15 (Fall):65-88. Revised as Jameson 1987.
  1987   "World Literature in an Era of Multinational Capitalism." In Clayton
          Koelb and Virgil Lokke, eds., *The Current in Criticism,* 139-58. West
          Lafayette, IN: Purdue University Press.
Karamcheti, Indira
  1995   "Academic Differences: Postcolonial African-American and American
          Studies." MLA conference, Chicago, IL (December).
Land, Ray, ed.
  1994   *Invasion and After: A Case Study in Curriculum Politics.* [Brisbane]:
          Queensland Studies Centre, Griffith University.
Lawson, Alan
  1995   "Whose Island Is It Anyway? The Uncontainable Other: A Post-
          colonial Paradigm." Association for Commonwealth Literature and Lan-
          guage Studies, Colombo, Sri Lanka (August).
Mills, Sara
  1995   "The Discontinuity of Postcolonial Discourse." *ARIEL* 26, 3:73-88.
Obeyesekere, Gananath
  1997   "The Im(moral) [*sic*] Economy: Cannibalism and the Trade in Heads."
          Captivity Narratives and the Captive Body: A Symposium to Honour
          Gananath Obeyesekere. Magnetic Island, Qld., 26 September.
Reynolds, Henry
  1996   "Frontier History after Mabo." *Journal of Australian Studies* 49:4-11.
  1998   *This Whispering in Our Hearts.* St. Leonards, NSW: Allen & Unwin.
  1999   *Why Weren't We Told? A Personal Search for the Truth about Our His-
          tory.* Ringwood, Vic.: Viking.

3

Looking in from "Beyond": Commonwealth Studies in French Universities

Jacqueline Bardolph

> ... the valuable advice and information we have
> received from scores of individuals and institutions
> throughout the Commonwealth and beyond.
> — "Introduction" to the Report of the Commis-
> sion on Commonwealth Studies, London,
> Commonwealth Secretariat (June 1996):9

In my reflection on Commonwealth studies in Europe and more particularly in France, I have found no help with the trinity of French thinkers, Derrida, Lacan and Foucault, not to mention Kristeva and Irigaray. I did find some theoretical guidance though: I have been thinking along the lines of what the stimulating sociologist Pierre Bourdieu defines as "un champ littéraire," a literary field: such a field is the locus of fertile tensions between socio-historical economic factors and literary creation. He analyzes the way the combination of publishing conditions, the nature of a given reading public and institutional powers, can not only facilitate works of art, but also grant them legitimacy, through academic recognition and through the conferring of sundry prizes and distinctions. This context can be a determining factor for a majority of works, accounting for their aesthetic and imaginary choices as well as for their explicit or implicit ideology; yet the movement is not consistent since some major works, by being inventive or transgressive, can modify the field and create new conditions for creation. In a conference I recently attended in Brussels, Africanists reflected on the various literary fields, national and international, that both define and are defined by African literatures, in French and in English. The debate was fruitful. Looking now at the relationship between European universities and Commonwealth literature, I have come across several questions: what is the interaction, if any, between writers from the Commonwealth and a body of scholars from a non-Commonwealth background, with a different working language? Are such academics intermediaries between new literatures and the reading public of the old continent? Are they mere outsiders, watching with a certain detachment the new production and the whole critical debate on postcolonial theories which has originated in North America and the old Commonwealth? Is there a two-way dialogue between research issuing from within the countries once linked by the British Empire, and those that have a different historical past, a different language? Any cross-fertilization? What kind of future will be made possible for such research by the academic institutions and publishing conditions?

I shall base my reflections on the example of France, with comparisons with other European countries—Germany, Italy, Spain, Belgium, whose situations I know best. I shall not include Great Britain or Ireland, where the conditions are altogether different. Yes, different because one has to keep in mind that, in all the countries I have chosen, English is not the mother tongue and has no official status. It is taught in schools and universities as a very privileged second language, a stronger status than French or Spanish would have in Canada. But most adults after their school days are reluctant to speak it. English or American books are difficult to get hold of, even in big cities, Australian novels more so, and in France banks will not pay your bills for books from Kenya, having next to no contact with some English-speaking countries—their network is Francophone. Academics teach literature in language departments, a permanently threatened portion of a syllabus that also features translation, linguistics and cultural studies. In a "bold" move in the 1970s the field of American studies was created, and some departments are reluctant to share the precious time devoted to the two cultural areas with a newcomer called "Commonwealth" or "New Literatures"—"When one thinks they have not read Milton!" One must also remember that, unlike German or Italian,

English as a second language is increasingly sought as *langue du pain*—a passport to a job—and not as a vehicle representing one or several cultures. Some smaller universities find it difficult to maintain a distinction in curricula and audiences between English for culture and commercial English. A specialist in Canadian or Indian authors may well have to teach translation or business English, or English to chemists, until the day when he or she can have access to part-time or, rarely, full-time teaching of Commonwealth literature. Never full-time on his or her chosen topic or author, as would be the case if he was in an Anglophone environment where research and teaching have a better chance to be fully matched. Finally, the field being new and resources and funds going to well-established subjects, preferably science or management, travelling is severely limited, especially for younger academics. The recent survey on Commonwealth studies notes that some European countries send more scholars than others to international conferences: it does not reflect on the level of interest in each one but basically on the allotment of travelling funds. Until a few years ago, the poor turnout of French academics—one in three hundred at an EACLALS conference in Graz in 1993—revealed that any research expenses for books, journals and conference attendance were entirely self-financed. Some countries, Canada in particular, have been extremely generous in helping new and established scholars to come and see the background for themselves, to use libraries and to initiate contacts. Nothing of the sort can be expected for those working on African countries for instance.

Summing up these few data is not meant to tell an apologetic hard-luck story (Western European universities on the whole have a fairly easy time if one compares them with others around the world), but to insist on the fact that the cultures of the Commonwealth are as a rule doubly foreign to the student or scholar. He has first to learn English, this treacherous language with its many accents, with its prepositions that slip out of place without warning. He has to learn about British history and culture, and then about how it has given a certain shape to life in countries that were once part of the Empire. In some cases, at a further remove, something has to be known about First Nation peoples and their histories and ways. As they acquire background knowledge in order to read fiction, some scholars get stuck on the way, immersed for good in Maori sculpture, Hindu gods or the successive constitutions of Nigeria. And an important difference with readers and academics from, say, New Zealand or Trinidad, is that all of this has to be learnt intellectually, not as a part of local culture or the mythical constructs one imbibes at primary school. The appreciation of cricket, of certain jokes, of what ANZAC or a "creek" or a "settlement" are or of what it meant last July for the yacht Britannia to leave Hong Kong harbour while the band played "Jerusalem"—all these have emotional undertones and connotations which are not given to the non-Anglophone European but which have to be learned.

This being said, if one looks at the early history of Commonwealth studies, it is no surprise that the history of research on the Commonwealth should have been initiated in Europe in the 1970s by two types of people: by Anglophones, mostly from the Commonwealth, and by people just returned from the colonies or the newly independent nations. Consider a few names in the first group: In Germany, Nelson Wattie, Gordon Collier, Geoff Davis; in Italy, Bernard Hickey, Jane Wilkinson; in Spain, Doreann McDermott with Susan Ballyn, Brian Worsfold, Felicity Hand; and, naturally, Anna Rutherford in Aarhus, to name but a few; all have been extremely active from the start. It was their combined energy that got the association going and established links with British and Commonwealth universities. In the early days—I am thinking of an EACLALS conference in Malta in 1976—a non-Anglophone member might well have the impression he or she was watching an expatriate club with its subtle unwritten rules. In each European country, some individuals had just returned from India, many from Africa, and were trying to find others with similar interests. I remember the joy at discovering, in 1975, that there were other people in France working on Anglophone African literatures, in spite of our institutions which wanted to place us in departments of anthropology. I remember the rainy Sundays we spent in unheated buildings in Montpellier, happily attempting to map out the as-yet-uncharted literary continent. Gradually, the isolated individuals met, and met again. In France a SEPC—Société d'Étude des Pays du Commonwealth—was founded with a journal that was to become *Commonwealth*, issued twice yearly, written mostly in English. Every year we meet on the occasion of the national conference of university specialists in English. Our workshop lasts for two and a half days, with a dense program of papers, increasingly submitted for selection beforehand. The association has produced a second branch, devoted to cultural studies on the Commonwealth: history, art, sociology, politics, etc. This group of academics is also thriving, with several annual meetings, in spite of the comparative difficulty of getting hold of primary sources and of finding common working topics. The history of the last twenty years would thus seem to be a success story, a positive evolution going from strength to strength. However, it needs to be looked at in more detail.

In particular, one must stress the importance of institutional factors in each country. Paradoxically, there was greater freedom in the early days: the academics were usually trained and recognized in a classical field, whether Faulkner or Austen, and afterwards could introduce a greater and greater proportion of Canada or India in their teaching as they grew in authority. Now, there have been many PhDs in specialized postcolonial areas, with the strong theoretical approach that goes with it. And this new generation of doctors find that no corresponding chairs have been created in sufficient numbers. This is particularly true in Germany, where posts offered by universities are precisely labelled and where three chairs at most exist on the topic in spite of strong recommendations by the national association of academics in English that a chair in Commonwealth studies should exist in each university. In France, chairs can be loosely defined as "literature" or "twentieth-century literature"—there is at the moment a shortage of applicants—and a specialty in Commonwealth is admitted as a good thing for the department, provided in most cases the new recruit promises to fill in with Hardy or Swift when necessary. One must say also that our French centralized system is a help so far. Two national teacher recruitment competitions—the "Capes" and the very prestigious "Agrégation"—shape every year what is taught throughout France at the postgraduate level, and the books chosen in the syllabus are bound to percolate down the pyramid in the following years. After much lobbying and information given to the jury by our association, several Commonwealth texts have been adopted over the years in the list of twelve texts assigned for the competition: Doris Lessing, *The Grass Is Singing*; Patrick White, *Voss*; Margaret Laurence, *The Stone Angel*; Wole Soyinka, *A Dance of the Forest*; V.S. Naipaul, *A House for Mr. Biswas*; Chinua Achebe, *Arrow of God*; J.M. Coetzee, *Waiting for the Barbarians*; and in 1997 Katherine Mansfield and Hanif Kureishi. In 1998 Margaret Atwood's *The Handmaid's Tale* was included. The jury nearly decided on Salman Rushdie's *Midnight's Children* and stopped because of the fatwa, and has been refusing over the years Wilson Harris's *The Palace of the Peacock* and David Malouf's *An Imaginary Life*. The books have to be dense reading as they are given the full treatment of hours of lectures and seminars—up to eighteen hours per book—on top of all the existing bibliography made available to the graduate students. In what we call "civilization," this year's topic is on the republican issue in Australia, and a few years ago there was something on the end of the Raj. In France, being given a space at the Agrégation syllabus is recognition indeed—Nobel, Booker and Goncourt all at once. It means that each university feels the need for specialized staff to avoid importing from other towns—remember the competitive aspect of agrégation which is also used to rate the efficiency of English departments. It means investing in primary and secondary sources and subscribing to journals. In short, it means that the field has acquired full recognition alongside Shakespeare and postmodern writers, as a third feature next to English and American studies.

Thus it has become licit to introduce courses from the first year onwards, which unfailingly prove very popular with students when they are optional. The choice of topics is left very much to the individual scholars. Several of us have been using short stories as a good way to introduce a wide range of styles and preoccupations for a given country or area. In undergraduate studies, the French tradition is to work on individual works, not reading lists, which is easier anyway, given the difficulties in obtaining even one work in sufficient quantity. Postgraduate studies, as separate from the national competition "concours," allow a great deal of freedom in the choice of topics, and this is true throughout Europe. This is the reason why, over the last years, a number of PhDs have been coming out on the New Literatures: they are now completed by good students, not just those who happened to stay in Ghana or Australia. In turn, this gives life to research centres which are either devoted to one country—in France, at least three centres on Canada, one on India—or form an important component of modern literature centres. Whether this flourishing situation will prove permanent, we shall question at the end of this paper. Anyway, one must take into account all these elements of reality to examine the characteristics of the research in universities.

The last element, in this overview of the conditions for research, is that specialists are not isolated in each country. Inside Europe and often in a wider worldview, one has the feeling of belonging to an invisible college where other specialists are not mere bibliographical footnotes but well-known faces and friends. There is the possibility of meeting in EACLALS and the remote possibility of travelling to a world ACLALS conference. Many more local events have taken place: in Milan on the Caribbean, in Barcelona and Paris on Australia, plus the more general topics in yearly national gatherings in Germany or

France. We may come across one another in the Commonwealth Institute Library in London, which has been an invaluable support in our research. In Europe, specialized journals are published: *Wasafiri*, the *Journal of Commonwealth Literature, Kunapipi* and *Commonwealth*. The last two do not reflect a particularly national approach. *Kunapipi* increasingly reflects the interests of its founder on Australia and gender. *Commonwealth* has one number each year devoted to the papers of the annual meeting of SEPC, not all by French people, and the other given to external contributors, mostly from outside France.

Looking at what has been published over the years in this last journal and at other sources, one can draw a rough sketch of the distinctive features of Commonwealth research in France. First, it is clear that the French have read postcolonial theory, use it in teaching, but do not use it much when it comes to their own reflection on texts. Just look at bibliographies. The tradition has always been one of close reading, the key discipline being the "explication de texte," an organized discourse on a short extract which has nothing of the running commentary. French scholars thus are interested in the definition and the evolution of literary genres: for instance, all the forms of the epic, the Baroque, the self-referential elements—*The Writer Written*, Jean-Pierre Durix—the non-realist modes which cannot all be labelled "magic realism." They rely a great deal on the findings of narratology, in the line of Gérard Genette who is still a staple in reading and teaching. They work on the "autobiographical pact" with Philippe Lejeune and its followers, on character with Jean Jouve, on metaphor and time with Paul Ricoeur, on reading with Michel Picard; they use linguistics or semiotics when it is handy. We can all happily spend a whole semester of minute examination of single pages from *The Diviners, Potiki, The Vivisector*, Walcott's poetry and so on. Students are trained in such methods and respond happily. Scholars enjoy reading good stylistic approaches, detailed analysis of a page or of a short story. This approach is considered essential in the training of critical capacities. People strongly believe that theoretical constructs cannot be separated from first-hand work on specifics. This type of discipline is considered threatened by loosely conceived cultural studies, as is testified in a recent paper by an Italian colleague.

This has several consequences. Apart from the small number of researchers narrowly specialized on one country—usually Canada—few focus their questioning on problems of national identity. The books are chosen for the pleasure and stimulation they give as literature. The students are taught early not to read works principally for their eventual referential value—although, naturally, they are given guidance as to where they can find relevant information. Cultural studies are firmly allocated a different space in the curriculum, different teaching methods and specialists. The same goes for research, increasingly so, even if naturally enough a great deal of background has to be filled in so that the creative works can be put into perspective. This approach, through a selection of major texts, combines with the demands made on academics to preclude narrow specialization: in France, Germany and Italy we have to cover a wide range of authors, whether for teaching purposes or to sit on the juries of the new PhDs: within one term we may have to read again all Atwood, all Wilson Harris, Caribbean poetry, Patrick White, Zakes Mda and Maori writing—a personal example, but the same goes for my colleagues. We contribute to local or national papers, radio or TV programs, cultural events of all kinds as well as to reviews in connected fields: political science, sociology. This precludes too narrowly specialized exposés. It follows somehow naturally, and out of choice, that our approach is often comparative: we often work in conjunction with other literature specialists, and the field itself of comparative literature is strong in France. History has provided us with grounds for parallels. The Association for the Studies of African Literatures, APELA, deals with texts in the three European languages and opens itself to texts in African languages. We have writing from the Mahgreb very much in our minds as we read some contemporary fiction from the Commonwealth. The same comparative approach goes for Caribbean studies, where some scholars compare the production in the three languages. Edouard Glissant is considered as a key figure to the understanding of the production from that area.

Such approaches do not look for coherence in overall theories. For instance, no all-inclusive "postcolonial theory" is produced in France; neither is it to my knowledge in Italy or Germany, although in the latter country some younger scholars are said to be increasingly interested in the debate. A book has been published in Denmark: *Teaching Post-colonialism and Post-colonial Literature*. It would not help us: we do not teach "postcolonialism" as such, only in relation with the various theories that help to apprehend a given text. Besides, a heading like "Anglophone postcolonial theories" would sound like an oxymoron, given the universalizing intent of most of the writing. As I mentioned earlier, we read with interest the literature on "postcolonial" modes, but do not use it much as a tool to explore texts. This may be partly due to a political history and background different from that of the countries in which it originated. In France, Germany and Italy the presence of socialist and Marxist thought has always been one of the elements of the debate as a matter of course, reflecting the political life on the campus and the nation at large. In countries like France or Italy which had an empire, the first analysis of the process of colonization or domination in the 1960s and 1970s was very much marked by thinkers like Frantz Fanon or Albert Memmi. One may add that since many scholars work on countries like Africa or the Caribbean, they tend to be more sensitive to neo-colonialism than to a so-called "postcolonial" era. Younger generations of scholars have not necessarily been submitted to a political debate in the same terms, but they are also more emotionally distant from the problems of national identity than Australian or Canadian critics. Rather than the problems of national or regional identity, what seems to attract readers in Europe are the issues around immigration, Diaspora, minorities and First Nations people—in short, all the texts by writers who can claim several loyalties and identities, not necessarily conflicting in what the philosopher Michaux calls "flexible identities." The Indian Diaspora, many Caribbean writers, Amitav Ghosh travelling to Egypt, the later Naipaul, who attaches more value to mobility than to roots, are such examples. A French graduate student from North Africa can relate easily to Michael Ondaatje and his refusal to be defined by maps.

French research on Commonwealth writing can be said to be more applied than theoretical. By contrast with the critical production from other countries, one can notice the absence of gender as an issue, apart from a few academics who have lived for long in Canada or in the United States. I pass no judgment; this is just a reminder that in the country of Beauvoir, Cixous, Kristeva and Irigaray—the latter mostly unheard of on French campuses—gender studies or feminist criticism hardly feature in the critical literature, even if we can appreciate it when we come across it. Maybe our reading tends to be myopic, but we do not on the whole find much help with Lacan, Derrida, Paul de Man, who seem oddly ill-adapted to the questions raised by our primary sources. In the early 1980s, when our fellow academics from American studies extolled the whole postmodern "anti-humanist" ethos, language as an arbitrary play of signifiers, the playful disarray of images meant to correspond to a contemporary vision, we sat on the edges of the debate, wondering how that could help us to deal with our angry writers, creating a feeling of urgency, even claiming like Chinua Achebe the outmoded role of teachers. Since then, the pendulum has started swinging with New Historicism, with the rebirth of the Author whom some said Barthes had killed for good. We are allowed to consider again what used to be dismissed as "carcan référentiel," referential straitjacket. In brief, even if we are not very clear on the meaning of the term postcolonial, it has been useful in giving legitimacy to our field in the eyes of fellow academics working on the "centre," be it Britain or the United States.

Whereas some generalizing approaches are less adapted to our tendency to focus on individual works, the works themselves are somehow selected by the approach itself. There has to be some meat for detailed examination. Experimental texts, in the modernist or postmodernist mode, feature recurrently. Some writers fit the bill: Wilson Harris, Wole Soyinka, Janet Frame, J.M. Coetzee, Patrick White, Salman Rushdie, Nuruddin Farah and now Michael Ondaatje are often quoted. Others, the kind of authors who benefit more from extensive reading, are overlooked or summarized in one so-called major work, Margaret Atwood by *Surfacing*, for instance. This obviously has drawbacks as some so-called easier writers, like Narayan for example, who do not lend themselves easily to exegesis, may be overlooked. According to the French expression, the novel or poem has to be dense enough to respond to close reading, "doit tenir à l'explication de texte." Does that mean that no research of an extensive nature is attempted by French critics? We cannot afford to keep to one topic only in our teaching life, but most of us in our research have specialized in one field where we have brought our contribution to the mapping of a particular area. In France, Italy and Germany, many have done works of erudition on African literature, joining our efforts to those of specialists from the United States, Canada and Britain. From the start, people have been gathering data on South African literature which is much studied in France, Italy and Germany. The same can be said about the Caribbean production, Maori writing, even New Zealand fiction. The mass and relevance of works done by nationals in Canada or Australia may seem daunting to surveys from outside, yet good specialists can be found on individual Australian authors, for instance. The contributions made by critics from Europe in reference books like the *Routledge Encyclopedia of Post-colonial Writing* or in critical collections edited by Bruce King or Douglas Killam show that in spite of the enormous difficulties we have in collecting primary and secondary material, we can feature honourably. It also shows, by the way, that it is not difficult to publish criticism outside your own country, due to the open attitude of editors, which is not the case in all academic fields.

What general conclusions can be drawn from this brief survey? First, one can notice that in one important instance, European academics do not feature in the literary field of the Commonwealth: there is little interaction with the writers themselves. They are not present in the juries where prizes are given, cannot offer writer-in-residence appointments nor write important reviews in the national press. In brief, they do not play any part in the legitimizing of works and writers, and have no say in canon formation in the countries where the books are published. Occasionally, they advise about translation, but this is a minor element in the reputation of an author. They are observers, but not actors. The system works one way only in another instance. European research knows all about North American criticism, but the reverse is not true. MLA and good library resources make it easy for a French student to get a bibliography on the Web or in a Canadian university on, say, Alice Munro. He or she feels no need to look up what has been published by research centres and journals in France and other countries closer at hand. I have the example of a special number on African literature issued by the venerable *Revue de littérature comparée*. The Francophone scholar asked to produce a bibliography of critical writing on Anglophone literature must have kept to North American sources. We need to collect our own data, make them available through modern media: a site on the Web has been started in Dijon, but we need now to establish a complete system of references different from the very useful guide produced for EACLALS. We also need to change attitudes, at home certainly, and over the ocean maybe. As for us, with the growth of the field, we cannot entirely rely on amateur initiative and the selfless commitment of some individuals.

What is the future? It is very much connected with the future of "Literature in English" as a topic in our universities. What if commercial English takes all the available resources? What if we produce brilliant PhDs, with no employment in their chosen field, and that, not just in Germany? What if a French minister one day decides teachers of English no longer need a competition based on literature, since they do not teach it in schools? What if in Italy research centres on Emerging Literatures, that is, African and Caribbean, are closed down by the central power because Development Studies are no longer fashionable? One possible change, if a reduction in options results from financial reasons, might be the creation of a strong field on twentieth-century literature, which might solve all our present problems of demarcation and labels. The writers heading the canon would survive and be studied. Commonwealth studies have helped to introduce them and there is no going back. Some national literatures will always be studied as such: Canadian, South African, for instance. But, in France, the concept itself of Commonwealth may become increasingly difficult to appreciate unless a clearer picture of the present-day identity of the polycentric association of nations comes across. Our own defensive approach to "La francophonie" is now proving more of a drawback than a help in the studying together of heterogeneous texts. Academics in that field wonder whether this geo-political label is an apt heading for the study of national and individual production loosely connected by the use of a single language. As for me and many of my colleagues, the heading of Commonwealth studies still makes sense. When all is said, I think it would be a pity to miss what the comparison brings to the reading of individual texts by writers who so far share something in their tradition, language, history, in some common values, as well as bringing a new vision to writing in English.

4

Climbing Mount Everest: Postcolonialism in the Culture of Ascent

Stephen Slemon

It scarcely needs saying that "Mount Everest" is *not* just "there."[1] As just about every book on Himalayas mountaineering likes to point out, "Mount Everest" was hoisted into physical—and cultural—ascendency through a prodigious act of imperial technology: the Great Trigonometrical Survey of India.[2] Mount Everest began as a theodolite measurement taken from a hundred miles away in 1847; it became a notation called "Peak XV" within an archive of survey records which reproduced the Indian subcontinent (or at least the parts the British could get at) as a vast grid of measured, crisscrossing triangles; five years later these measurements passed into the hands of two rows of mathematicians, or "computers" as they were called, seated at a long table in Calcutta, who refigured them through logarithm into the measurement of "29,002 ft."[3] After this, legend sets in.[4] The chief computer, Radhanath Sickdhar, is said to have sent a message to the Surveyor General of India, Colonel Andrew Waugh, saying, "Sir, I have discovered the highest mountain in the world" (Krakauer 1997:13; Bilham 1997:26). Colonel Waugh reported to the Royal Geographical Society in London: "here is a mountain,

---

Notes to chapter 4 are on pp. 67-70.

most probably the highest in the world, without any local name that
we can discover, or whose native appellation, if it have any, will not
very likely be ascertained before we are allowed to penetrate into
Nepaul and to approach close to this stupendous snowy mass." Waugh
therefore proposed that Peak XV be named "after his respected chief
and predecessor in office," Colonel George Everest (Richards, "Tea in
India" 1857). A political officer named B.H. Hodgson objected, writing
from Darjeeling to say that "although he agrees with Colonel Waugh as
to the fitness of the name of Mount Everest, and sympathises with the
sentiment which gave rise to it, he must add . . . that the mountain in
question does not lack a native and ascertained name; that the name is
Deodhunga, Holy Hill, or Mons Sacer" ("Tea in India" 1857). The President of the Royal Geographical Society thanked Mr. Hodgson for his
contribution but nevertheless concluded that "all who were present
would be delighted if this mountain should for ever retain the name of
th[at] distinguished geographer who . . . ha[s] been the means of
carrying on that magnificent operation" ("Tea in India" 1857). And so
it was that the mountain that Nepalese speakers now call Sagarmatha,
which is usually translated as "Goddess of the Sky," and that Tibetans
call Chomolungma, which is almost always translated as "Goddess,
Mother of the World,"[5] became universally known as "Mount Everest,"
"the roof of the world." Later, when George Leigh Mallory was asked
by a U.S. reporter in 1923 why it was that he wanted to climb Mount
Everest, Mallory produced the legendary reply: "Because it is there"
(Unsworth 1989:100).

   What put Mount Everest "there" at the top of the world was technology and a powerful act of colonial naming, but what put the discourse
of mountaineering into play—what it was that added the language of
climbing the mountain to the meaning of "Mount Everest"—was Mount
Everest's geopolitical location on the frontier of colonial control in
British India. The act of naming "Mount Everest" took place squarely in
the historical period which mountaineering literature now calls the
"Golden Age of Alpine climbing"[6] (Unsworth 1989:73); but in this mid-
nineteenth-century "Golden Age" the summits coveted by mountaineers were all in Europe. The Himalayas belonged to Tibet and Nepal—
boundary sites for British colonial administrators. These were secret
kingdoms to the British, places defined by their inaccessibility and by
the burgeoning need to *know* about them as the competition between
British and Russian interests in imperial expansion intensified in the
region (Hopkirk 1982; Richards 1993:11-22). Thomas Richards has

argued that a dominant mode for managing a developing sense of crisis over the actual administration of an expanding British Empire in the latter nineteenth century was a specific form of symbolic management that he calls "archival confinement" (Richards 1993:11)—that is, the act of amassing data about colonial regions at both a physical and an ethnographic level, tabulating that information, storing it, building up the "imperial archive," finding new and increasingly complicated ways of filing and indexing the archive, and all this as a way of managing— but only on a *symbolic* plane—a sense of administrative drift in the actual practice of British imperial control. Tibet and Nepal, Richards argues, were crisis sites for the imperial archive: they were framed within a discourse of absent information[7] at precisely the moment that the armature of surveillance and knowledge construction was being made to stand in for actual administrative colonial control. As I read it, the inaccessibility of the highest mountain in this secret region on the colonial frontier took on *allegorical* purchase: it became an allegory for the inaccessibility of that information which would provide the material for knowledge construction in the symbolically controlling imperial archive. The English regarded Everest as "the British mountain" (Morris 1993:xiv);[8] and though it was obvious that actually climbing to the top of it would mean little to the imperial archive in terms of useful scientific data, and absolutely nothing to the archive in terms of ethnographic or human information, the idea of a British climber triumphantly *on* Everest—one foot in Nepal, the other in Tibet (Krakauer 1997:5; Gikandi 1997:19), symbolically "the-monarch-of-all-I-survey" (Pratt 1992:201, 205-206)—sutured mountaineering to the principle of imperial paramountcy, and "Everest" became the inevitable site for an allegory of colonial continuance. "English being the first mountaineering race in the world," wrote Lord Curzon, Viceroy of India, "an Englishman ought to be the first on top" (Unsworth 1989:18).

Later, after Peary bagged the North Pole in 1909 and Amundsen the South in 1911, this imperial allegory took on universalizing dimensions. Everest came to be talked about as the earth's "third pole" (Krakauer 1997:14). Francis Younghusband—the famous "Great Game" political officer—called Everest "the embodiment of the physical forces of the world" and said that the attempt to climb it tested nothing less than "the spirit of man" itself (Unsworth 1989:125). George Leigh Mallory claimed that "there is something in me which responds to this mountain and goes out to meet it; . . . the struggle is life itself, upward and forever upward" (Morrow 1986:63). But the original grounding of what it means to climb Mount Everest in the allegory of colonial authority—in a discourse in which symbolic management stands in for the handling of an actual crisis in colonialist information and administration, but can only ever be *symbolic* management—has specific consequences for what the literature of climbing Mount Everest will come to look like.

The first of these consequences is that triumph on the mountain, getting to the top, calls the apparatus of allegory into play—and allegory, as every reader of Edmund Spenser knows, traditionally associates mountaintop vision with the principle of revelation. The principle of revelation informs just about all descriptions of the first sighting of Everest, and it comprises one of the structuring principles of the writing: "We had seen a whole mountain range, little by little, the lesser to the greater," writes George Mallory, "until, incredibly higher in the sky than imagination itself had ventured to dream, the top of Everest itself appeared" (Coburn 1997:23). What remains foundational in the literature of climbing Mount Everest, however, is the extent to which the motif of revelation needs constantly to be *staged*. Mallory's description is characteristic of how writers describe their first sighting of the Mountain—the organizing category is "the sublime" (MacLaren 1984: 58-59; 1985, 90-101)—but what is remarkable about the topos of revelation concerning Mount Everest is the extent to which the revelation of triumph on the mountain is physically overproduced in order explicitly to allegorize the principle of colonial continuance.

The paradigmatic moment of this staging, of the claiming of Everest as an allegory of imperial continuance, is the brilliant First Ascent of Everest in 1953. (This paper will address three "great" moments in which climbing on Mount Everest becomes world news, and this moment historically is the second of those three.) Everyone knows the story: Edmund Hillary of New Zealand and Tenzing Norgay of Nepal summiting from the south col route on 30 May; the news reaching the young Queen Elizabeth the night before her coronation on 2 June; word passing along the street as people gathered patriotically in the postwar early morning to watch the Coronation procession go by; newspapers around the world reporting the triumph—"The Crowning Glory"; "Everest Is Climbed"; "Tremendous News for the Queen"; "Hillary Does It!"; Everest not only conquered, but conquered by the "new Renaissance Men" "of British blood and breed" (Tiffin and Lawson 1994:1; Morris 1993:xi-xii). It hardly needs to be said that "in Britain at least the linking of the two events was regarded almost as an omen, ordained by the Almighty as a special blessing for the dawn of a New Elizabethan Age" (Unsworth 1989:340). What Jan Morris makes clear in her astonishing book entitled *Coronation Everest* (1993), however, is the extent to which this remarkable coincidence between mountaineering paramountcy and imperial coronation depended upon a conscious, staged manufacture and manipulation of this moment of allegorical revelation. James Morris, then a correspondent for the *Times* (and later to become the famous travel writer Jan Morris) writes here about how, in anticipation of stage-managing the Coronation Everest coincidence, he left Base Camp on the morning of 29 May and climbed up to Camp IV, how on the next day he met the triumphant climbers descending to their tents, how he raced down to Base Camp and in a state of exhaustion sent a runner to the transmission office at Namche Bazar, how the transmission went out to the world, but in cipher—"snow conditions bad stop advanced base camp abandoned yesterday stop awaiting improvements"[9]— and thus how it was that triumph on Everest was stage-managed in coincidence with the great imperial moment of Elizabeth's coronation, and why it was that the *Times* of London had its scoop.

My thesis is that this language of triumphalism in climbing Mount Everest is predicated on an allegory of symbolic management for actual colonial relations. The association of this language of triumphalism with the literary device of allegory accounts for the ubiquitous figuration of revelation in the discourse. The practice of symbolic management, however, depends on the assumption that the social and political field is organized by representations—not merely on the assumption that representations have social and political effects—and this assumption gives rise to the anxiety that symbolic management can only ever be symbolic management. This anxiety, when it takes root within the language of triumphalism, has generative purchase: revelations of triumph on Mount Everest are anxiously overproduced, or staged, in the writing. The language of triumph on Everest is grounded in colonial allegory, and this structure of predication accounts for the curious undercurrent of nostalgia that inhabits the writing. For underneath the language of triumph in ascent runs a constant murmur of awareness that symbolic imperial management can never actually do its real political work: nostalgia is the effect of this awareness of crisis in the discourse of colonial continuance. Early figurations of this nostalgia pertain to the space of Mount Everest itself— this is the general tenor of an editorial that appeared in the *Evening*

News in 1920, opposing the idea of the first British attempt on Everest on the grounds that "Some of the mystery of the world will pass when the last secret place in it, the naked peak of Everest shall be trodden by . . . trespassers" (Unsworth 1989:24). But later the focus of nostalgia changes: it becomes not so much the mountain that is to be lamented but the mountaineer who attempts to claim it. This suturing movement—this surrogation of the climber for the place to be climbed, the self for the site of otherness—is in my view precisely what it is that defines the cultural work of mountaineering literature and gives it its social force. To ground this argument, I want to turn to the first of the three great historical moments in which the climbing of Everest made world news.[10]

In 1924 the British made the third of their consecutive attempts at a First Ascent of Everest, this by the north ridge through Tibet. All eyes were on George Leigh Mallory—a vain and careless climber, but wildly handsome, a *Boy's Own Paper* figure adored by Lytton Strachey, and regularly called "Gallahad" in the British press (Unsworth 1989:41-43; Wainright 1997:9-14). On 8 June, this time wearing the oxygen mask that he had previously dismissed as "unsporting, and therefore un-British" (Unsworth 1989:78), Mallory, accompanied by the young and inexperienced Andrew Irvine, set out from Camp VII on the North Shoulder into what has become without doubt the most famous failed summit bid in mountaineering literary history. Noel Odell, clearly the strongest climber of his day, but left behind by Mallory at Camp V to watch,[11] recorded his last sighting of Mallory and Irvine before they disappeared into the mountain, and his description of this last sighting has become the most famous paragraph in mountaineering literature. Notice how Odell employs the language of revelation and then of loss to capture his sense of the moment:

> as I reached the top there was a sudden clearing of the atmosphere above me and I saw the whole summit ridge and final peak of Everest unveiled. I noticed far away on a snow slope leading up to what seemed to me the last step but one from the base of the final pyramid, a tiny object moving and approaching the rock step. A second object followed, and then the first climbed to the top. As I stood intently watching this dramatic appearance, the scene became enveloped in cloud once more. (Unsworth 1989:127)

This passage, I believe, marks the tropological centre of mountaineering literature in its classic, colonialist mode. It fixes the moment of passage from revelation to nostalgia, the passage of the human climber *into* the mountain he tries to climb, the moment where revelation of the mountain becomes coterminous with revelation pertaining to the mountaineering self. This is the moment where the mountain becomes *peopled*, and this by death: this is the transformation that sits at the figurative centre of mountaineering writing. "If anything could mitigate our sorrow in the loss of Mallory and Irvine," wrote a mourning team member, "it is the knowledge that they died somewhere higher than any man has ever been before, and it is possible for their relatives to think of them as lying perhaps even at the summit" (Unsworth 1989:133).[12] The news of Mallory's death, along with Irvine's, produced a national display of mourning in England. The deaths, inevitably, produced fierce debate over the question: Was the sacrifice worth it? An editorial in the *Morning Post* on 24 June 1924 gave the following answer:

> In the days of peace England will always hold some who are not content with the humdrum routine and soft living. The spirit which animated the attacks on Everest is the same as that which prompted arctic and other expeditions, and in earlier times led to the formation of the Empire itself. Who shall say that any of its manifestations are not worth while? Who shall say that its inspiration has not a far-reaching influence on the race? It is certain that it would grow rusty with disuse, and expeditions like the attempt to scale Everest serve to whet the sword of ambition and courage. (Unsworth 1989:141)

In a recent article in *Harper's Magazine*, Bruce Barcott argues that mountaineering has become "the most literary of all sports," and the only participatory sport that ritually insists that some of "its players die" (1996:65). This narrative need for death, in my view, is grounded to the suturing of nostalgia for the mountain to nostalgia for the mountaineer, and in order to locate the ideology of mountaineering literature with a bit more precision I want to identify some additional features, which seem to me definitive of the genre. First, the classic literary texts of mountaineering focus on first ascents and new routes: the values they extol are self-discipline, privation, training, technical knowledge, the ability to improvise and the capacity to carry teamwork to its absolute limit. Second, the organizing genre of these texts is travel, but mountaineering literature differs from imperial travel writing in that mountain climbers journey towards fetishized arrival points that are by definition *unpeopled* by cultural others. Third, mountaineering literature almost uniformly suspends the generative agency of the enabling, "native" guides on climbing expeditions. "Native" figures in climbing writing never really stop being just coolies or porters, and even when they climb as team members on the final pitch, they are never route finders, and they never get there first. Collectively, these features define mountaineering literature as a travel genre in which all transformations are entirely internal: the genre never breaks with the Manichaean logic of separate spheres that Syed Manzurul Islam, in his excellent book *The Ethics of Travel* (1996), sees as the primary obstacle to the latent transformative potential of actual self-other cultural encounters. Instead of cultural encounter, classic mountaineering writing articulates a map; it charts an assault line. But it is axiomatic to the genre that *great* climbing writing produces a map that virtually no reader, as a physical traveller, could ever actually follow.

If the text of "climbing Mount Everest" has an originary grounding in an allegory of colonialism, it should come as no surprise that when colonial political relations reformulate themselves into neo-colonialism, and when most of the potential routes for a first ascent on Everest come to be exhausted, the meaning of "climbing Mount Everest" is going to have to change. The turning point for this change came in 1985 when a wealthy Texas oil tycoon and resort owner named Dick Bass, a man with "limited climbing experience" (Krakauer 1997:21), "cliented" his way up Everest at the age of fifty-five—accompanied by his climbing partner Frank Wells, president of Warner Brothers—under the wing of one of the world's best mountain guides. Bass and Wells thus became the first human beings to reach the top of each of the highest mountains on each of the seven continents on earth, and their climb of Everest became the first in a new line of Everest climbing identities, and the last of the old firsts—though the first Everest paraglider, the first father-and-son success, the first husband-and-wife team to summit remained just a little in the future (Coburn 1997:249). Bass and Wells's book, *Seven Summits* (1986), foundationally changed the meaning of climbing Mount Everest (Dowling 1996:40). As Jon Krakauer puts it, the book "spurred a swarm of other weekend climbers to follow in his guided bootprints, and rudely pulled Everest into the postmodern era" (1997:22).

Bruce Barcott locates one of the central changes in this shift *beyond* colonialism into the neo-colonial moment in mountaineering writing when he notes that "the early Everest books were driven by the climb; now the climbs tend to be driven by the books" (1996:66). In the spring of 1996—and this is the third of those three moments when climbing Mount Everest became world news—300 climbers from thirty separate expeditions gathered at Everest Base Camps, sixteen of those expeditions planning to summit via the Hillary-Tenzing route of 1953.[13] Ten of these expeditions were commercial ones, with clients paying up to $65,000 U.S. apiece for a crack at the top. Two others were national teams seeking their first national ascent. In recent years, with the globalization of sports competition, it has become de rigeur for countries seeking to relocate their position on the postcolonial world stage—for countries hoping to send out the message that they have redefined themselves in relation to a colonial past and have fully arrived within the ambit of unquestionable self-determination—to invest very heavily in trying to put a national team of climbers on Everest. The Canadians did it in 1982: the picture of the Canadian flag on top was given a fanfare in the press, and the two climbers who summited had lunch with Trudeau (Morrow 1986:96). In the spring of 1996 a South African and a Taiwanese team were attempting to stage *their* moment of postcolonial nationalist triumph on Everest (Wilkinson 1997:45). The following year an Indonesian national team and a Malaysian national team would try for their own picture of the flag on the summit, but those teams would be clienting their way up under the tutelage of highly paid Western climbing guides (Child 1997; Wilkinson 1987:45). In the spring of 1996, several of the Everest climbing clients arrived at Base Camp with publishing contracts already in hand. One of those clients—a wealthy social climber, Sandy Hill Pittman— posted daily messages to the *Today* show through the NBC Interactive website (Dowling 1996:36). School children across the U.S. followed Hill Pittman's progress on the mountain by clicking on the "KidsPeak" icon on the Global Schoolhouse Net homepage, and carried out a series of integrated pedagogical activities across the curriculum which were designed to help them identify with Hill Pittman as she bagged the summit.[14] Hill Pittman's was already, as *Outside Online* reported, "the most-watched commercial expedition of all time" (Balf et al.).

Climbing Everest by the Hillary-Tenzing route has become big business. Nepal now charges $70,000 U.S. per expedition for a permit, plus an additional $10,000 for each climber after the seventh (Coburn 1997:38-39). Climbing Mount Everest by the Hillary-Tenzing route has also become blasé. The route gets called "the yak route" (Unsworth 1989:514), and it involves only forty feet of technical climbing, this near the top of the mountain at the famous "Hillary Step." Difficult climbing on the route takes place just above Base Camp, however, in the Khumbu glacier icefall. By 1996 the Khumbu icefall had been transformed into a toll route: a British team had it roped and laddered, and other expeditions paid the British $2,000 apiece in order to pass through (Krakauer 1997:76). Beyond the icefall, the significant difficulties on Everest are really the height and the weather: climbers on Everest cover more vertical feet above 25,000 feet, in the oxygen-scarce "Death Zone" (Krakauer 1996:5), than they would on any other mountain, and storms can come on suddenly. To deal with this problem, the commercial expeditions employed top-notch Western climbing guides and paid them between $20,000 and $25,000 each; they also employed top-notch Sherpa climbing guides to do exactly what the Western guides were doing, but for a tenth of the salary (Coburn 1997:33; Krakauer 1997:44-45). Jon Krakauer records how Scott Fisher, expedition leader of the commercial outfit called Mountain Madness, promoted the yak route: "We've got the big E figured out, we've got it totally wired. These days, I'm telling you, we've built a yellow brick road to the summit" (1997:66).

On 10 May, twenty-nine climbers from three separate expeditions attempted a summit bid. But Lopsang Jangbu Sherpa, who was supposed to fix guide ropes on the summit ridge on the morning of the final assault, did not arrive at the summit ridge before the client climbers: he had exhausted himself the day before carrying Hill Pittman's satellite phone from Camp III to Camp IV (where it no longer worked), and by short-roping Sandy Hill Pittman on summit day up the slope like a water skier.[15] With their expedition leaders lagging behind, client climbers waited too long at the South Summit for permission to forge ahead, then clustered in long traffic jams at the Hillary Step, and then partied too long on the top of the mountain waiting for the expedition leaders to come up and tell them that it was O.K. now to get off; an unpredictable storm blew in; eight people died in the blizzard, two others lost their fingers and their noses to frostbite; and for the third time Everest became genuinely global news once again.

In the riot of condemnation, rumination and debate that followed May 1996 on Everest—in *Life* magazine, *Men's Journal*, *Vogue*, *Outside*, *Time*, *Newsweek*, on web sites, in townhall debates, and in Jon Krakauer's best-selling book *Into Thin Air*[16]— a central problematic emerges, and the general tenor of this problematic marks the moment at which mountaineering writing about Everest enters into the ambit of discursive *post*coloniality. "The commercialized trips and the over-crowding are what caused this thing," said Edmund Hillary: "it was inevitable"; it showed "disrespect for the mountain" (Dowling 1996:41; Krakauer 1997:34). Special condemnation accrued to the practice of taking guided clients beyond the point of self-sufficiency—past the point where they were able to get down from the death zone if their oxygen ran out. Much was made of the fact that clients paying $65,000 apiece thought they were paying for the summit, not for the opportunity of doing the work that would get them there. Professional mountaineers pointed out again and again that clients who did not haul loads, did not prepare camps and did not *plan* not only became dependent on their guides but lost the enabling sense of teamwork. Much criticism focused on the cavalier attitude displayed by a Japanese team on the mountain's north side, which continued on to the summit without stopping to assist three dying climbers from Ladakh—"morality," said one mountaineer, "goes away when it becomes a commercial enterprise." Everest, it was agreed, had fallen subject to what one commentator called "Disney-fication." Blind, ambitious "me-firstism" had become the mountain's dominant mode.[17]

My argument to this point has been that what makes Everest the paramount object of mountaineering desire within popular culture is not simply its height but its history. In classic mountaineering mode, to climb Mount Everest is to enter the space of narrative—narrative that allegorizes colonial continuance and control. This is because the inaccessibility of Everest stands in for the paucity of information that can be captured for the imperial archive about a "last secret place" located in a power vacuum on the colonial frontier; and so to triumph on Mount Everest is allegorically to know this information and to deploy it in a structure of symbolic management for colonial anxieties about administration and control. But this is *only* symbolic management; the triumph of imperial revelation has to be anxiously staged, and it produces nostalgia for the place that triumphalism has transformed. The social role of classic mountaineering literature is to suture that nostalgia for the mountain to nostalgia for the mountaineer. Death on the mountain becomes the paradigmatic and paradoxical figure for the consolidation of imperial authority in a narrative of triumph and information. Since Everest climbers seek their triumphs at a point above human dwelling, in a place defined by its exclusion of cultural others, Everest travel writing also ensures that all transformations of the imperial traveller take place only within the contained and culturally unconnecting ambit of the self.

But when Everest gives way to "Disney-fication," a new climbing subjectivity emerges, and writing about Everest abandons the narrative of imperial allegory for the genre of critique. The old colonial question—Who does Everest belong to?—becomes postcolonial, self-reflective and brooding: "Who belongs on Everest?" (Cahill 1997:17). Everest's paradigmatic inaccessibility, its figuration of otherness without cultural others, becomes violently translated—by commodification, by commerce, by the staging of postmodern nationalist arrival—into exactly its opposite: Everest becomes a main street, a traffic jam, a ship-of-fools party on the rooftop of the world. Triumphs remain stageable, but triumph allegorizes nothing: triumph on Everest is too easily staged. Unsurprisingly, a recent $65,000 Everest client is now suing for his money back because his expedition leader *failed* to get him to the summit (Krakauer, "Into Thin Air":23; "*Outside* Symposium on Everest"). Nostalgia for Everest also remains rampant—but it takes two forms, and they are incommensurable. The first is a nostalgia for Everest's return to the imperial archive: it was as though the summit was "like some children's storybook paradise," writes Tim Cahill (1997:17), "where only the pure of heart and the well-intentioned were admitted." The second is a nostalgia for an Everest *before* imperial history. But for mountain climbers, this second form of nostalgia is impossible and self-annihilating: it is nostalgia for a perfect, untravelled, non-signifying Everest—an Everest before mountaineering passed through its mirror phase into desire and the Symbolic order, before climbing consolidated its self into a "culture of ascent" (Krakauer 1997:20). Even death on Everest has lost its suturing power. The bodies of dead climbers now litter the standard assault routes on Everest, and climbers take photos; but dead mountaineers now can never quite *become* the mountain—mourning is trivial and the suture will not take place. Climbing Mount Everest still carries enormous symbolic capital— the capacity to consecrate—but only for those benighted national administrators and those calculating corporate entities sufficiently distant from contemporary Everest realities to know what climbing Mount Everest, now, really means. Mountaineering professionals are fast deserting Everest—not at the level of their labour, for there is still money to be made from guiding. Their desertion takes place at the level of meaning. Everest, as imperial allegory, no longer carries a capacity to transform.

My thesis for this paper is that this current moment of suspended allegorization—this moment that frames the question "What does it means to write about Mount Everest?"—is capable of lending unusual, and disturbing, clarity to the inescapably contingent but nevertheless oppositional concept of "postcolonialism" itself. What defines this moment is its predicative stasis—for the genre of mountaineering literature, that is, but not for the many other modalities in which "Everest" can be thought about and represented. This predicative stasis rests on a structural opposition, one that seems unresolvable from within. On the one hand, it is impossible for mountaineering literature to ground a critique of present (neo-colonial) climbing practices on Everest without drawing on the discourse of classic mountaineering: to critique the present is implicitly to endorse the imperial allegory of Everest's colonial past. On the other hand, it is impossible for mountaineering literature in its current postcolonial moment to frame a critique of classic Everest climbing practices without implicity endorsing the neo-colonial discursive contract that underwrites the dominant idea of "Everest" in the present. Critiques of *present* modalities for being on Everest—that is, critiques of present forms of commodification, of postmodern nationalism and of privileged individual access on Everest—cannot help but reiterate the logic of a *past* colonialist discourse: a discourse of "Western" prerogative, of border patrolling, of exclusivist professionalism and the grand narrative of imperial meanings. At the same time, critiques of the *past*, high-imperial modalities for being on Everest cannot help but underwrite a narrative of presentist permissiveness, where cross-culturalism by individual volition, and by the wealthy, becomes definitive of travel in the contact zones, where nations join together in the making of freely negotiated but profoundly unequal commercial relations that produce overwhelming environmental damage and translate entire populations into service-industry providers and where a class-based identification with a surrogate, travelling self in the virtual community of Internet participation becomes foundational and normative in a new, postmodern pedagogy for engaging with the world.

In postcolonial critical theory, one of the terms now being used to identify a predicative stasis of this kind is the term "complicity/ resistance dialectic" (see Gikandi 1996:123-25)—a schema in which resistance against a single and specific axis of domination within the multiple and interwoven axes that comprise a discursive formation (race, class, gender, sexuality, etc.) entails complicity with at least one other axis of domination within that discourse. And one of the most urgent debates within postcolonial critical theory is over how we are to understand the social productivity of writing that seems framed within this complicity/resistance dialectic—a zero-sum game, or an ambivalent but generative way to the production of social change? In closing this paper I want to suggest that this postcolonial moment of predicative stasis, of complicity and resistance, in the genre of Everest mountaineering literature might itself allegorize the structure of at least one form of professional postcolonialism as it seeks its own triumphs in university institutions today. In this allegory, the "native guide" that Helen Tiffin (1978:147-48) places at the centre of the paradigmatic colonialist travel narrative—the journey from the "sick heart of Empire" to the transformative colonial frontier—has become translated by institutional postcolonialism into the "non-native" *academic* professional, whose job it is to client students up the slopes of cultural otherness, breathing theory as they reach for the top. In this allegory, the idea of marginality has been transformed into a mountain: it is marginality itself, says Spivak, that postcolonialism has commodified (Young 1995:163). Cultural difference, in this allegory, has been translated into a celebration of the borderless. Cross-culturalism has been made virtual on the Internet frontier. The pedagogy of cross-culturalism has surrendered into travel writing. And genuine, postcolonial encounter has frozen on the mountainside—a photo-opportunity for social and literary criticism, and then criticism climbs on.

It is conventional to end a paper that describes a problem by volunteering a solution, but in lieu of that difficult work I want to provide four very brief snapshots of how the complicity/resistance dialectic of climbing Mount Everest has actually been navigated. In what follows, I will draw only on Canadian examples—not simply "because they are there" but also because, collectively, they say something about the curious compromises that can attend a rhetoric of oppositional self-emplacement, and about the unexpected fissures that can fall out of a rhetoric of seamless compliance, when the locus of representation is that ambivalently positioned middle ground between the massive binaries of colonizer and colonized—a middle ground which currently supports many critical discussions of how Canadian invader-settler cultures might be positioned within the binaristic tropologies that are commonly used to articulate imperial relations. In what follows, one might trace the beginnings of my own allegory of disciplinary postcolonialism in its current seizure of narrative contradiction.

The first snapshot comes from 1997, and features two Calgary climbers—Jamie Clarke and Alan Hobson—who managed to fund their Everest expedition through sponsorship from a multinational real estate company and a U.S.-based computer firm. The "Colliers Lotus Notes Everest Expedition" of 1997 maintained a daily website that permitted "subscribers" to follow the climbers' progress towards triumph:

Clarke and Hobson summited on 23 May, two of twenty-two climbers to summit on that day. Twenty-five employees of the real estate firm holidayed at Base Camp as the Canadians reached the top. "Everest," said the Chairman of Colliers International on the promotional web page: "the teamwork, commitment and dedication it involves—is symbolic of the challenges we face day-to-day in our business. Overcoming obstacles, using weaknesses to find strength, operating as a team in pursuit of a grand vision—this is what the Colliers Lotus Notes Everest Expedition is all about." "Through team work," added the Everest project manager for Colliers International, "we are well positioned to provide our clients with first-rate commercial real estate services in markets worldwide" ("Colliers Lotus Notes"). After the climb, *Macleans* magazine did an exclusive feature of the Canadian ascent. "The story of the climb by Clarke and Hobson is one of determination, bravery, teamwork—and very high danger," wrote *Macleans*. Hobson and Clarke contributed a brief piece of their own to *Macleans*: "Our adventure safely concluded," they declared, "our goal will be to demonstrate how the lessons we learned on Everest can be applied to the world of business and the business of life" (Gikandi 1997:20).

The second snapshot comes from 1986, and it features the second Canadian to summit on Everest—Patrick Morrow. Morrow was also the second, after the Dick Bass and Frank Wells team, to climb to the top of the highest mountain on each of the seven continents in the world, and he wrote about it in a book entitled *Beyond Everest: Quest for the Seven Summits* (1986). In that book, Morrow argues persuasively that Bass and Wells bagged the seven summits first because they had no need to seek corporate sponsors. "Bass and Wells brought to the project the type of élan that had been lacking in the climbing world since the days of steam, when climbing was a rich man's sport," wrote Morrow. "[They] were able to take an important time-saving shortcut because they did not have to search for sponsors. They surrounded themselves with the best climbing guides available, who led them in safety up the mountains and prepared their camps and meals" (1986:96). Morrow also argues that Bass and Wells's *idea* of the seven summits was faulty. Morrow argues that, instead of climbing Australia's highest mountain, Kosciusko, Bass and Wells should have climbed the highest mountain in Austral*asia*—Carstenz Pyramid, on Irian Jaya. Morrow went on to climb Carstenz Pyramid: left to the vagaries of implication is the argument that Morrow's placement of "second" in the "seven summits" competition should retroactively now be upgraded to a "first."

The third snapshot features a 1997 novel by the Halifax writer J.A. Wainwright: its title is *A Deathful Ridge*. Wainwright retells the story of George Leigh Mallory and Andrew Irvine's famous 1924 climb, but this time with a difference. In Wainwright's retelling, the narrative of a glorious British failure on Everest explodes into a cluster of alternative narrative possibilities about what really happened on the mountain, each of them opening into new ways of thinking about colonial history and the "rock of Empire" (1997:30). The most interesting of these narrative possibilities, for my purposes, is the suggestion, made early in the book, that on Everest Mallory actually *didn't* die: instead, he went crazy with the mixture of ambition and elevation, whacked his iceaxe into Irvine's head and had to be squired away by his expedition leaders to a secret hideout in Wales.

The fourth and final snapshot comes from 1947 and features Earl Denman, a Canadian engineer who made his way to Rhodesia and then, with no real climbing experience behind him, nonetheless decided to climb Mount Everest, alone and in secret (Unsworth 1989:246-50). "[I]t was always the distant heights which fascinated me and drew me to them in spirit," wrote Denman in his 1954 book *Alone to Everest*. "[I was] determined to see at least one major dream through to fulfilment" (cited in Unsworth 1989:246). And so without a permit and with scarcely any credible climbing equipment, Denman made his way to Darjeeling, hired just two Sherpas—one of them the young Tenzing Norgay himself—and actually managed to climb with them to the foot of the North Col, before being driven back by the inevitable storms. Denman set out to climb Mount Everest again the next year, but this time the authorities were on to him about his lack of permit and none of the Sherpas was willing to risk another maniacal run at the mountain, even though Tenzing Norgay, it is said, still found the idea of an unofficial attempt deeply attractive. Walt Unsworth, author of the book *Everest: The Ultimate Book of the Ultimate Mountain* (1989), describes what happens next. "He returned home to Rhodesia," writes Unsworth (1989:250), "wrote a book about his adventures, and was planning to attempt the mountain through Nepal in 1953 when the news came through of the British success. He turned his back on the mountain for ever."

Notes

1 This paper was originally given at the "Commonwealth in Canada" Conference, sponsored by the Canadian Association for Commonwealth Literature
and Language Studies, and held at Wilfrid Laurier University, November
1997. My thanks to Rowland Smith and Gary Boire, organizers of that conference, and to Guy Beauregard, Alan Lawson, Ian MacLaren, Nima
Naghibi, Cheryl Suzack, Paul Tiessen, Asha Varadharajan and Jo-Ann Wallace for helpful commentary along the route. The paper was subsequently
published in a special issue of *Canadian Literature* (58 [Autumn 1998],
15-41), edited by Neil Besner and dedicated to Bill New, who always summits. For guidance into the practice of mountain climbing, and thus into its
literature, I owe enormous thanks to two extraordinary mountaineers,
Kerry Best for introducing me to climbing and to David Cockle for thereafter being my mentor and guide. The phrase "the culture of ascent" is Jon
Krakauer's (1997, 20).

2 The definitive document on the Great Trigonometrical Survey is Edney
(1997). Bilham (1997) provides useful information on the technical measurement of Mount Everest's height. Jon Krakauer's chapter "A Mountain
Higher than Everest" (in 1990:116-29) offers background information on
the Everest legend (much of it repeated in Krakauer, 1997:13-14); see also
Unsworth 1989:especially 2-24, 541-50). Hopkirk discusses the political
background. Baber (1996:147-51, 246-49) provides a history for trigonometrical survey in India going back to the early eighteenth century, and
explains the relation of this practice to topographical and statistical surveys
in the building of an empire of science for British India. Bayley (1996:
307-309) discusses the "extraordinary bureaucratic chaos and conflict" that
attended the Great Trigonometrical Survey and points out that it did little
to serve utilitarian aims in British administration in India—instead, according to Bayley (1996), the Survey was "a huge exercise in Newtonian triumphalism."

3 Krakauer (1990) points out that the height of Everest was "pegged" in
1975 at 29,029 ft. by a Chinese team; Bilham notes that an Italian/Chinese
team in 1992 corrected this to 20,023 ft.

4 Edney makes clear that this narrative of Everest's "discovery" as the world's
highest mountain is indeed legend, and that Radhanath Sickdhar's role in
this "discovery" was not as Krakauer, Bilham and others have described it.
"[T]radition incorrectly describes the computations which established
Peak XV in the Himalayas as the world's highest mountain," he writes
(1997:262).

5 Morrow mistakenly reports that Sagarmatha means "Churning Stick of the
Ocean of Existence" and that Chomolungma means "Goddess Mother of the
Wind" (1986:62-63). Unsworth concludes that "the evidence rather suggests that the Survey of India knew all about Chomolungma [as the mountain's name] but chose to ignore it" (1989:548); he further notes that the
name Sagarmatha is a very recent invention, promoted by the Nepalese
government.

6 Irwin notes that the British Alpine Club was formed in 1858, and that "the growth of a literature of mountaineering was contemporaneous with the growth of the sport." He also notes that the association of mountaineering with scientific study, which begins with the natural philosophers in the early nineteenth century, continues to prevail in the literature: "*The Alpine Journal* has retained its original subtitle, 'a record of mountain adventure and scientific observation'" (1950:xv-xvi).

7 Bayley elaborates the concept of the "information order" for British India, and he examines the processes by which "information" about India—"observations perceived at a relatively low level of conceptual definition"—was transformed under various colonial modes into units of "knowledge"—"socially organised and taxonomised information" (1996:3-4, n. 9). Bayley argues that in India between 1780 and 1870, the British "could not count on an inflow of 'affective knowledge' and so were forced to manipulate the informational systems of their Hindu and Mughal predecessors" in order to manage their crisis of authority: this involved a range of procedures for gathering information and translating it into knowledge, such as the creation of "a new type of native informant." "The statistical movement, which gathered pace after 1830, had a powerful impact" (Bayley 1996:7-8) on the making of that "information order."

8 Sir John Hunt, leader of the successful 1953 British expedition to Everest, writes: "It was as if an agreement existed in those years, by which it was tacitly understood that certain of the big peaks were the special concern of climbers of a particular nation" (1954:6).

9 This was code for the message: "Summit of Everest reached on May 29 by Hillary and Tenzing" (Morris 1993:117).

10 Although I have attempted in note 1 to map out the trajectory of this paper's progress, I want at this point to acknowledge, and to thank, the two anonymous readers who refereed this paper for its first publication in *Canadian Literature*. I have found their comments extraordinarily helpful. These readers located a number of alternative routes by which this paper might have attempted its theoretical assault on Everest writing: specifically, through a meditation on melancholia and mourning (in the footsteps of Freud and Lacan); through an examination of the generic affinities between mountaineering writing and both "the wider stylistics of exploration" and the "production of visual images through sketching and photography"; through a consideration of masculinities and homoerotics in mountaineering and exploration writing (see Lisa Bloom's excellent monograph *Gender on Ice* [1993]); and through the "complex spaces of transculturation involved in portering" (see Butz 1995). One reader, accurately I think, argues that the concept of "symbolic management," in the paper, needs belaying: "for Bordieu symbolic power is to be taken as seriously as administrative or bureaucratic power." Clearly, the troublesome and powerful relations between productivity and constraint within narrative acts of symbolic management, and between narrative representation and broader modalities of social management, remain very big questions for critical theory, but my own thinking on symbolic management—thinking which has yet to summit—has been advanced by Mary Poovey's examination of

the structure of "corrective substitution" in Dickens's *Our Mutual Friend*. Poovey considers the ways in which social anxieties about financial instability and race, for example, are addressed through symbolic stabilizations of "woman as other," and she argues that at a certain point the "neat parallelism" of Dickens's narrative founders in productive contradiction. Exactly how such forms of narrative contradiction are to be read as productive is not so clear, and the elaboration of this problematic obviously needs to be grounded and theorized. Homi Bhabha's speculations on the productivity of narrative contradictions through their circulation in the "time-lag" of social-symbolic ordering" (1995:337ff.) may provide a useful place to begin this theoretical work.

11 Unsworth argues that Mallory's insistence that Irvine accompany him in the summit bid, rather than Odell, cannot be accounted for in the logic of climbing. "Mallory," Unsworth claims, "chose Irvine partly on aesthetic grounds" (1989:124).

12 Everest is a changing text; its stories submit to constant rewriting. In May of 1999 a commercial expedition, led by the U.S. guide Eric Simonson, and sponsored by the BBC, the PBS television show *Nova* and Lincoln-Mercury, climbed to 27,000 feet on Mount Everest's northeast ridge in order to follow up on a clue, dating to 1975, on the location of Andrew Irvine's body. Instead, climbing guide Conrad Anker found the astonishingly well-preserved body of George Mallory. The discovery scarcely provided comfort to Mallory's surviving relatives, especially after photographs of Mallory's frozen corpse, its head fused into the mountainside, appeared in *Newsweek*. Mallory's seventy-eight-year-old son John excoriated the climbers; Sir Edmund Hillary voiced his disgust. Simonson is reported to have responded as follows: "We all think this is a totally cool picture. . . . We were kind of surprised people were bummed" (Burrough 1999:284-95, 347-50; see also the special issue of *Climbing* Magazine [1999]).

13 The most comprehensive, and most interesting, account of the 1996 Everest "tragedy" is Krakauer's book *Into Thin Air* (1997), which contains important corrections to his 1996 article of the same title. Beidelman (1996), Dowling (1996), Kennedy (1996) and Wilkinson (1997) tell different facets of the story, and I have drawn the information in the following paragraphs from all of these sources.

14 The GlobalNet Foundation's webpage—"Linking Kids Around the World!"—is "a virtual meeting place where people of all ages and backgrounds can collaborate, interact, develop, publish, and discover resources." Its main objectives are to promote Internet use in schools, with a view to teaching "students to become active learners and information managers" and to "encourage business, government, school, higher education, and community partnerships for on-going collaboration" (http://www.gsn.org/who/gshistory.html). "Education today," claims the GSN web page on the GSN Program Vision, "is severely missing the mark. We suspect that one solution to having a more effective school lies in a more advanced communications system, including the use of electronic tools." The GSN is a "non-profit consortium comprised of educators around the world," and it "provides its services to all schools *free* of charge." Its "Executive Sponsors" are Advanced

Network & Services, Cisco Systems, MCI Corporation, Microsoft and Network Solutions; its "Associate Sponsor" list includes Canon Communications, Eastman Kodak and Pacific Bell (http://www.gsh.org/who/partner/spon.html). The GSN KidsPeak web page offered "a real-time, day-by-day virtual web adventure of climber Sandy Hill Pittman and her team as they try to ascend Mount Everest along the same route of Sir Edmund Hillary (http://gsn.org/past/kidspeak/index.html). The list of the Virtual Field Trip activities for Kidspeak included the following: "Imitate the distance of Sandra's trek: track how far Sandra Hill Pittman has trekked, round trip, and translate that to a number of times around the school track"; "Develop a [web] page that tells how you are using the information you learn from Sandy's reports"; "Have students research the cost of an expedition. Who are the Sherpas? What are the costs associated with feeding all the trekkers? Where does the food come from? Does it generate revenue for the local merchants?"; "Tell students to consider the amount of money put into the local economy as a result of the expeditions" (http://www.gsn.org/past/kidspeak/procon.html).

15 Sandy Hill Pittman was attempting to be the first woman to claim the "seven summits," and had a contract with Chronicle Books (Mitchell) for a book entitled *Seven Summits of My Soul*. In the debate about what went wrong in May 1996—a debate carried out almost entirely by men—Hill Pittman became "a lightning rod for criticism" (Mitchell): the "Susan Lucci of the continuing Everest soap opera" (Wilkinson 1997:101-103). Wilkinson correctly points out that the debate was—and is—inflected with "more than a hint of sexism" (1997:101). I have not engaged with the dynamics of gender in this paper; but in anticipation of the allegorical relation this paper later posits between Everest in May 1996 and the field of postcolonial studies, I cite the following from Gikandi: "students of colonial discourse and postcolonial theory do not know what to do with the women of empire—whether these women are European or native. They don't know how to read them within the project of the Enlightenment and colonial modernity, nor do they know how to explain or rationalize female subjectivity and institutional function beyond the existence of women as objects of male discourse of desire" (1996:121).

16 See Wilkinson 1997:43. An ABC "docudrama" on the climb aired on 9 November 1997. The *Edmonton Journal T.V. Times* writes: "It was the deadliest ascent of Mount Everest in history—claiming eight lives, including two renowned mountaineers. The 1996 saga is now chronicled in *Into Thin Air: Death on Everest*, a TV movie based on the book by Jon Krakauer (1997). The drama teams *Veronica's Closet*'s Christopher McDonald (as Krakauer) with Peter Horton (*thirtysomething*) and Nathaniel Parker (*David*), as ill-fated expedition leaders Scott Fisher and Rob Hall. An IMAX film entitled *Everest*, shot by David Breashears and narrated by Liam Neeson, has made the 1996 Everest "tragedy" one of the best-known international stories of the 1990s. The film has become the most popular IMAX movie ever made.

17 The information in this paragraph is drawn from the "*Outside* Symposium on Everest," involving climbers Alex Lowe, Charlotte Fox, Ed Visteurs, John Cooley, Al Reed and Todd Burleson, and moderated by Mark Bryant.

References

Baber, Zaheer
  1996   *The Science of Empire: Scientific Knowledge, Civilization, and Colonial Rule in India.* New York: SUNY Press.
Balf, Todd, with Martin Dugard and Alison Osius
  1995   "Climbing: Race You, Pops." *Outside Magazine* (June). http://outside. starwave.com/magazine/0695/6di_clim.html
Barcott, Bruce
  1996   "Cliffhangers: The Fatal Descent of the Mountain-Climbing Memoir." *Harper's Magazine* (August):64-68.
Bass, Dick, and Frank Wells with Rick Ridgeway
  1986   *Seven Summits.* New York: Warner.
Bayley, C.A.
  1996   *Empire & Information: Intelligence Gathering and Social Communication in India, 1780-1870.* Cambridge: Cambridge University Press.
Beidleman, Neil
  1996   "The Last Step: A Mount Everest Survivor Tells His Story." *Climbing* 163 (15 September-1 November1):102-103.
Bhabha, Homi K.
  1995   "In a Spirit of Calm Violence." In Gyan Prakash, ed., *After Colonialism: Imperial Histories and Postcolonial Displacements*, 326-43. Princeton: Princeton University Press.
Bilham, Roger
  1997   "The Elusive Height of Everest." In Broughton Coburn, *Everest: Mountain Without Mercy*, 26-27. New York: National Geographical Society.
Bloom, Lisa
  1993   *Gender on Ice: American Ideologies of Polar Expeditions.* Minneapolis and London: University of Minnesota Press.
Burrough, Bryan
  1999   "The Riddle of Everest." *Vanity Fair* (September):284-95.
Butz, David
  1995   "Legitimating Porter Regulation in an Indigenous Mountain Community in Northern Pakistan." *Environment and Planning D: Society and Space* 13:381-414.
Cahill, Tim
  1997   "Sorrow on Top of the World." In Broughton Coburn, *Everest: Mountain Without Mercy*, 13-17. New York: National Geographical Society.
Child, Greg
  1997   "Everest a Year Later: Lessons in Futility." *Outside Magazine* (May). http://outside.starwave.com/magazine/0597/9705fechild.html
Climbing Magazine
  1999   Special issue, no. 188, September 15.

Coburn, Broughton
1997 *Everest: Mountain Without Mercy.* New York: National Geographical Society.
"Colliers Lotus Notes Everest Expedition." http://trerice.imicro.com/ OVERVIEW/EVEREST

Dowling, Claudia Glenn
1996 "Death on the Mountain." *Life* (August):32-46.

Edney, Matthew H.
1997 *Mapping an Empire: The Geographical Construction of British India, 1765-1843.* Chicago: University of Chicago Press.

Gikandi, Simon
1996 *Maps of Englishness: Writing Identity in the Culture of Colonialism.* New York: Columbia University Press.
1997 "High Drama: Two Canadians Take on Everest—and Live to Tell the Tale." *Macleans,* 7 July:16-20.

Hopkirk, Peter
1982 *Trespassers on the Roof of the World.* Los Angeles: Jeremy P. Tarcher.

Hunt, Sir John
1954 *The Conquest of Everest.* New York: Dutton.

Irwin, William Robert, ed.
1950 *Challenge: An Anthology of the Literature of Mountaineering.* New York: Columbia University Press.

Islam, Syed Manzurul
1996 *The Ethics of Travel: From Marco Polo to Kafka.* Manchester and New York: Manchester University Press.

Kennedy, Michael
1996 "By the Book." *Climbing* 163 (15 September-1 November):94-101; 147-56.
"KidsPeak: For Kids Who Want to Be Part of Everest Assault '96." http://www.gsn.org/past/kidspeak/index.html

Krakauer, Jon
1990 *Eiger Dreams: Ventures among Men and Mountains.* New York: Anchor.
1996 "Into Thin Air." *Outside Magazine* (September). http://outside. starwave.com/magazine/0996/9609feev3.html
1997 *Into Thin Air: A Personal Account of the Mt. Everest Disaster.* Villard: New York.

MacLaren, I.S.
1984 "Retaining Captaincy of the Soul: Response to Nature in the First Franklin Expedition." *Essays in Canadian Writing* 28 (Spring):57-92.
1985 "The Aesthetic Map of the North, 1845-1859." *Arctic* 38, 2 (June):89-103.

Mitchell, Deborah
"Pitons are served." http://www.salonmagazine.com/june97/media/ media970611.html)

Morris, Jan
  1993 *Coronation Everest*. London: Boxtree. Originally published in 1958.
Morrow, Patrick
  1986 *Beyond Everest: Quest for the Seven Summits*. Scarborough: Camden
        House.
        "*Outside* Symposium on Everest." *Outside Online*. http://outside.
        starwave.com/peaks/fischer/slesymp.html
Pratt, Mary Louise
  1992 *Imperial Eyes: Travel Writing and Transculturation*. London: Rout-
        ledge.
        "Real Estate Firm on Top of the World." http://www.infotech.co.nz/
        february_10/nxcoll.html
Richards, Thomas
  1993 *The Imperial Archive: Knowledge and the Fantasy of Empire*. London
        and New York: Verso.
        "Spaulding & Slye, Lotus Help Scale Mt. Everest." http://www.sfbt.
        com/boston/stories/052697/tidbits.html
  1857 "Tea in India—Deodhunga, the Highest Mountain in the World." In
        The Illustrated London News (15 August). Rpt. http://www.dataindia.
        com/darj.htm
Tiffin, Chris, and Alan Lawson
  1994 "Introduction: The Textuality of Empire." In *De-scribing Empire: Post-
        colonialism and Textuality*, 1-11. London: Routledge.
Tiffin, Helen
        "Towards Place and Placelessness: Two Journey Patterns in Common-
        wealth Literature." In C.D. Narasimhaiah, ed., *Awakened Conscience:
        Studies in Commonwealth Literature*, 146-63. New Delhi: Sterling.
Unsworth, Walt
  1989 *Everest: The Ultimate Book of the Ultimate Mountain*. London: Grafton.
Wainright, J.A.
  1997 *A Deathful Ridge: A Novel of Everest*. Oakville: Mosaic.
Wilkinson, Peter
  1997 "Everest: The Aftermath." *Men's Journal* (May):40-46, 101-105.
Young, Robert
  1995 *Colonial Desire: Hybridity in Theory, Culture and Race*. London and
        New York: Routledge.

5

Afrikaners, Africans and Afriquas: *Métissage* in Breyten Breytenbach's *Return to Paradise*

Johan U. Jacobs

In a speech at the University of Stellenbosch in 1990, Breyten Breytenbach identified himself as an "Afrikaner, South African and African" (1996:32). At a conference on the theme of "Identity and Differences" in Senegal the previous year, he had defined identity in terms of place; he said: "Perhaps the deciding factor is not *who* you are, but *where* you find yourself. Which . . . implies that identity is circumstantial and relative" (1993:73-74). Breytenbach has since qualified his claim to a triple identity by describing himself as "an Afrikaans-speaking whitish male South African African temporarily living outside the continent" (1993:xiii). At a conference on "Home: A Place in the World" in New York in 1990, he again asserted his Africanness:

> Exile has brought it home to me that I'm African. If I live in Europe most of the time, it is not as a participant but an observer, an underground activist for Africa. . . . I consciously try to shape my work, even the expressions of a private or peculiar idiom, as contributing to the awareness of Africa. (1996:47)

Breytenbach has admitted, however, that "[t]o write about Africa is to go on a journey, to be confronted by the endlessly unfolding conjugations of an elusive reality" (1996:124). In *A Season in Paradise* (1985) he describes his three-month return visit to South Africa in

1973 after thirteen years of exile from the country of his birth. During the flight from Paris to Johannesburg he rhapsodizes over the thought of the continent below. In contrast to the Cartesian mind of Europe, he postulates a homogeneous Africa of primary orality:

> Africa is eternal. . . . Man has always been in Africa. The African has no need to know his origin or his destination. He has no need to know because he has never labored under the misapprehension that he doesn't know. To know, to discover, to conquer and to tame and to rule—these are European illnesses. (1985:42-43)

Also in contrast to Africa, Breytenbach describes South Africa, the apartheid state symbolized by Robben Island, the prison off its southernmost tip, as an excretion: "In history," he says, "there was a country with the name of Africa. Between the feet of that country, on the ground, like an unmentionable thing . . . there was a region named Shit Africa. . . . And even shittier than that, like an aborted fetus, there was an island . . . The Island of the Robbed" (1985:82).

Breytenbach's idealization of Africa and his abhorrence of South Africa are, however, by no means absolute. Although in his writing he has configured South Africa variously as *"No man's land"* (1996:160), "Nowhere Land, Utopia" (1996:135) or "St Albino . . . land of Whiteness, the prison of laws and taboos" (1986:55), he has also projected the country of his birth as a paradise from which he has been barred. South Africa, he has said, is for him therefore "a paradoxical space . . . a zone of pain and conflict" (1996:160). A comparable ambivalence can be seen in Breytenbach's view of Africa; rather than simply representing a cultural topography of myth and magic and epistemological wholeness, Africa too has become a paradoxical zone for him. In 1982, he wrote:

> I feel at one with Africa, with the African peoples, with the resilience and the absurdity and the fragility and the poverty and the decadence and the inadaptability and the garishness of her cultures. . . . Africa humiliated. African in exile. Africa with rotten and greedy rulers, and beggar economies. (1986:209)

In June 1992, at a conference in Leiden, he still subscribed to his essentialist—and uncomfortable—view that "to the Africans the world is a complex but unchanging environment into which you are born and where you adapt, posited on metamorphosis, because we are interchangeable with the land and vegetation and animals and spirits" (1996:89). But four months later, in a speech in St. Louis, Missouri, he felt compelled to acknowledge and address the Western "depiction of present-day Africa as a continent where dying is a mass pastime, best left alone to its starvation, desertification, tribal wars, AIDS, and the implosion of its social structures" (1996:99).

An important agenda in Breytenbach's writing since *A Season in Paradise* has been his attempt to reintroduce South Africa into Africa, and to reconcile his claim, "I am an African" (1985:84), with his identity as a native Afrikaner—a people of whom he says, "We are in Africa and we are not Africans" (1985:157). This integration of complex, conflictual and conflicting texts informs his prison memoir, *The True Confessions of an Albino Terrorist* (1984), in which he tells of his clandestine return to South Africa in 1975 and his subsequent arrest, trial and seven-year imprisonment. In *Memory of Snow and of Dust* (1989), Breytenbach attempts to articulate himself, by means of an elaborate fictional counterpointing, as a South African into an African text and as an African into a South African one. The reinscription of South Africa into Africa also forms the substance of the third volume of his autobiographical triptych, *Return to Paradise* (1993), which describes another three-month-long journey to and around South Africa during 1991. Like *A Season in Paradise*, *Return to Paradise* begins with a reflection on Africa during the flight to Johannesburg. Breytenbach prepares his reader for his arrival by describing some of the other airports through which he has entered various African countries during the past number of years: Ouagadougou, Dakar, Tripoli, Accra, Entebbe, Dar-es-Salaam, Algiers, Lusaka, Abidjan, Nairobi, Lagos, Harare:

> So many fly-palaces, so many dreamers who have hit the jackpot, so many portraits of dictators dirtying the walls, so many panels carved from precious indigenous wood, so many impatient ministers with fat bellies and swollen rings and hangers-on with imitation club ties and empty briefcases. (1993:8)

Although Breytenbach's disenchantment may now smack of cynicism, these African place names which he compulsively rehearses direct one to the true goal of yet another narrative journey into the locations of his own identity—as he explains in the last chapter: ultimately, "Africa was the subject" (1993:217).

What might it mean to claim that Breytenbach has tried to write South Africa back into Africa—an act which, as he expressed it in a lecture in Amsterdam in 1995, means to be "involved in *writing . . .* the present and a possible future for ourselves" (1995:17)? His works exemplify his belief that writing itself constitutes *"points of transition"*

(1985:97) which signal stands taken by the writer. *Return to Paradise* represents Breytenbach's most self-conscious attempt to bridge the gulf between his Afrikaner origins and the African filiation he claims. He admits that these two texts seem incompatible: "I own up to the discrepancies. I am of a people who are the mortification of Africa, a people of colonists without a metropolis, with whom nobody wants to share history" (1993:75). Nevertheless, he states, for him "to be African is not a choice, it is a condition." Nor does he deny his integration in Europe. To accommodate these paradoxes, Breytenbach poetically revives the ancient term "Afriqua" to designate an African-Afrikaner identity for the future. Afriquas, he explains, was the name by which "the mixed offspring of Khoi (Hottentots) and passing sailors were known. Later the word was deformed to 'Griquas.' The suffix -*kwa* (-*qua*) to Hottentot names indicated 'the people, the sons, the men of'" (1993:v). The name "Afriqua," Breytenbach maintains, provides "the only opening [he has] for making use of all [his] senses and capabilities" (1993:75). It provides a conduit from the early African past to a new African future. "Afriqua" conveys the true mongrel nature of Afrikaner culture that developed in South Africa over three centuries. He argues in *Return to Paradise* that "the unwritten history and customs and attitudes of the vanished Khoi and San constitute an invisible presence in the make-up of South Afriquas"; similarly, the disappeared Malay-Portuguese spoken by the "slaves, political exiles and convicts from Africa, Madagascar, Ceylon, India and the area today known as Indonesia" survives as a core element in the Afrikaans language (1993:210-11). Hybridization, Breytenbach has repeatedly said, is the way to reconciliation (1996:35). In the "process of *métissage* and metamorphosis" out of which Afrikaans developed, he believes, "not only new cultural identities . . . but also more sensitive moral criteria" may emerge (1996:15). He has therefore appealed to his fellow Afrikaners:

> we Afrikaners ought to look closely at themes such as: bastardization as motivation for an intellectual, cultural and political renaissance; or a more sensitive definition of South, and an attempt to see where we fit in the Third World; from there an effort to outline our function in the North-South relationship, and therefore a theological, political, ideological and practical enquiry into the methods and contents of Africanization. (1996:35).

In *Return to Paradise*, South African identity is better approached as a contrapuntal cultural ensemble, and best analyzed in terms of Said's principles of "complementarity and interdependence" (1994:115).

"We are in Africa and we are not Africans" (1985:157). The chiasmus used by Breytenbach provides a still more precise way of understanding his act of South African-African cross-cultural translation. He displays, I would argue, what Sanford Budick, following Nietzsche, calls "a manifold of mind," whose elements are best expressed in the interactive binarisms of chiasmus (1996:225). Budick argues that chiasmus, a reversal of syntactic elements, or signs which together form an X or *chi* in the pattern AB:BA, "is necessarily the figure of a mind that cannot make up any kind of mind except by being beside itself" (1996:227). While it is generally true "to think of chiasmus in terms of antithesis or negation," he says, it is

> more accurate to say that a chiasmus is a movement of two sets of opposed signs (two binarisms) in which the pattern AB:BA is only one interim possibility. Because of the multiple meaning of all signs, any one reading (at a given junction of possible combinations) of any sign—or syntactic element or binarism—is always to some extent an arbitrary decision. Within the fourfold network of signs, each binary term is always poised for a change of its sign (A into B, B into A). (1996:227)

In connection with "this feature of shifting signs within the structure and movement of chiasmus," Henri Suhamy has pointed out that "in their mirror arrangement, the binary terms, passing from one syntactic element to the next, as much *reflect* as oppose each other" (in Budick 1996:227). Budick suggests that

> more than any other figure of language, chiasmus inevitably embodies the problem of other minds. In fact, what we picture in the AB:BA of chiasmus may only be the experience of the limit of (our) being within thought itself: that is, we think *our being* [A] only at the limit of *what is not our being* (or *death*) [B]. Yet no sooner are we lost in this movement of thought, than we de facto reverse direction, now thinking from *what is not our being* [B] toward the limit of *our being* [A], and so on. (1996:227-28)

Budick goes on to argue the usefulness of chiasmus for any discussion of "a shared thinking or a mutual fit of cultures" (1996:229) and he proposes the matching chiasma of different individuals as presenting "a picture of shared (divided) thinking—and of mutuality of culture" (229-30). Chiastic configurations are both oppositional and reciprocal, and, in their continual creation of potentialities of relation, are premised on co-subjectivity.

Many of Breytenbach's views on writing define the chiastic cast of his mind and art. When he speaks, for example, of the need for self-invention as "keeping alive the creative tension between sharedness and differences: if only to keep alive a sustainable balance" (1996:9), or of writing as "the line contouring if not synthesising the known and the unknown, a frontier between decency or tolerance, and barbarity" (1996:15), or of having "to imagine the syntax of reconciliation" (1996:83) to build the new South African nation, it is just such a "manifold of mind" that he is expressing.

Return to Paradise demands a contrapuntal reading of its travelling subject in his different personae, of its narrative structure and of its diverse discourses. To begin with Breytenbach's personae: in *A Season in Paradise* Breytenbach first fully articulated his imaginative strategy of what he called *"The self-image in the eye of the I"* (1995:197). He explains this concept in terms of a mask, or, more accurately, *imago*, which writers in particular create and project as a substitute or even a shield for the "I." Others perceive it differently from ourselves and they also help to determine its shape. The relationship between self and mask can turn into one of tension as gradually the mask becomes inseparable from the self which takes the shape it is constrained under by the community. Breytenbach expresses this interplay between the image and the "I" chiastically as: "I create Image; Image makes 'I'" (1995:149).

In *Return to Paradise*, Breytenbach projects himself into four additional personae who can best be understood in oppositional yet reciprocal relation to him and to each other. It may be more accurate to regard these *alter egos* as akin to Fernando Pessoa's *heteronyms*. The figure of Ka'afir, familiar to Breytenbach's readers from his other works, is reintroduced here. Ka'afir, whose name is an anagram of "Afrika," is the "[p]oet, student, world wanderer, stray dog, dealer in thises and thats with North America" (1993:19) whom Breytenbach first met on the slave island of Gorée. Breytenbach describes his life as entwined with that of his African acolyte, who instructs him in the art of "us[ing] illusion to pin down reality" (1993:74). Breytenbach's footsteps are also dogged by the figure of Walker, a wheeler and dealer from his political past, an international adventurer without home or identity documents, but someone "bitten by the Africa bug" and whose ambition to write his life story is complicated by the fact that in his travels he has lost one hand. Breytenbach is further burdened in his South African journey by the figure of Mr. Ixele, the carved "bust of a man with a long head and bearded mouth" (1993:50), red-painted face and bulging eyes, which he buys in the former homeland of Venda.

The African-sounding name he gives the bust converts into an anagram of "exile," as does the name of Elixe, the "whitish" young hitchhiker who clutches a tourist souvenir toy windmill and winks knowingly at Breytenbach in the rearview mirror, and who later tries to steal and bury Mr. Ixele. Each of these co-travellers features in Breytenbach's narrative reflection and self-reflection as an attempt to answer the question by Pessoa quoted as an epigraph to the book: "in what mirror did I lose my face."

Return to Paradise is the paradoxical text in which the Afrikaans poet who has become in his own words a "nomadic nobody" is constituted (also in his own words) as the mirror-like "lair of a collection of impressions, sentiments, afterthoughts" (1993:74). Breytenbach describes his travel book-cum-memoir as "a tissue of fiction stitched together with ruptures," a story "neither of the past nor in the present" but "wind[ing] its way through words in lost time" and "consist[ing] of many futile paradoxes" (1993:xv). The personal journey it records was for Breytenbach "a passage towards the making and unmaking of memories," in the course of which he admits that he also looted and adulterated other people's recollections and imaginations (1993:217).

Breytenbach's peculiar South African-African "manifold of mind" is apparent in the intricately cruciform structure of the narrative which alternately maps antithetical and inverted topographies. In his discussion of the use of topography in literary and philosophical writings, J. Hillis Miller argues that narrative and place have converged in place names: "Place names make a site already the product of a virtual writing, a topography, or, since the names are often figures, a 'topotropography.' With topotropography, the act of mapping, goes topology, the knowledge of places" (1995:3-4). On the one hand, Miller says, the (toponymically) "encrypted place generates stories that play themselves out within a topography" and "narration is the only way to talk about it" (1995:8); on the other hand, he says, every narrative in turn provides an exercise in spatial mapping in the way it "traces out in its course an arrangement of places, dwellings, and rooms joined by paths or roads" which could be mapped (1995:10). In the case of fiction, Miller suggests, this figurative mapping of its physical landscape is implicitly done in the mind of the reader in the act of reading.

Return to Paradise begins its spatial mapping with the series of African toponyms, but its "figurative mapping" of South Africa begins with the string of Western Cape toponyms which Breytenbach has recited like well-worn prayer beads to map his South African past:

Riviersonderend, Bredasdorp, Swellendam, Stormsvlei, Halfaampies-kraal, Reisiesbaan, Dekriet, Suurbraak. "Listen," he says, "there's a story buried behind each and every one of them" (1993:27). Whose history, he asks? That of his Afrikaner, Dutch and German forebears, or that of his "other ancestors" (1993:28), the imported slaves and the nomadic people who had roamed the country for centuries before the colonists arrived? The narrative is further characterized throughout by Breytenbach's detailed recitation of the scientific and popular names, in Afrikaans with English translation, of plants, mammals and birds, the various digests retracing the cognitive map of his land of birth. It is, however, by means of the detailed lists of toponyms that signpost his present and past travels in South Africa and elsewhere in Africa that he invites his reader to enter via these topotropographies into a new South African-African topology. The text offers hundreds of names of cities and towns, rivers and dams, farms and mountains, to be savoured by author and reader alike as part of a wider epistemological recovery. By reciting them, the postmodernist Breytenbach's narrative paradoxically reveals behind the "spatial history" (to use Paul Carter's term) of colonial South Africa a world of orality; for, as he says:

> Africa is the domain of the spoken word. Words have a magic dimension, they are spun out to ensnare time, to delay it, to annul it, to perpetuate it. Words constitute the nearly visible tissue of relationships, the creation of patterns of congress. Although speaking is patterned and ritually stereotyped, it leaves room for subtle shifts, adaptations and accentuations. It is furthermore an activity which can cast a spell and physically take on shape through structure—a reference field, a history, finally a reality. (1993:39)

The most obvious example of this is in chapter fifteen, entitled "Guide," where Breytenbach, recalling an earlier journey by car from Swaziland to Grahamstown in 1989 when he was allowed only a four-day visa to take leave of his dying father, rehearses the names that marked the route, obliging his reader also to "read the land" through "the resting-places of the tongue, the intimate symbiosis between shape and sound" (1993:175):

> This is the way we came. From where the Phophonyane Falls thunder above the Hhohho Valley, in the distance the purple Lebombe and closer Kobolondo or Gatoorkopberg (Arse-over-Kettle). Through Mhlambany-atsi and Bhunya to the Nerston border crossing. Then Amsterdam, Piet Retief (Hondkop to the left), Kwamandlangampisi, Wag-'n-bietjie (oh, Wait-a-while), Wakkerstroom and Volksrust with the glorious battle-hill

of Majuba on the horizon. On to Vrede (Peace). Not for long. Jakkalskop, Leeukop, Roadside, Kaalkop (Bald Hill), Pramkop (Udder Head), Skuinshoogte, Warden (hard by Kafferstad), via Kruispad (Crossroads) to Bethlehem. Slabberts, far in the distance Mount Horeb, Fouriesburg, Appelkooskop (Apricot Hill) and Wonderkop, Kommandonek, Ficksburg, glancing right to the killing fields of Spioenkop and Vegkop, Eerstekamp, Modderpoort (Mud Gate), Gethsemane lies over the mountain frontier in Lesotho. Marseilles, Faust, Thaba Phatswa, Kommissiepoort, Hobhouse, Jammerdrif (Sorry Passage) and off to the right Skiethoek, Wildekophond, Kafferskop, Wepener. Elandsberg. Zastron. Aasvoëlberg (Mount Vulture). Genadeberg (Mount Mercy). Dansters and Winnaars (Dancers and Winners) are railway sidings. Houtkop, Rouxville, Beestekraalnek, Aliwal North, Jamestown with away to either side Swempoort and Predikantskop (Preachers Hill). Laggende Water (Laughing Water), across Stormberg direction Molteno to Syfeergat (Seephole), Carrickmore, Boesmanhoekpas, Malabarsberg, Sterkstroom to Queenstown. Over the Black Kei. Goshen left. Katberg, Outyd (Old Times), Fort Beaufort, Koonapshoogte, Grahamstown. (1993:174)

Encoded in this oration is a history of settlement and conflict, and of dispossession and defeat. It speaks to Breytenbach of his rich patrimony and its corruption by apartheid, and it brings into focus the identities both by which he is constrained and from which he is exiled.

This recollection is contained within the frame narrative: Breytenbach's account of his travels in 1991, after the release of Mandela, around a South Africa in troubled transition from the old order to a new democratic identity—a country which Breytenbach typifies as "the favoured terrain of double-think, double-talk, double-do" (1993:138). What emerges from his elaborate tracing, not only of his various journeys in South Africa in 1991 but also of his previous journeys that are enclosed in the main narrative, is a picture of South Africa in terms of what Foucault would call its heterotopias—sites "in which all the other real sites that can be found within the culture are simultaneously represented, contested, and inverted" (1986:24). Heterotopias are those sites where radically incommensurable worlds of discourse can coexist, and in Breytenbach's text there are as many as there are place names: in Johannesburg, the squalid township of Alexandria bordering on the conspicuous consumption of Sandton; in Cape Town, shack settlements crawling inexorably over the dunes towards manicured suburbs; in Lebowa, tension between traditional healers and witchdoctors and the "comrades" of the liberation struggle; in Thohoyandou, "mutual parasitic dependence" (1993:53) between racist Boers and

Vhavenda; in KaNgwane, a democratically elected Chief Minister who is the sole exception to the incompetence and corruption of the other "homeland" leaders, but who has been overtaken by history; in the Kruger Park, social dislocation and human destruction as a result of the civil war in Mozambique adjacent to the animal "world of gorging and guzzling and foraging and copulation and breeding, of stalking and being stalked, and of hiding" (1993:68); in the Natal Midlands, killing fields with their ANC and Inkatha death squads which subvert any political optimism and reduce politicians to incoherence; in Pretoria, Breytenbach's own implication in this heterotopian world: receiving a literary award in the city he had cursed as the home of "the codes of total evil" (1993:100); in Montagu and Sedgefield, his closeness to his brothers despite the ideological divisions between them; and everywhere, his absorption into the beauty of the land together with his despair at the politicking and the ongoing bloodletting. The lesson of his journey through South Africa, Breytenbach concludes, is to have learnt "the complexities of everything and its opposite being true" (1993:138).

Dovetailed with this South African topotropography are numerous descriptions of visits undertaken to other countries in Africa. The narrative crosses over from its South African itinerary to various African ones which were motivated mainly by Breytenbach's opposition to apartheid over the years. Each of these African toponyms, however, signposts a comparable site of paradoxical inversion: in Mali, a vision of Timbuktu as symbol both of the wisdom and education that had been unequalled in Africa in the twelfth to fifteenth centuries, and of its loss; in Burkina Faso, assassination of Thomas Sankara two days after he had hosted in Ouagadougou a Pan-African meeting on apartheid; in Lagos, a meeting of writers the occasion for observing the corruption in Nigeria; in Accra, a conference of African writers, organized by a swindler, degenerating into a shambles; in Tripoli, summary execution of army officers who had attempted a coup while Breytenbach was feasting there with international jurists; and in Senegal, the first unlikely meetings in 1987 between South Africans and the exiled ANC in Dakar, and the Institute for Democracy in Africa founded on the slave island of Gorée by Breytenbach and Van Zyl Slabbert.

Finally, also woven into this composite South African-African narrative are extracts from the encyclopaedic *Description of Africa*, published in 1668 by the Dutch historian, Olfert Dapper, without his ever having left Holland, but knowing everything he needed to know through his reading. The lists of place names constituting Dapper's seventeenth-century African topography combine half-truth with pure fantasy. They merge with Breytenbach's actual South African and African ones in a text that is itself a paradoxical site of antithetical and yet reciprocal discourses, and, in pointing towards the potential reconciliation of Afrikaner and African, demonstrates something of the "Afriqua," Breytenbach's belief that "[a]ll meaning is making, a blending, a bastardization, a metamorphosis" (1996: 143).

References

Breytenbach, Breyten
  1985 [1980] *A Season in Paradise*. London & Boston: Faber and Faber.
  1986 *End Papers*. London: Faber & Faber.
  1993 *Return to Paradise*. Cape Town: David Philip.
  1995 "Africa Needs to Reinvent Itself in Order to Survive." Dr. J.M. den Uyl-lezing, 27 January 1995, Amsterdam.
  1996 *The Memory of Birds in Times of Revolution*. Cape Town: Human & Rousseau.
Budick, Sanford
  1996 "Cross-Culture, Chiasmus, and the Manifold of Mind." In Sanford Budick and Wolfgang Iser, eds., *The Translatability of Cultures: Figurations of the Space Between*, 224-44. Stanford, CA: Stanford University Press.
Foucault, Michel
  1986 "Of Other Spaces." *Diacritics* (Spring): 22-27.
Miller, J. Hillis
  1995 *Topographies*. Stanford, CA: Stanford University Press.
Said, Edward
  1994 *Culture and Imperialism*. London: Chatto & Windus.

6

Inheritance in Question: The Magical Realist Mode in Afrikaans Fiction

Sheila Roberts

What I hope to do in this essay is take some of the liberty provided by magical realism's broad and sometimes conflicting hermeneutics to address the ways in which this mode has been employed in some recent Afrikaans fiction. My discussion of novels and stories in this malleable mode (also touching on fantasy and allegory) produced during the 1980s and through the past decade—the most violent yet hopeful transitional moments in South African politics—might serve to clarify the purpose of a South African drift away from the naturalist pastoral mode to the use of many-layered textures of surrealism and its shifting meanings.

Some of the works, such as Etienne van Heerden's *Toorberg* and *Kikoejoe* and Marita van der Vyver's *Entertaining Angels*, I would posit, are responding with anxiety, yet optimistically and humorously to political change. They reject governmental sanctioned forms of history and memory in their creation of new stories, new memories or in a reworking of the old ones. Such novels, in effect, challenge the fixity of any received ideas, truths and systems—even as they construct a new foundation for historiography and myth-making Their characters express guilt and dread for past decades of damage, yet at the same time insist that acknowledged remorse plus cheerful self-confidence in the future will be the means to restoring peace to the land for all South Africans.

In other words, these fictions, as well as the low-keyed novels of Karel Schoeman, such as *Another Country, Die Uur van die Engel* and *Hierdie Lewe* (to which I can only give marginal attention within the confines of this paper), all written before or during the establishment of the Truth and Reconciliation Commission in South Africa, present testimonies on new variations of historical truth, personal memory and moral meaning.

Working metatextually and "magically," with imaginative arabesques of plot and characterological improvisations, some of these novels reach their own moment of reconciliation, however open-ended. In *Toorberg,* for instance, that moment demonstrates how powerful and generationally established Afrikaner landowners may begin restoring South Africa to its ancient indigenous peoples through acceptance of a repatterning of their common history. *Another Country* provides a sombre prescription, lit up by moments of epiphany and clairvoyance, on how to live by sharing and how to die without shame in the Country-To-Be. Marita van der Vyver's character Griet in *Entertaining Angels* would add that what the country also needs is more happy-ending stories and, in the interaction of all people, more comedy and laughter. As Griet would ask, When last did anyone read a funny Afrikaans book?

In his essay "Magic Realism as Postcolonial Discourse," Stephen Slemon asserts that "In none of its applications to literature has the concept of magic realism ever successfully differentiated between itself and neighboring genres such as fabulation, metafiction, the Baroque, the fantastic, the uncanny, or the marvelous, and consequently it is not surprising that some critics have chosen to abandon the term altogether" (1995:407). As phrased in my first paragraph, I am fully aware of the shifting meanings of the concept. Be that as it may, for my own purposes I choose to use the term magical realism specifically for those texts where the author presents us with a material world, familiar and recognizable, most importantly to *us* the readers, as well as to the characters who inhabit it, but a world able to support the inexplicable and strange. In the many genres Slemon mentions, a world strange to the reader may not be uncanny to the characters peopling it. In magical realism, those elements of the uncanny, the supernatural or the fantastic that interweave themselves seamlessly through the mundane fabric of the characters' lives do not surprise them or us. Some phenomena may be annoying or startling, but the prosaic foundational world remains the same—ghosts, nocturnal beasts, dreams, the sixth sense and optical illusions being no more than proof that the material has multiple ways of revealing its meanings to us. "[W]hat lies beyond the known does not necessarily lie beyond the *real*" (Fink 1998:17). In other words, the antinomy between reality and fantasy is underplayed by presenting super- or preternatural events as if they did not contradict reason or the sensual evidence of the material.

In support of my use of this definition of magical realism, I should like to turn to an earlier Afrikaans novel which would not fall under my rubric; this is *Seven Days at the Silbersteins* by Etienne Leroux, a novel which appeared in Afrikaans in 1962 to heightened attention, most of it admiring but some very damning. Leroux's fantastic imagination contorts the plot unremittingly and playfully, a plot which involves a visit by Henry van Eeden to a huge Baroque farmhouse in the midst of wealthy vineyards (the first of several farmhouses looking like Transylvanian castles which will loom through the mists and half-lights time and again in later Afrikaans texts). The farmer, Jock Silberstein, has invited Henry for seven days of pleasure and entertainment, during which time, as Henry understands it, he will get to know Jock's daughter, Salome, with a view to marriage. Over the course of the week, Jock stages all manner of parties: discomforting ones where a group of guests swimming naked in the pool have the water suddenly drained away from under them; an uncanny pastorale where all are disguised in animal heads; a *Walpurgisnacht*; and a pavane for the Salomes where all the young women look alike. Henry, described as the "flawless little robot deliberately produced by the sexual act and properly conditioned" (Leroux 1967:7), does not finally meet Salome nor is any engagement arranged.

As Jack Cope pointed out, "Everything . . . is not quite what it seems to be. Neither dream nor fancy, it remains a remarkable *tour de force. . . .* [T]he narrative grips one's interest to the last page, intriguing and frankly amusing" (1982:115). I would add that everything is not quite what it seems to the initially unsuspecting reader and the bewildered characters. But the reader soon catches on that some malicious, very human agency is at work on the farm. That agency, so it emerges, is Jock Silberstein.

Jan Rabie termed *Seven Days at the Silbersteins* "the most brilliant and strange . . . firework display yet in South Africa." He objected, however, to the "subordination of MAN to the idea of symbol [in Leroux's corpus] and to the author's view of the black man as an emblem of chaos" (Cope 1982:116). While almost all of the works I am discussing owe something to *Seven Days*, and while most of them do invest their characters with some symbolic status, a radical change among later writers is in their portrayal of black characters as not chaotic but as eminently reasonable or angrily rational as against the unreasoned behaviour of whites. There is, by the way, a difference between a character constructed to be so unstable that his or her thoughts and actions are chaotic (as might be the case of Magda in Coetzee's *In the Heart of the Country*, 1978), and the distortion of the "known" by an author so that while the characters remain rational and mystified "the known" grows unreal or chaotic. Good examples of this form of distortion appear in some of the South African anti-border-war stories, such as *My Kubaan* by Etienne van Heerden, and his more recent collection *Mad Dog and Other Stories*; in the work of Ivan Vladislavic; and in M.C. Botha's stories, *Belydenis van 'n Bedrieer* (*Confessions of a Deceiver*).

In any event, even though the characters in *Seven Days* are largely flat or merely emblematic and there is much talk of devils and evil, the whole affair is, as I have pointed out, staged by Jock Silberstein, a wine farmer, who is staged by Leroux, the author, charged by his own fantastic dislikes and desires. *Seven Days* is like a series of engaging if rather unSouth African *tableaux vivants*, the ugliness of the flesh beneath the fancy dress showing through. The supernatural or the magical do not here interest Leroux, but shocking the bourgeoisie does. Of course, shocking the bourgeoisie in a South Africa of the 1960s was viewed by the Censor Board as indeed an act of political subversion, a view difficult to comprehend now, so long afterwards.

Leroux's work, often self-reflexive and metafictional, was, incidentally, part of the *Sestigers* or Sixties movement, which was "a loose combination of Afrikaans writers embodying the concept of artistic individualism as opposed to the . . . expectation that all should embrace some kind of mythical loyalty or obligation to the 'volk'" (Cope 1982:99). Some critics have considered that the Sestigers' emphasis on the individual, on the myths being attached to the Afrikaner people and on modernist/postmodernist technical experimentation reduced its value as an effective political and social challenge, unlike, for instance, the force of the almost contemporaneous magical realist experimentations of Latin America.

Criticism of a similar sort has been directed at the novels of J.M. Coetzee, particularly for their lack of South African specificity. When Coetzee is geographically specific, as in *Life & Times of*

Michael K. (1983), he takes the reader on a journey through a war-torn South Africa with Michael K., a small, impoverished, coloured garden worker able to survive for long periods without food, that is, *the* food he needs for body *and* soul, even if this is sometimes pumpkins. Here Coetzee himself dips his pen briefly into the fantastic or the magical, particularly at the end when Michael K. believes he can repeat his journey provided he has a teaspoon with which to scoop water.

To return to what I consider authentic Afrikaans Magical Realism: in Etienne van Heerden's *Toorberg* of 1986 (translated as *Ancestral Voices* in 1992), most of the characters recognize ghosts visually, or by traces such as footprints, a smell or the sensation of a breeze arising out of nowhere. Early in the novel a Magistrate arrives in the area to collect testimony regarding the death of a small boy, Noah Trickle du Pisani. At the train station he senses the presence of Abel Moolman, the last of the mighty Moolmans who had built up the farm Toorberg—a veritable Magic Mountain. The Magistrate has a brief and bitter dialogue with Abel and then respectfully walks around his shadow and goes to attend to his business. The Magistrate is in no way surprised; indeed he had expected that Abel Moolman would come to meet him to discourage him from investigating. That the Magistrate is indeed a magistrate is later called into question when his resemblance to dead De la Rey Moolman (and by extension to the Boer War hero Jacobus De la Rey) is noted by Abel Moolman's widow. As the novel progresses "the reader senses . . . as does the Magistrate that no amount of testimony will yield the 'real' guilty party in Trickle's death" (Fink 1998:10). To digress slightly but also, in fact, to *place* the novel, this sentence has been reverberating again and again over the past years in the court-rooms of the Truth and Reconciliation Committee.

Trickle, the dead child, was the last of the children produced by a Moolman and a coloured person. His death has called forth a gathering of the clans, a coming together of Moolmans alive and those dead four generations back, the ghosts serving almost as a (silent) Chorus in a tragedy. Also arriving as witnesses are members of the so-called "shame-family," those coloured people whom Moolmans over many years had cohabited with and then rejected, leaving them to subsist on the most arid section of the Toorberg farm. The ancestors of the family of shame, TameBushman and Jan Swart, a Khoikhoi, also arise from their graves.

The issues circle around one another. The first is how uncon-scionably the Moolmans have treated one another as well as members of their so-called shame-family. That conflict takes on immediate political force when two of the younger men, Oneday, a coloured man, and CrossAbel Moolman, his cousin, adopt divergent political positions— Oneday as an activist and CrossAbel as a riot policeman in love with violence. Both men are, however, sterile and, with the loss of Trickle, the Moolman line is likely to die out.

Backgrounded but troubling everyone is the fact that the Seven Eyes, the sources of the river to water the lands, have dried up one after the other. The land is being laid waste: something is rotten on the Moolmans' Magic Mountain. Abel Moolman, clinging absurdly to the material, therefore, brings in John Deere machinery to drill for water. It is in this situation of racial resentment and fear for the survival of the farm that Trickle goes playing among the red machinery and falls down a borehole. Or he is pushed by one of his ghostly uncles loitering on the farm, or by the wraiths of Founder Abel or Old Abel. But the hopeful implication of Trickle's falling is that he may become the sacrificial godling who will bring rain and healing to the farm.

Watched by all, Abel Moolman does all he can to get Trickle out of the hole alive. But Trickle dies. Abel then does something untoward. He goes from person to person among the shame-family and greets them all, acknowledging them as equals. Abel then disappears and, it is discovered, commits suicide. Thus Abel is already dead when, in the early pages of the book, the Magistrate arrives on the scene to investigate the boy's death. Arguably, Abel's death reveals his remorse for the harm done to the shame-family and specifically to little Trickle. However, his only inheritor now, CrossAbel, sterile and violent, does nothing thereafter but ride his motorcycle wildly in circles around the farm reduced to dust, "symbolically destroying the work of his ancestors and nullifying his own presence in Toorberg" (Fink 1998:16).

Perhaps Abel Moolman could not bear to live and observe the changes coming to Toorberg. On the last page, old Katie Danster, the matriarch of the shame-family, struggles home in the wind. But "She imagined she could hear the wild geese crying and see Noah standing in the footpath ahead of her listening to the wind . . . then suddenly, as though they would never again be able to come to rest, the wild geese clattered up out of the poplars. Crying, they flew over her head, dived through the wind and swung away into the white mist that was tumbling down over the head of the Toorberg" (Van Heerden 1992:260).

The ending alerts us that the powerful Moolmans are receding into the past, the last dusty image being of CrossAbel on his motorcycle.

The shame-family will inherit the farm and there are signs of rain coming to fill the rivers and streams. However, to avoid any suggestion that the Moolmans, as representatives of Afrikaner dynasties of old, will be effaced from the South African "narrative," Van Heerden arranges for their spirits to remain on the land, benignly to haunt it. To erase them would simply be to repeat a National Party history that attempted to erase the voices, memories and stories of other populations.

Before going on to examine further novels, I should like to point to what seems something of a contradiction in the texts I am examining. In their introduction to *Magical Realism: Theory, History, Community*, Parkinson Zamora and Faris make some excellent observations—e.g., "Almost as a return on capitalism's hegemonic investment in its colonies, magical realism is especially alive and well in postcolonial contexts and is now achieving a compensatory extension of its market worldwide" (1995:2); and, mentioning the many practitioners of the mode (Marquez, Paz, Toni Morrison, Kawabata, Walcott, etc.), they suggest that "magical realist practice is currently requiring that we [re]negotiate the nature of marginality itself" (1995:4). The contradiction or ambiguity that emerges from the choice by Afrikaans writers to avail themselves of the mode is that since 1948 Afrikaners have never been a marginalized group in South Africa. As this mode of novel-writing continues to proliferate in South Africa, one explanation for its strength and popularity is that it *foretells* by comfortable imaginative means the Afrikaners' own coming marginality; this helps them face the evidence of their once-proud language reduced to the status of any of the other languages reinstated in South Africa. In *Kikoejoe*, for instance, everyone speaks a crazy Afrikish or Anglikaans. Moreover, this mode of fiction prepares for a reparceling of biblically sacred lands as a form of reparation, following the "truth" of its stories—stories that might "trickle" (apologies for the pun) down into the common consciousness and become stabilized.

Apart from Karel Schoeman's *Another Country*, all of the novels I am discussing have particularities in common: the discovery that the wealthy family in its farmhouse, whether merely grandiose or Gothic or Baroque, has African, coloured, Khoikhoi or San ancestors, heretofore held secret. In *Toorberg* the contribution of various ethnic groups to the building of the family is clear from the beginning, though the "others," the coloureds, are kept at a distance. In *Griet Skryf 'n Sprokie* by Marita van der Vyver (translated as *Entertaining Angels* in 1997) the grandmother of the protagonist Griet is darker than she should be, but no one pays that fact much attention in the mid-1990s. In Etienne van Heerden's *Kikoejoe*, set on a vacation farm constructed more like a series of Hollywood sets than anything else, large, gay Aunt Geertruida with her motorcycle has discovered through research in Amsterdam that the proud Latsky family indeed derives from coloured ancestors.

Is this strategy on the part of Afrikaans writers to "recolour" their ancestry born of a desire to alter their whiteness, to camouflage their emerging "otherness" in a post-1993 South Africa? I think so. I think also that this strategy is an acknowledgment, if not a confession, that the coloured population of South Africa derives largely from Dutch exploitation of slaves and indigenous populations.

To digress: with a wonderful fairy-storyteller's touch, Van Heerden begins *Kikoejoe*'s opening chapter with

> Far in Africa, at the foot of a mountain, lies a vacation farm where the stuffed heads of wild deer are mounted against the verandah walls. During the cicada-singing summers bats explode from out of the eaves of the bighouse at twilight, and shortly before the punishing frost-winter arrives swallows sit on the telephone wires. They look northward and bounce in the wind. (My translation; 1996:1)

He ends the novel with the image of Reuben, the efficient black man who really runs the farm, standing with "His tray sparkling against his chest: a shield against what is coming" (my translation; 1996:294).

In André Brink's *Imaginings of Sand*, the protagonist, Kristien, discovers on returning home from London to speak to her grandmother as the old woman lies dying that there were women of every skin colour and ethnicity in their family. She greets this information and the elaborately improbable stories of these women with great pleasure. Again, the setting for most of this novel is an enormous farmhouse of multiple unmatching architectural styles from which the grandmother establishes a matriarchal dynasty for Kristien. A question relating to the one above about the "recolouring" of skin is whether, by defamiliarizing the familiar Cape-Dutch farmhouse, writers are preparing themselves and their readers for geographic and spatial alterations and for the inevitable marginalization of Dutch-Afrikaans history? Or are they merely doing "a Leroux"—creating a mockery of the familiar farmhouse by transforming it into a replica of the castle of someone like Robert the Devil in Normandy?

Brink tries to wear a feminist cap and adopt the voice of a liberated, liberal woman, but can do no better than provide Kristien with no power to beat off men who want to paw her and with generations of foremothers who were defined by how they treated or were treated by men, and, worst still, who were obsessed with their menstrual cycles. In effect, Brink offers a dynasty of wombs, and even provides in the farm's deep dark basement sacks and sacks of used sanitary napkins stored by the grandmother—a grotesque twist of plot no woman writer would have thought up. At the end, when free elections are being held, Kristien, a former ANC activist in London, takes her justifiable place among ANC leaders, and even becomes a spokesperson—a pale, half-Britishy copy of Gordimer's Hillela in *A Sport of Nature*.

Related to the use by Afrikaans writers of a mode of fiction generally associated with those who have suffered personal or political sub-jugation is the frequent assumption of the female voice, insultingly manipulated by Brink, but generally put to good use by Schoeman, Van Heerden and Van der Vyver. To simplify, these writers, while castigating Afrikaner Nationalist power and damage, also reject the authoritative pronouncements of the father, and give voice to those normally never listened to: grandmothers; rejected wives on the point of breakdowns; wizened, coloured matriarchs; a crippled German missionary woman; a lesbian woman on a motorcycle; and a half-blind little boy whose father, the farmer in *Kikoejoe*, hallucinates and chatters in his bed, under the influence of psychiatrically prescribed doses of marijuana.

In *Another Country*, set in the 1870s, the matter of the disinheri-tance and inheritance of the earth becomes an intense issue in the debates between the Scheffler family of German missionaries and their friend Versluis, a Hollander come to Bloemfontein in hopes of finding a cure for his tuberculosis in the dry climate. The idea of South Africa as a life-giving country, capable of bestowing material and spiritual wealth to its multi-ethnic and cosmopolitan population, is the major theme of *Another Country*. The secondary but equally powerful theme is how to live so that dying on South African soil provides a meaning that reflects back over the lived life and forward into future genera-tions.

Marita van der Vyver's *Entertaining Angels* "embraces the absurd, if not the magical," according to Christopher Fink (1998:19). Griet, the protagonist and narrator, is grieving over a broken marriage, a string of miscarriages and a contemplated suicide when an angel unexpectedly presents himself at her door and literally makes the earth move for her. However, I would suggest that Van der Vyver, the author, did not have the courage of her own imagination, for Adam, first accepted by the reader as an angel, is later converted into an ordinary but beautiful blond English fellow who drops in on his way to go surfing and then later sends her messages from London. Griet herself seeks solace in the magical during this time of personal crisis and great but violent change in South Africa by telling herself fairy stories. The stories, reflecting on Griet's personal life and the violent public events heralding the arrival of the New South Africa, are significant subtexts, but they are not magically nor profoundly integrated into the pattern of the plot, remaining semantically and stylistically distinct from the larger narrative. They are Griet's spontaneous and meaningful but disconnected inventions, and serve as alternatives to the miseries of the status quo. They have a value similar to that of the Magistrate's never-mailed letters to his wife in *Toorberg* and, in reverse form, to the "writer" who appears in *Kikoejoe*, a first-person narrator but not one of the residents at the vacation farm. Each novel offers us, therefore, a form of *mis en abime* of authorial frames filled by a narrating first person who then creates other frames and voices to move the text thematically along.

To begin to answer (or to refute) my own questions as to why there has been, since the mid-1980s, a drift away from naturalism in Afrikaans fiction, I should refer to the epigraph on the opening page of *Toorberg*, a quotation by Judge Lucius, one of the ghosts within the novel. It reads: "It is of course true that there are many similarities *ex analogia* between the testimony and that to which the testimony refers; but then life itself, and death as well of course, is really a fable endlessly repeated." As Christopher Fink has brilliantly pointed out,

> It is as if, through questioning the validity of testimony in the novel, Van Heerden is calling into question his novel *as* testimony, and thus questioning . . . a literal exegesis of history. . . . [T]hrough the incorporation of a fictional epigraph, the novel has no historical referent other than itself. The novel is grounded firmly in its own myth making. (1998:10-11)

To add to Christopher Fink's statement and that of Malvern van Wyk Smith that "In the space, the liberated zone, left free by or wrenched from the oppressor, the imagination of the oppressed can only repeat, like a litany, its own history" (1993:82), I would say that a liberated zone has also opened up for Afrikaners (inevitably regarded wholesale as oppressors) in which their writers can rewrite mythologically (even as a litany) their past history and their future in South Africa.

In a South Africa that has been preoccupied with examining its past before the Truth and Reconciliation Committee and discovering (as the backlog of work continues to accumulate) that within narratives, written or spoken, the truth becomes protean or disappears altogether under blankets of abstractions or doublespeak, I would suggest that the process of a new, enabling myth-making gesture towards important "truths" is crucial to the ongoing energy and creative life of all South Africans.

References

Brink, André
1996 *Imaginings of Sand*. New York: Harcourt Brace.

Cope, Jack
1982 *The Adversary Within: Dissident Writers in Afrikaans*. Cape Town: David Philip.

Fink, Christopher
1998 "Magical Realism in South African Fiction." Unpublished doctoral essay, Department of English, University of Wisconsin–Milwaukee.

Leroux, Etienne
1967 *Seven Days at the Silbersteins*. Translated by Charles Eglington. Boston: Houghton Mifflin. First published as *Sewe Dae by die Silbersteins* (Cape Town: Human & Rousseau, 1962).

Parkinson Zamora, Lois, and Wendy B. Faris, eds.
1995 *Magical Realism: Theory, History, Community*. Durham, NC: Duke University Press.

Schoeman, Karel
1991 *Another Country*. Translated by David Schalkwyk. London: Sinclair-Stevenson.

Slemon, Stephen
1995 "Magic Realism as Postcolonial Discourse." In Lois Parkinson Zamora and Wendy B. Faris, eds., *Magical Realism: Theory, History, Community*. Durham, NC: Duke University Press.

Smith, Malvern van Wyk
1993 Review of *Perspectives on South African English Literature* (Johannesburg: Ad Donker, 1980), edited by Sarah Christie, Geoffrey Hutchings and Don Maclennan. In *Current Writing: Text and Reception in Southern Africa* 5, 1 (April).

Van der Vyver, Marita
1996 *Entertaining Angels*. New York: Plume.

Van Heerden, Etienne
1992 *Ancestral Voices*. Translated by Malcolm Hacksley. New York: Viking. First published as *Toorberg* (Cape Town: Tafelberg, 1986).
1996 *Kikoejoe*. Cape Town: Tafelberg.

7

Natal Women's Letters in the 1850s: Ellen McLeod, Eliza Feilden, Gender and "Second-World" Ambi/valence

Margaret J. Daymond

A distinction between the positionality felt in settler writing and in imperialist writing has recently become crucial in postcolonial studies; in support of this distinction, Stephen Slemon and Alan Lawson have both argued that settler writing is properly positioned as a "middle ground" (Slemon 1990:34). While the settler writer may depict the same geographical locale and even the same set of events as the imperial writer, the former inhabits a distinct realm inasmuch as his or her sense of margin and centre, while including the perspective of the imperialist, becomes an "inherent awareness of both 'there' and 'here'" (Lawson 1994:76). In this way, settler writing "not only has to encounter 'the other'; it is constrained by the discourse to *be* 'the other' as well" (Lawson 1991:68). In this condition of "ambi/valence" the settler feels herself "caught between *two* First Worlds, *two* origins of authority and authenticity" (my emphasis; Lawson 1994:72). Slemon argues for this fundamental ambivalence from his sense that resistance in all postcolonial

---

Notes to chapter 7 are on pp. 111-12.

writing is inevitably compromised; this view leads him to disagree with a critic such as Timothy Brennan who has argued that writers like Nadine Gordimer and J.M. Coetzee are to be placed within the line of the European novel of Empire rather than within a postcolonial line. Slemon counters this first-world positioning of settler writers (white South Africans in this case) by pointing out that reserving post-coloniality for the resistant black writer may only reverse and so perpetuate the binaries of imperialism, and that this may, ironically, re-centre Empire and leave the resistant black writer forever marginalized. Lawson posits a middle ground in order to explore the conflicted subject position of recent Australian and Canadian postcolonial writing. While both critics seek to establish settler writing as a proper part of the field of postcolonial studies, and while Lawson wishes to examine "the very place where the processes of colonial power as negotiation, as transactions of power, are most visible" (1995:22), neither critic has so far related the concept of ambi/valence to writing which comes from a moment of settlement itself.

Furthermore, while Lawson's suggestion of the doubleness of the middle ground, which positions the settler as both agent and subject in colonial relations of power, gives valuable flexibility to the field of study, neither he nor Slemon have extended this account of doubleness by incorporating feminist analyses of the double consciousness to be found in women's writing. This line of analysis can be traced to Virginia Woolf's observation that "if one is a woman one is often surprised by a sudden splitting off of consciousness, say in walking down Whitehall, when from being the natural inheritor of that civilization, she becomes, on the contrary, outside of it, alien and critical" (1974:96). It was not by chance that Woolf placed this "sudden splitting off" as happening at the heart of England's whited sepulchre; for women at the remove of the colonies, the experience may well have been rather less surprising and rather more frequent. By incorporating this gendered sense of being in but not of a place and its "civilization" into my account of writing from the middle ground, I wish to release two possibilities. First, attention to the unsettled place of women will help to expose ambi/valence as present in colonial discourse from its earliest days. Second, it will show that, in the colony as in the metropolis, gender stereotypes are both seductive and dangerous for a woman writer in that they are so readily usable to ratify male-favouring relations of power. As the historian Joan Scott puts it, because gender differences have been "[e]stablished as an objective set of references, concepts of gender structure . . . the concrete and [the] symbolic organisation of all social life" (1986: 1069). In establishing gender and settler ambi/valence in the writing of Ellen McLeod and Eliza Feilden, I will show how their writing both represents and rejects the authority of Empire and both desires and repudiates the authenticity of the indigene.

In her study of travel writing by metropolitan women in the nine-teenth century, Sara Mills has argued that although their work emanated from the imperial centre, it was often inflected by gender in ways which complicate currently influential views of imperial dis-course. Had writing about the margins by women such as Mary Kings-ley been taken into account, the picture that emerges in, for example, Edward Said's *Orientalism*, would not have had "the same clear-cut qualities" (1991:62).[1] Mills's point that it "is more difficult to analyse women's colonial writing" (1991:62) because their work reveals such a variable alignment with the discourses of colonialism and femininity and is never straightforwardly "orientalist," is supported by Dorothy Driver. In Lady Anne Barnard's journal of her sojourn in the Cape, 1797-98, for example, "her continually splitting subject-position gives a different tenor to colonial discourse than one hears in its male propo-nents" (Driver 1993:8). When this discursive difference is extended from metropolitan to settler women, the gap between male and female positionality is even greater. In frontier discourse, opposed categories, such as colonizer/colonized, self/other, white/black, male/female, are more evident because more polarized than they need be in the metropolis (Driver 1988). On the frontier, the privileged poles are also, in their hierarchical ordering, made to reinforce each other despite the conceptual difficulty arising from aligning, for example, black and female. Because white is aligned with male, thereby excluding female, the settler woman functions simultaneously as the sign of a subordina-tion which underwrites white male domination and as a superordinate sign which ratifies the subjugation of black colonized people. White women mark a doubled boundary, sexual and racial, and in their limi-nality are perhaps the most unruly, ambi/valent of figures in the colo-nial social and symbolic tapestry.

The instability of the settler woman's positioning is likely to emerge most strikingly when she takes up her pen to write because writing can, in a colonial as well as a metropolitan context, release the agency of an authoritative subjectivity, but at the same time the need to be heard requires the woman writer to inhabit, or at least to work from within, a socially agreed feminine speaking position. Again this is evident in Barnard's negotiations as she strives to "secure for her observations and opinions a kind of authority which she feels may not be granted to a woman's accounts" of what she saw at the Cape (Lenta 1996:171). Driver has argued that as well as the doubleness that these negotiations with imperial authority required, Barnard was sometimes capable of a comparable bifocality in relation to the indigenes: her writing sometimes reveals a "self-othering" (1993:11) which enabled her to see herself as the Other of the indigenous people who had been Othered by colonial domination.[2] This oscillating doubleness in relation to both centre and margin is sometimes consciously undertaken, becoming a form of elegant duplicity in Barnard's writing; at other times she has clearly not questioned her own assumptions.

The two settler women, Ellen McLeod and Eliza Feilden, whose letters I will discuss, come from a different century and a different class from that of Lady Anne Barnard and consequently show little of the witty self-regard of which she is capable. The extent to which their letters reveal and even manipulate the aspects of a female settler doubleness that I have outlined is what I now wish to examine. Thirty years after returning to England, Eliza Feilden herself gathered her letters and, with extracts from a journal which she kept while in Natal, published them in London as *My African Home; or, Bush Life in Natal when a Young Colony (1852-7)* (1887). Ellen McLeod's letters were preserved by her family but remained unknown until 1970 when they were edited by Ruth Gordon and published in Pietermaritzburg as *Dear Louisa*. Louisa is the sister to whom McLeod wrote throughout the thirty years that she lived in Natal.

George and Ellen McLeod left England after the family brewery failed and they came to Natal in 1850 under the Byrne scheme for immigrants.[3] They lost all their possessions when their ship, the *Minerva*, was wrecked at the entrance to Port Natal. After camping for a month at the port, the family of seven (there were five children, all under ten years of age) arrived destitute in the Byrne valley where they had purchased a small tract of land. Theirs was an isolated spot, some thirty miles as the crow flies from Pietermaritzburg, and hardly accessible to wagons. Provided with only a tent, they had to build their own hut; for the first few years they had no clothing except what relatives in England could spare and they ate only the potatoes, mealies and pumpkins that George was able to grow. The focus of McLeod's early letters is thus on survival and this minor miracle, as she viewed it, seems to have provided her with all the justification she needed for her presence and her endeavours in Natal. At no point does she question their right to buy and occupy the land that J.C. Byrne had appropriated to sell to prospective immigrants.

Eliza and Leyland Feilden's circumstances were much more comfortable. The youngest son of Sir William Feilden of Feniscowles Hall in Lancashire, he had also first come to Natal in 1850 as a Byrne immigrant. Besides buying his immigrant's quota of land, he purchased farmland in the Richmond area and near the Bay at Port Natal; his first intention was to invest in cotton, but he soon turned his attention to sugar. When he brought his wife to Natal in 1852, they lived at first in what Eliza Feilden describes as "a little red brick house" (1887:12) in Pine Terrace. Then they moved four miles from the Bay, to higher land which Leyland had purchased from the Dunn family, and they named their farm, which bordered the Umbilo River, "Feniscowles" (Spencer 1992:93-94). The move was made advisable by the unhealthiness of the Bay area, but also seems to have served the Feildens' sense of themselves as British landed gentry. A month before the floods which ruined his second farm and sugar mill at Springfield in April 1856, Leyland wrote to his mother: "I have a fair prospect of realizing a good fortune . . . and you may still see us again in England, occupying the station in life to which we belong" (Feilden 1887:278). A year later, having lost money, they left Natal and did not return.

Ellen McLeod's letters were never intended for publication and they remain securely in the private realm which women were thought to inhabit by nature. There is little sign of her wish to negotiate any discrepancies between what she spontaneously felt and thought and what she might have known would be publicly acceptable, and she shows a certain artlessness in her willingness to leave all but domestic life to her husband's opinionated reporting. This reliance on the discursive division between male and female matters allows McLeod both a certain freedom in her relation to indigenous people and a certain protection from the imperial framing of that relationship. Because the narrowly domestic realm from within which she writes was in some ways the key site from which colonial dominion was extended, the structured ambi/valence of the settler in relation to Empire and indigene is, however, pervasive if not actively recognized in her reports of family life.

The comparative freedom with which her self-confinement to the domestic and her simplifying struggle for survival allowed her to approach her new world is evident in the first published letter from

Byrne. In it she shows an openness to difference and a reciprocity in her dealings that is unusual:

> George has dug up his acre and half . . . and planted it with Indian corn, potatoes, peas, beans and all other sorts of vegetables which are coming up very nicely. . . . We have not been able to get a cow yet so do not often get milk as the natives do not often bring it round and sell it very dear: the smallest amount of money they take for anything is the three penny piece. They will not take any coppers. (McLeod 1970:16)

Although Ellen McLeod needed as much milk as she could get for her infant children, she shows no impulse to censure or to patronize the native people for their trust in silver. This nascent neighbourliness is still present in her letters a year later, although the economic factors which will push her awareness of difference into the processes of Othering are beginning to harden. She writes: "We had a tremendous hailstorm today . . . and had the pleasure of giving food and shelter to a Kafir woman with a baby on her back. . . . The basket the woman had on her head was so heavy that George could scarcely assist [her] to lift it on her head again" (1970:34). Despite the kindliness, the earlier "native" has been replaced by "Kafir"; this discursive shift seems to have occurred once the family was able to employ local people as occasional labourers. With its religious origins, the term was not at that time in Natal simply a racist one, but its use by McLeod does suggest that once she is in a class relationship to indigenous people, she needs to support her position by assuming her Christian superiority over those whom she employs. But even here, her own poverty and her focus on survival rather than profit seems to have exercised some restraint on the hierarchical implications of her word. Her letters of this time register what all settlers thought of as the primary problem in Natal: the difficulty of getting cheap labour. But, unlike most, McLeod does not attribute the indigenous peoples' reluctance to take regular employment to their laziness, ingratitude or barbarity. Instead she recognizes their right to the concerns which keep them at home:

> I have had a great deal to do lately as we have been without a Caffir [sic] for some time. They will not work for you just at this time; it is near the Indian corn harvest and they are all at work about their beds, but I hope when it is all gathered in that we shall get one again, for I do very badly without. The wood fire is so troublesome to attend to. George has made me a pair of bellows or I should not be able to cook anything. (1970:22)

Later in 1851, she records that the family has "been without a sixpence for more than a month now" (1970:28) and acknowledges that labour's being obtainable only by the month actually suits them very well under such circumstances.

The way that gender inflects McLeod's attitudes, differentiating them from the locally authoritative view, is exposed when she touches on settler claims that access to cheap indigenous labour was their right. In the 1850s in Natal the category of "refugee" was bestowed on all those African people who lived south of the Thukela River, the boundary between Natal and Zululand, on the grounds they had fled the wars of succession in the Zulu kingdom. This decision involved the dubious claim that the land was uninhabited before the arrival of the settlers and it enabled them to treat all African people as newcomers to the colony, and as being obliged to pay for the colony's protection with their labour. A letter of 1859 shows that McLeod has absorbed this view, but even here her attitudes are not those of her husband. She writes:

> George has the assistance of a Kafir, a refugee from the country where they have been fighting. From those beaten many have fled into Natal, when they are taken by the Magistrates and bound to the settlers to serve there a certain number of years. Ours is bound to us for three years at 5/-a month. His wife also comes to assist me in my washing one day a week, of which I can assure you I am very glad. She washes and cleans my room with her little baby always tied to her back. (1970:101)

Even as she accepts the colonizing relationship in which the refugee argument places her, McLeod resists it by presenting the wife who works for her as her assistant and in remarking on the infant on this mother's back. It seems that the relations of power that obtain in the colony at large are not quite the same in the kitchen.

This gendered difference is confirmed whenever George's voice sounds in the letters. Ellen explains that employer and labourer are governed by a contract (however unjust the imposed obligation), but her husband seems to have been much less inclined to recognize a mutual obligation. When Ellen writes at his dictation in order to advise her sister and brother-in-law against emigration to Natal, this is the language she records: "The work is too hard . . . and he [her brother-in-law] would make a worse hand than even George in driving about black naked savages to do the work for him" (1970:91). The change is great. The brutality is probably not habitual even for George—he seems intent on shock tactics in order to deter their relatives from emigrating. But the complacency of "do the work for him" does suggest the norm which guides George. It is strikingly different from Ellen's use of "assist" when she speaks with gratitude of her washerwoman's help.

In many ways, Ellen McLeod can be seen as an example of the settler woman who, in limiting herself to the realm of the feminine, negatively exposes the rougher, male aspects of power. Her later letters sustain her concentration on children, her house, her garden and the daily life of the Byrne valley, and she hardly ever lifts her head to comment on the colony's public issues. She was, for example, a devout churchgoer, but even the controversies around Bishop Colenso, which directly affected the holding of services in her valley, are treated as her husband's concern. Her chosen speaking position enables her to continue to show an unusual degree of concern for native people. For example, in 1878, while she participates in the settlers' angry sense of trespass when they hear that Cetewayo is threatening to cross the Thukela and violate the boundary they have set up (1970:116), she is full of sympathy for his people when she hears that they are threatened with famine, following a drought (1970:131). Her references to crises such as the 1873 Langalibalele uprising and the 1879 Anglo-Zulu war is again confined to their effect on the daily life of the valley's inhabitants. After the battle of Isandhlwana she reports that "the Kafirs in Natal are in a terrible fright" (1970:219) and their common plight leads her to pray for black and white Natalians alike that God will "preserve us from these dreadful savages" (1970:219). As her inclusive "us" for those south of the Thukela River suggests, the chosen narrowness of her world leaves Ellen McLeod both more free to respond to the personal identities and needs of indigenous people and less free to question the conditions of Empire which contain them all. Even in her private realm, McLeod's inclusive tolerance is narrow in range. She lives in harmony with the rhythms of the land they farm but, as was said earlier, questions of ownership do not arise for her; this means that she cannot entertain questions about the history of the land's habitation. She acknowledges her indigenous neighbours, and the claims of their daily lives, but she never wonders about their past. Like all settlers, McLeod lives within the imperial myth of previously empty land and treats her arrival as the originary moment. On the other hand, because she never feels the pressures of self-justification, her sympathies are fair; the defensiveness of colonial selfhood is not an active feature of her letters.

Eliza Feilden's book, *My African Home*, reveals a somewhat different speaking position. For one thing, it is imbued with her consciousness that her writing is for public consumption in Britain and that she has to engage with metropolitan expectations of the imperial enterprise. Her speaking position is, in this respect, closer to the public voice of the woman travel writer than to the private voice of family letters. And this more conflicted position is not produced simply at the time of publication for Feilden's writing began as private correspondence, and in what the internal evidence suggests are her actual letters there are indications that from the first she sought to represent, and so to control, the divides of class and of race on which the imperial enterprise was founded. It is the power to command which derives from her comparative affluence that leads to the more overtly ambivalent energies with which she writes. As with other settler women, the indigenous people whom she meets are those who come to work for her as domestic servants; in order to preserve Empire's justificatory barriers of difference, she presents these people as curiosities who will delight and amuse (but not terrify) her readers. In the colonized world, settler women's determination to be amused by their domestic trials stands as the equivalent to the frontier myth of indomitable male courage.

The interacting codes of class and gender which Feilden brings with her from England shape most of her account of her servants—white as well as black. Yet when it comes to her African servants, there are signs that she is somewhat less inclined to impose her metropolitan expectations on them than she is on the white people whom she employs. This is not quite the self-othering that was seen in Barnard, but Feilden does occasionally indicate that she cannot claim to know a people whose culture does not participate in the complex agreements which give cohesion to the society from which she has come. At these moments she begins to reach for ways of figuring her world that go beyond the self-justificatory Othering of imperialism. Her search for appropriate figures of speech, and the ways in which these prove unstable and even at times betray her purposes, is evident in one of the retrospective passages of reflection on the hardships of her life in Natal:

> my husband . . . had not calculated on taking me to such a life of labour, neither had I counted on the kind of life I went through. I had looked for a sort of Abrahamic life, with flocks and herds, field and garden produce, a comfortable farmhouse &c. &c.; in short, a simple working life and easy style, with all things requisite about us. I did not count on the tiger[4] taking all our fowls and calves; the hawk, our chickens; the something else burrowing under the iron house and devouring our pigeons; and the wild pigs ploughing up our vegetables; and no respectable female servant to be had to help me in the house. (1887:250)

Her need as she writes is to reassure herself, and her readers, that she did not cease to be a gentlewoman in her new, primitive conditions. To recapture her once innocent hope of a life of pastoral dignity and ease, she uses the phrase an "Abrahamic life." The invocation of an Old Testament patriarch is however both supportive and disruptive of this woman's effort to report on her life. It enables Feilden, writing as a privileged settler, to surmount one of the questions which did not occur to Ellen McLeod—her right to invade another people's land—for reference to Abraham allows Feilden to validate her presence by invoking the great movement of a chosen people towards their promised land. But at the same time Abraham, as an embodiment of male authority, serves to occlude the female in Feilden's presentation of her new world.

The exclusion of the female from her metaphor is not the only source of its instability; the way in which Feilden figures the black population also challenges the resources of her discourse. An "Abrahamic life" expresses the metropolitan "authority" of her class, but it does not equip her to convey what she half knows is the "authenticity" of indigenous life in Natal. The domestic arrangement that Feilden had expected was that a competent white woman housekeeper would run her household and exercise control over the black servants engaged as "hewers of wood and drawers of water" (1887:259). What she found was that most white immigrants had left Britain in order to escape, not retain, their "station" in life and, concomitantly, that the indigenous population regarded working for the white settlers as, at most, a transient necessity. As with the McLeod family, no black servant stayed for long and three months seems to have been the average stretch. Rather than turning to the seasonal requirements of farming to explain her servants' mobility, as McLeod does, Feilden reassures herself with the generalization that the Zulus "are a wandering tribe, and stay not long in one place" (1887:48). The biblical word order indicates that an "Abrahamic life" still hovers in her thoughts, but this time it is to the black people that she accords its simple dignity.

The first African servant whom Feilden represents in detail is a young mission-educated woman called Louisa, who is also the only African woman she employs. The general scarcity of black women servants in the colony (Cock 1990) is a matter into which Feilden's narrative gives some insight when Louisa, who is about to leave on a visit to her mother, explains that there are no women to take her place: "No, ma'am, no girl, they all wife" (1887:37). Reasons why, in precolonial societies in southern Africa, there would have been a rigorous control over a wife's agricultural and domestic labour have been advanced by Jeff Guy (1990), but while indigenous economic practices clearly affected the settler's difficulties in obtaining labour, they are not something into which these people chose to inquire. Their needs as invaders were better met by the generalization that African people were fundamentally lazy and selfish (Atkins 1993; Coetzee 1988). Feilden participates in this view, but it leads her into difficult waters for she often also records her disapproval of African men compelling their wives to "do all the work required at the craals [sic]" (1887:16) and she attributes the desire for a second wife to African men's laziness.[5] On the other hand she does not record finding it strange that it is African men, not women, who come to perform her own household chores. For example, when a young man she calls Ginger presents himself for work, her attention is given to his arriving at the moment of Louisa's departure—not to his being a man who will undertake domestic work.[6] In Ellen McLeod's letters, the rights and wrongs of labour in the colony are at issue by implication when she takes some interest in the individual women who work for her, but the issue is not examined because she places it in the male sphere of concern. In Feilden's case, although she exposes the issue through her interest in the position of black women, she goes no further because her class habits of superiority seem to occlude the questions she might have raised.

Feilden finds Louisa to be sufficiently an object of curiosity for her to grant the black woman a speaking presence in her narrative.[7] In doing so, she is not allowing the black woman her own voice, but she is representing the ways in which, in the 1850s, people such as Louisa thought and spoke for themselves. Besides her explanation of the shortage of female domestic labour, Louisa's words are recorded when she refuses to travel with the Feilden's white manservant, Gudgeon, from the Bay to Feniscowles; when she reads aloud from a Zulu translation of Genesis; when she laughs at Feilden's sketch of people squatting under a tree and recognizes them as "Caffres"; when she declares that she would rather go to church than work on a Sunday; when she agrees that she would like to pass on to her people what the missionaries have taught her, but regrets that "they not like to learn" (1887:26-28); when she lifts her employer by the ankles so that Feilden may see her returning husband (1887:34); and finally when she explains to her employer that she is leaving because she wishes to be near the man who is courting her (1887:45).

Louisa's is a vivid presence and, however mediated, these exchanges from the 1850s may well be the first record of a Zulu woman's point of view.[8] Matching Louisa's vigour, however, is the kind of control that Feilden attempted to exert over her subject. When Louisa leaves to marry, Feilden's report is that although her servant "was very sorry . . . selfishness prevailed, and she set off there and then" (1887:45). Feilden's regret is that Louisa's domestic training and lessons in English will end, but this is outweighed by her class-based and settler-oriented criticism that Louisa "talks of love to God, but does not strive to please her mistress" (1887:32). Feilden's class attitudes also allow her a quite contradictory enjoyment of the scene when her white housekeeper, Mrs. Welsh, is told by Ginger that work will not make him servile: "You are poor people, but me is a gentleman; me have plenty cows, plenty mealies, and plenty oats. When me in craal me do no work; me wife make fire, gather wood, cook food, and she say 'Now you come eat'" (1887:56). When Ginger eventually leaves Feilden's employ because he does not like taking orders from Mrs. Welsh, Feilden's comment is that "he carried his head like an independent man, and was as proud in his own barbarous way as Mrs Welsh herself" (1887:61). It is an extraordinary moment in the readjustments of relationships demanded by life in the colony, but the implied conflicts in Feilden are immediately foreclosed. Her metropolitan class attitudes allow her to enjoy Ginger's standing up to Mrs. Welsh; her gender interest allows her to observe with some concern the work expected of Zulu women but her settler racism, evident as she passes the verdict "barbarous" on Ginger, protects her from exploring the second-world ambi/valence to which the tensions in her discourse might have led her.

It is probably an inkling of the full meaning of Ginger's self-respect which led Feilden to speculate on the origins of the people who would speak of themselves in this way. She turns, as she did when first imagining the pastoral life she would lead in Natal, to the Old Testament, and she writes that the local Africans may well be

> true descendants of Ishmael, who were to live in the presence of their brethren, but of whom nothing is said of their being brought into the fold. There are many Jewish casts of countenance and feature among the Caffres. . . . The Ishmaelites may have Abraham's features, as they have him for their father. What are the prophecies regarding the African races? Ham's descendants spread over Africa, but these Caffres are neither negroes nor Hottentots. (1887:91)[9]

Her musings on origins and those who "spread over Africa" do not crystallize into questions about land rights because, as with McLeod, the "refugee" argument seems to have blocked Feilden's arrival at any sense that African people had an originary claim to the land (Atkins 1993). But while Feilden is shielded from the full implication of the questions she raises, she is still, perhaps not fully consciously, affected by the authenticity that indigenous people can claim. Again it is her figure of speech that exposes her predicament; her speculations that the African people in Natal have their origins in Ishmael, sharing a paternity with the Israelites, expose and then clash with the idea of her own membership of the "chosen people" in which she had cloaked her arrival in the colony.

   In her efforts to understand her relationship to her black servants, the discourse most readily at hand for Feilden was that of the patriarchal traditions of Christianity which had served the ruling-class interests of the British for centuries and which imperialism readily transported to the colonies. Against this rhetoric, her interest in her own role as a settler woman in the colony and her nascent concern for Zulu women had little chance of untrammelled expression, let alone of leading her to a radical questioning of her position. What emerges from the comparison between her patronizing interests in the indigenous people and McLeod's less conflicted but more circumscribed responses to them is that gender in the discourses of both writers is a significant factor in the emergence of a settler (as distinct from an imperial) point of view. As an apparently "objective set of references" gender also allows us to understand why settler discourse remained bifocal, deriving from but not remaining of the metropolitan centre.

Notes

1 Mills's target could equally have been Patrick Brantlinger who, in his account of how the "altruism of the antislavery movement" had, by the 1884 Berlin Conference and Europe's official carving up of Africa, given way to the "cynicism of empire building" (1985:166), concentrates almost entirely on writing by male missionaries, travellers and novelists. He does include one nineteenth-century woman novelist, Sarah Lee Wallis, but he implies that her attitudes were shaped by her more famous husband, Thomas Bowdich (1985:175).

2 Driver gives as an example of this "self-othering" Lady Anne's "fleeting" recognition that she is looking at slavery from "free born eyes" and Driver argues that this recognition is "substantially if subtly different from feeling 'sorry' for slaves" (1993:12).

3 The Irishman "J C Byrne, arranged with the Government that, for £10-00, each adult immigrant should receive a free passage to Natal and from 20 to 50 acres of land on arrival. . . . [T]he land had been divided without any

regard to the character of the soil, and the allotments were often only rocky hillsides, utterly unsuited for tillage" (Russell 1899:204-205).

4 Leopards were frequently referred to as tigers at this time.

5 Feilden's only direct comment on polygamy is that the Natal government is duplicitous in not prohibiting it. Her point is that because each wife has a separate hut, and African men are taxed according to the number of huts in their homestead, the government protects polygamy as a source of income (1887:253-54).

6 Conversely, the settlers seem not to have considered women for agricultural labour: "the Natal Natives were not agriculturists: they were hunters and pastoralists. Cultivation of the soil was women's work. Although African women at the present day assist materially in the cultivation of the cane-fields, no one seems to have thought of them as a source of labour in the 1850s" (Brookes and Webb 1987:81).

7 Although Feilden's interest is in Louisa as a "strange, untutored creature" (1887:34), she does not exhibit the "refusal to be aware of the other areas" of her servant's life on which "the ability to exploit depends" and which is depicted in South African writing from the present century (Lenta 1989:239).

8 This comment is made with regard to the date of Feilden's letters (the 1850s), not that of the publication of her book. Other Zulu women are also heard at one remove in Feilden's narrative, as when Ginger's friends and family visit him. His three sisters are intrigued by Feilden's small waist and, by gesture and laughter, compare her slenderness with their own figures (1887:55).

9 Feilden reports that Henry Francis Fynn is her informant on this matter.

References

Atkins, Keletso E.

1993   *The Moon Is Dead! Give Us Our Money! The Cultural Origins of an African Work Ethic, Natal, South Africa, 1843-1900.* Portsmouth: Heinemann; London: James Currey.

Barnard, Lady Anne

1993   *The Cape Journals of Lady Anne Barnard 1797-1798.* Edited by A.M. Lewin Robinson with Margaret Lenta and Dorothy Driver. Cape Town: Van Riebeeck Society.

Brantlinger, Patrick

1985   "Victorians and Africans: The Genealogy of the Myth of the Dark Continent." *Critical Inquiry* 12:166-203.

Brookes, E., and Colin de B. Webb

1987   *A History of Natal.* Pietermaritzburg: University of Natal Press.

Cock, Jacklyn

1990   "Domestic Service and Education for Domesticity: The Incorporation of Xhosa Women into Colonial Society." In Cherryl Walker, ed., *Women and Gender in Southern Africa to 1945,* 76-96, 352-54. Cape Town: David Philip.

Coetzee, J.M.

1988   *White Writing: On the Culture of Letters in South Africa.* Sandton: Radix; New Haven and London: Yale University Press.

Driver, Dorothy

1988   "'Woman' as Sign in the South African Colonial Enterprise." *Journal of Literary Studies* 4, 1:3-20.

1993   "Literary Appraisal." In *The Cape Journals of Lady Anne Barnard 1797-1798*, 1-13. Edited by A.M. Lewin Robinson with Margaret Lenta and Dorothy Driver. Cape Town: Van Riebeeck Society.

Feilden, Eliza Whigham

1887   *My African Home; or, Bush Life in Natal when a Young Colony (1852-7).* London: Sampson Low, Marston, Searle, & Rivington.

Guy, Jeff

1990   "Gender Oppression in Southern Africa's Precapitalist Societies." In Cherryl Walker, ed., *Women and Gender in Southern Africa to 1945*, 33-47, 348-49. Cape Town: David Philip.

Hattersley, A.F.

1949   *The Natal Settlers 1849-1851.* Pietermaritzburg: Shuter and Shooter.

Lawson, Alan

1991   "A Cultural Paradigm for the Second World." *Australian-Canadian Studies* 9, 1-2:67-78.

1994   "Un/settling Colonies: The Ambivalent Place of Discursive Resistance." In Chris Worth, Pauline Nestor and Marko Parlyshyn, eds., *Literature and Opposition.* Clayton, Vic.: Centre for Comparative Literature and Cultural Studies, Monash University.

1995   "Postcolonial Theory and the 'Settler' Subject." Special issue of *ELW*—"Testing the Limits: Postcolonial Theories and Canadian Literature"—56:274-86.

Lenta, Margaret

1989   "Intimate Knowledge and Wilful Ignorance: White Employers and Black Employees in South African Fiction." In Cherry Clayton, ed., *Women and Writing in South Africa.* Marshalltown, SA: Heinemann.

1996   "The Art of the Possible: Lady Anne Barnard's 'Cape' Writings and Their Survival." In M.J. Daymond, ed., *South African Feminisms: Writing, Theory, and Criticism 1990-1994*, 169-84. New York: Garland Publishing.

McLeod, Ellen

1970   *Dear Louisa: History of a Pioneer Family in Natal: Ellen McLeod's Letters to Her Sister in England from the Byrne Valley.* Edited by R.E. Gordon. Pietermaritzburg: Shuter and Shooter.

Mills, Sara

1991   *Discourses of Difference: An Analysis of Women's Travel Writing and Colonialism.* London and New York: Routledge.

Russell, George
   1899   *History of Old Durban*. Durban: P. Davis and Sons.
Scott, Joan W.
   1986   "Gender: A Useful Category of Historical Analysis." *American Historical Review* 91, 5:1053-75.
Slemon, Stephen
   1990   "Unsettling the Empire: Resistance Theory for the Second World." *World Literature Written in English* 30, 2:30-41.
Spencer, Shelagh O'Byrne
   1992   *British Settlers in Natal 1824-1857: A Biographical Register*. Vol. 6, *Eagle-Fyvie*. Pietermaritzburg: University of Natal Press.
Woolf, Virginia
   1974   *A Room of One's Own*. Harmondsworth: Penguin.

8

Rural Women and African Resistance: Lauretta Ngcobo's *And They Didn't Die*

Cherry Clayton

> How was it that laws were so clear cut, when the lives they governed were so muddled? — Ngcobo 1991:226

> The hand that rocks the cradle should also rock the boat. — South African women's slogan

Culture, Ideology and Representation

Debates about the relationship of culture, ideology and the politics of literary representation are complex. Frantz Fanon wrote in *Toward the African Revolution* that the process of industrialization camouflaged racism: "the perfecting of the means of production inevitably brings about the camouflage of the techniques by which man is exploited, hence of the forms of racism" (1967:35). These essays evoke the spirit of the 1958 Accra conference on African strategy and unity as a historical unravelling of the 1884 Berlin conference, which carved up continents in the name and spirit of European imperialism. Fanon goes on to say that "The advent of peoples, unknown only yesterday, onto the stage of history, their

---

Notes to chapter 8 are on pp. 126-27.

determination to participate in the building of a civilization that has its place in the world of today give to the contemporary period a decisive importance in the world process of humanization" (1967:146). A black South African writer, Lauretta Ngcobo, echoes this thought when she says: "there is another victory to be won, if South Africa is to be restored to her space in Africa. The cultural battle. There is no other place in the continent which is less African than South Africa" (1994:570).

The humanist discourse which emerges in relation to the decolonization of Africa now co-exists with a deconstructive discourse which problematizes cultural identity, critiques the development and enlightenment paradigms for Africa, and insists on contradiction and difference in the cultural articulation of African and Afro-American identities.[1] Henry Louis Gates, Jr., argues that the heritage of each black text in a Western language is "a double heritage, two-toned" and that writers of African descent "occupy spaces in at least two traditions: a European or American literary tradition, and one of the several related but distinct black traditions" (1984:4). While "the very act of writing has been a political act for the black author (Gates 1984:5), the structure of the black text has been repressed and treated as if it were transparent (Gates 1984:6). Black people have always been "masters of the figurative"; saying one thing and meaning another has been "basic to black survival in oppressive Western cultures" (Gates 1984:6).

Critics working within African and Afro-American feminism have also wanted to stress repetition and revision in black women's texts. Barbara Johnson, writing on Zora Neale Hurston, argues that Hurston's protagonist needs to "assume and articulate the incompatible forces involved in her own division. The sign of authentic voice is thus not self-identity but self-difference" 1984:212). Houston Baker, Jr., situates narration within "a world that is itself constituted by a repertoire of 'stories'" (1984:224). Susan Willis, writing on Toni Morrison, says that "sexuality converges with history and functions as a register for the experience of change, i.e. historical transition" (1984:263). Morrison, like Ngcobo, "develops the social and psychological aspects that characterize the lived experience of historical transition" and its consequences, "the alienation produced by the transition to wage labour" (Willis 1984:265). Domestic service constitutes only a marginal incorporation as wage labour, and in Morrison's fiction "individual genealogy evokes the history of black migration and the chain of economic expropriation from hinterland to village, and village to metropolis"

(Willis 1984:265). Individual differences between women function to test the social dynamic within the group and society at large (Willis 1984:279). Jane Bryce, discussing African women's writing in a "post-Negritude, post-colonial reading of culture" suggests that recent writing is marked by a "self-conscious disjunction" (1994:619) between tradition and modernity. African women writers' use of English and of the novel genre "may be seen as an implicit assertion of distance from the nostalgia for origins, a recognition of the need for a revisioning of culture and their relationship to it from a postcolonial perspective" (Bryce 1994:620-21).

When Lauretta Ngcobo contextualizes her own literary production, she also points to multiple, often conflicting allegiances. Born in 1931 in rural Natal, she was forced to flee South Africa in 1963 after persecution by the South African government and police harassment.[2] Her husband was in the first executive of the Pan-Africanist Congress, a radical group that broke away from the African National Congress in 1959 and organized the pass resistance that led to the Sharpeville massacre in 1960. He was sent to jail along with people like Sobukwe (leader of the PAC) and Mandela. Ngcobo's husband was involved in the lengthy Treason Trials which began in 1956. He was then in prison between 1960 and 1963, and a militant activist until 1969, when the couple eventually settled in England with their three children, and where Lauretta began her first novel, *Cross of Gold* (1981), a novel in which she found it difficult to keep her female protagonist alive as a focal centre (Hunter 1994:102). Sindisiwe dies because at the time "death and destruction" were all-pervasive; "such has been the history of our struggle in South Africa" (Hunter 1994:107). At the time of writing her first novel Ngcobo found it difficult to see African women as capable of effecting change:

> In South Africa . . . a black woman is oppressed by law, which has calcified around the old traditional customs. Under the Natal Code, for instance, a woman is a perpetual minor who cannot perform at law even when her husband is dead. She's equally incapacitated socially, economically, all round. (Bush 1984:7)

Ngcobo has also expressed ambivalence about feminism and the freedom that Western women aspire to, while being agents of racial oppression themselves, whether in South Africa or England: "I am not referring to the structure of institutionalised power, but to the yoke of daily injustice, to the bitterness of everyday living" (Vivan 1989:111). She calls attention to a range of levels of oppression and draws a comparison between oppression by African men and white women: "through our man we feel the weight of the system, as well as that of law and tradition. An analogous thing happens to us in respect of the white woman: it is through her that a variety of oppressions befall us" (Vivan 1989:112). Yet she acknowledges that white women have won rights which will benefit African women after democratization. This has been the case in South Africa, where women represented in Parliament now constitute 33-1/3 percent of the total, moving from 130th in the world to 10th place (Davis 1994:587).

In attempting to define her place in relation to Western and African traditions, Ngcobo admits that "Our women are caught up in a hybrid world of the old and the new; the African and the alien locked in the struggle to integrate contradictions into a meaningful new whole" (Ngcobo 1986:82). African women had been cardboard figures in a written tradition that created contradictory images of idolized mothers and the realities of wifehood.[3] The oral tradition, though she cites a moving instance of its performance by her grandfather at her own birth, also "extolled the virtues of humility, silent endurance and self-effacing patterns of behaviour for our girls" (Ngcobo 1986:81). During her growing years and education she was made to feel marginalized in the educational system (35 women to 500 men when she attended university) (Ngcobo 1986:85). At school and university she observed the cultural clash between rural and city ways and people: "I began to feel a disfigurement of outlook, a mutilation within" (Ngcobo 1986:85). This may account for the strong presence she gives to rural women, and their powers of resistance, in her later novel, *And They Didn't Die*, in which the title signals defiance and survival.

In her autobiographical writing, essays and interviews Ngcobo relates the fragmentation of cultural traditions to political processes, especially industrialization and migrant labour. The introduction of scripted literature divided society into an educated elite and an uneducated mass, and became a source of alienation. The system of migrant labour "altered beyond recognition the structures of our societies" and affected women who had traditionally played a prominent role in the transmission of oral literature (Ngcobo 1986:84). Urbanization in the gendered form of migrant labour for men "created . . . hardened divisions between men and women" (Ngcobo 1986:85). The story of *And They Didn't Die*, which relates the different but politically inflected trials of an African couple, Jezile and Siyalo, sundered by multiple factors deriving from poverty, migrant labour, political activism and prison, customary law and gendered oppression, becomes the vehicle for conveying this process of "hardened division" between the sexes. The stories of their different trajectories into city life, patterns of disillusionment, economic struggle and politicization, become representative stories illuminating the complex intersections of capitalism, race and gender in South African life and their effects on rural people.[4] Ngcobo's self-positioning in relation to literary traditions is also complex, acknowledging hybridity and multiple affiliations. She acknowledges her special feeling for Thomas Hardy's fiction, and this may have affected her creation of dignified rural people who are crushed by political and economic conditions as if by fate, and the passing away of rural communities (Vivan 1989:106). She has also mentioned the attraction of the novel form: "The only form that I get on well with is the novel, but I want to capture the feel of South Africa at this particular time of transition" (Daymond 1996:85). However, she feels that her emphasis on one central character and action is derived from an African tradition:

> our folklore which always pivots around the story of an individual, an important person of our tradition. The importance of the plot is created around one single character. . . . Each character has a certain gamut of options, which are drawn from an objective reality, even if it is then partly invented in the story. (Vivan 1989:109)

Thematically African novels are restricted, because topics like land or factory ownership have no relevance, so the themes of European fiction become "arid, senseless, useless material" (Vivan 1989:110). "The black writer is forced to limit himself to a few themes which deal with a society scarred by poverty and restrictions" (Vivan 1989:110). But there is a broader theme of historical suffering: "the fundamental themes which are for us of common interest, and ask for an answer to the feelings of our people" (Vivan 1989:110).

In her introduction to Miriam Tlali's *Footprints in the Quag* (1989), Ngcobo traces the movement in black South African writing from a literature of cultural assimilation to protest. As literature tried to deal with industrialization and migratory labour, writers were bewildered: "These writers were faced with the paradox of creating or fashioning a new indigenous character, while the dynamics of the situation pointed to the destruction of the culture in which that character had to be rooted and flourish" (Ngcobo 1989:xi). The consolidation of white power with the Union of the provinces in 1910 "marks the Africans' first awareness of themselves as an oppressed people" (Ngcobo

1989:xii). A new spirit emerged dramatically in the 1970s and within that mood Miriam Tlali "writes from the heart of those turbulent cities" (Ngcobo 1989:xv), expressing "the wounds sustained in the collapse of our societies" (Ngcobo 1989:xvii), especially through women's eyes. As a result, Tlali tends to see tradition as a salvation for African people, whereas Ngcobo is much more critical of African custom. With regard to political purpose, Ngcobo says that her writing is "a social/political comment": "I believe books by the oppressed people can, ever so subtly, restore the desire for freedom and the will to achieve this" in the face of the psychological introjection of colonial images of inferiority (Bush 1984:8).[5]

Rural Women, Gender and Racial Politics

In *And They Didn't Die* Ngcobo's purpose was to show "how country women cope and resist the pressures of the law, how the laws of the country disadvantage them" (Bush 1984:6). Rural women, the traditional food producers, have been without tilling and land tenure rights. Yet women have often rallied to oppose injustice: they fought against the imposition of passes in the late 1950s; against the problem of dipping their dying cattle (dipping tanks were introduced to control disease), and the government's policy of building beerhalls for men, while not providing facilities for child care (Bush 1984:8). Multiple grievances led to defiance by women, erupting in different regions of Natal in 1959. About 1,000 women were arrested. These events, the context for the first section of the novel, record the emergence of "a vast new political constituency. No understanding of the radicalisation of black politics in those years would be complete without a knowledge of the emergence and behaviour of this constituency" (Lodge 1983: 150).[6] Jezile's husband is in Durban while she struggles with her mother-in-law's persecution for her infertility. Siyalo is politicized in Durban by the evidence of social injustice, overcrowding and exploitation of labour, and is soon identified as a troublemaker. During Jezile's visit she experiences the humiliations of her husband's hostel life, but is also given a glimpse of the activism of urban women who storm the beerhalls in protest. She feels a bond with city women: "how similar their situations were" (Ngcobo 1991:30).

Historical activities by the ANC Women's League are represented in a woman doctor and leader, Nosizwe, who illuminates aspects of political leadership during the build-up of popular resistance. The problems of traditional lifestyles are illustrated by Jezile's friend Zenzile, who dies in childbirth. We see the contradictions of Jezile's life and her growing awareness of her husband's involvement in an African patriarchal system. The difficulties of parenting are shown when both parents are imprisoned for periods of time. The contradictions of government policy, destroying rural communities while trying to preserve them artificially, are shown in intimate detail, as are impossible economic conditions in the countryside.

In the second phase of Jezile's life she is incorporated into urban domestic service while her husband is in prison. The transition from a fairly stable though distant family life to a single-mother household suggests the contradictions of human sexuality and family life in rural and urban South Africa. Jezile is accused by her mother-in-law (the custodian of customary law) of infidelity when she returns pregnant from a brief prison sentence. After Siyalo's prison sentence she is drawn into a single women's culture which supports her. She takes on domestic service in a white household and is then raped by her employer, who sends her home with the child to protect himself from arrest. Once back in the village she is disowned by her in-laws for having mothered a "white" child. After Siyalo's release from prison he claims his daughters, but he and Jezile are separated by customary law. The compounded force of racial oppression and customary law is vividly illustrated in these ironic plot twists.

In the last, compressed section of the narrative, Jezile and her children move through the turbulent political clashes of the 1976 countrywide insurgency and the emergency period of the mid-1980s. Jezile's daughter Ndondo becomes a political activist and flees the country. Her son Lungi, the child of mixed race, becomes a leader at his coloured school and is paralyzed from the waist down in a police shooting incident. When her daughter Ndondo visits her secretly during the emergency period, a soldier storms their house and attempts to rape Jezile's other daughter, S'naye. Jezile kills the soldier. Jezile now goes to her husband with an account of her own rape by her employer and they realize that at the moment of a possible reunion they will be sundered by another prison sentence. The final scene is complex in its evocation of a historical abyss, the abyss of the combined historical damage of industrialization, the apartheid system and racialized sexual abuse: "He swung around to face her, carnage in his mind, and looked at her wordlessly, penetrating those eyes, mind to mind, heart to heart. Together they drifted back in reverse into a vortex beyond recovery, in a kind of falling away" (Ngcobo 1991:245). This ending also counters any emancipatory or enlightenment narrative, constituting a critique of the liberal ideology which sees modernization as inevitably progressive.[7] Ngcobo's narration during the transitional period in South Africa thus involves a memory of the complexity of historical damage to individuals, the family and the collectivity of the oppressed. Her novel is an implicit answer to the question Said poses as central to a decolonizing imagination: "How does a culture seeking to become independent of imperialism imagine its own past?" (Said 1993:214).

While the narrative moves toward a violent crisis and sense of historical loss, the seizing of subjectivity by those who have traditionally been seen as objects and a "subordinate race despised by all" (Wicomb 1992:18) manifests "the material reality of people's lives" in a way which Wicomb calls moving beyond "the legacy of victims" (1992:15). Ngcobo's novel demonstrates a complex relationship between social structures and subjectivity, particularly in Jezile's fully rendered consciousness as she struggles with the changing political and cultural contexts that surround her, with what Belinda Bozzoli calls "the changing material world" as "a decision-making existential being" (Bozzoli with Nkotsoe 1991:236). The novel is well suited to displaying the tension between internal and external struggles, conflicts between generations and genders. *And They Didn't Die* is thus anti-essentialist in effect, recognizing, like Foucault, "the manifold structures of power" with their varied forms and multiplicity of "localized resistances and counter-offensives" (Escobar 1984-85:381) and thus also recognizing that "women, far from being powerless, are agents in their own fates" (Udayagiri 1995:161). In Jezile's successful defence of her daughter's body the materiality of women's oppression is recognized and partly resolved. Female sexuality mediates systems of power, but the generational progression from Jezile to S'naye shows how self-defence is the lesson of female experience. In defending her daughter, Jezile defends herself in an action that testifies to the consciousness-raising she has undergone in both racial and gender politics.

Discourse, Labour and African Renewal

Ngcobo has argued that in South Africa women's quarrel is primarily with the state, and that this differentiates their feminist struggle from many others (Bush 1984:8). Because of her characters' involvement in radical political action her fiction could be said to be part of the discourse of the Pan-Africanist Congress. Graham Pechey characterizes two counter-texts to the Freedom Charter of 1955 and its

broad universalizing humanism: the Pan-Africanist Congress and Black
Consciousness (1994:28). The PAC critique of 1959, he argues (the
point in time where Ngcobo's second novel begins) "is founded in an
anti-modernist narrative that reduces everything to a story of reposses-
sion" (1994:28). *And They Didn't Die* could be said to participate in this
anti-modernist discourse and in the radical politics of the PAC, but it
feminizes this discourse and offers a critique of liberal discourse and
earlier women's writing in South Africa by revisioning key tropes.
Instead of the seduced and abandoned white settler women who characterize the novels of Olive Schreiner and Pauline Smith, and whose
stories are played out in terms of white settler hegemony and patriarchal social codes for settler women, Ngcobo's protagonist Jezile is
politicized by multiple forms of gender and racial oppression to the
point of militancy and an act of violence. Seduction is replaced by
rape, indicating the structural and personal violence the state inflicts
on African women, and their economic and personal vulnerability in
domestic labour.[8]

The liberal use of the adoptive situation in Schreiner's novel *From
Man to Man* (1926), where a white woman adopts the child of her husband's liaison with a coloured servant, is also revised when Jezile bears
a coloured child from her employer's rape and the child becomes an
activist in radical clashes with the state and the military. This situation
allegorizes the national situation: European interbreeding with an
indigenous and slave population produced the people whose partial
alliance with Black Consciousness helped to oust them from power.
Ngcobo's reworking of this narrative trope inverts Sarah Gertrude
Millin's notorious use of mixed blood as the sign of laxity and degener-
ation (see Coetzee 1988). The revised adoptive family evokes the spirit
of non-racial resistance that marked the 1980s in South Africa and the
rise of associations such as the United Democratic Front.

And They Didn't Die thus evokes the existential dimension of the
cultural dislocations, land expropriations and economic disempowerment imposed by colonialism, industrialization and migrant labour. By
appropriating narrative, one of the forms of cultural control, and sub-
verting it to oppositional purposes, South African writers circulate new
histories, in this case making rural women's consciousness in previously "hidden struggles" available to new readerships (see Beinart and
Bundy 1987). The intersections of customary law, African patriarchy
and apartheid legislation are revealed in the detailed emotional texture
of family life.[9] The destructive personal effects of migrant labour are

graphically presented: sexual loneliness, enforced adultery, arrest for those politicized in the cities, the degradation of the physical and social environment, "a hopeless patchwork of effort, determination, and failure" (Ngcobo 1991:221; see Ramphele 1991). The slow collapse of subsistence agriculture is the context of the opening chapters, and the women's grievances are related to the extension of influx control legislation in the Bantustan (homeland) policy designed to prevent permanent African settlement and thus political franchise in the cities (Walker 1982).

At the same time the novel provides a fictional record of the construction of patterns of resistance and solidarity, the ways in which currents of freedom rippled through rural communities and in moments of private reflection and understanding:

> she knew she had taken a decision that she should have taken ages before. Nobody would ever take that power away from her—not his mother, not her own mother, not anyone. Both mothers had had such a hold on her precisely because they had never had that power over their own lives. (Ngcobo 1991:11)

The lifting of women's local resistance to new levels is shown in the prison experience of the village women:

> Then suddenly, somewhere in the deepest part of that jail, they heard a different kind of song. It pierced the prison air and shattered the silence of the vast corridors. The women in the cells listened for a few moments. Then they knew it was Nosizwe. They picked up her song and sang it with gusto. Her song was not a hymn, it was a political song that throbbed in the gut. Their voices returned to them full of strength and defiance. They grew strong and threw off the feeling of inadequacy that had gripped them. (Ngcobo 1991:100-101)

The links between the 1950s decade, which Ngcobo describes as the beginning of "political confrontation with the oppressor" (1989:xii), and thus of a new type of literature, and the township uprisings of the 1970s and 1980s are telescoped in the last section of the novel, in the story of Jezile's children (see Mzamane 1985). Ngcobo's position within the generation of writers produced by Sharpeville and its political contexts is unique, as Mzamane has pointed out, because she carries to an English-speaking audience the rural experiences and subjectivities usually produced in indigenous languages or in the liberal, patriarchal, morally recuperative format of Alan Paton's *Cry, the Beloved Country* (Mzamane 1985:40). The English language and the multi-generational realistic family saga are adapted to become the vehicles of a South African narrative of dispossession and resistance. Ngcobo adopts the documentary devices of incorporating political speeches, lists of grievances, historical dates and protests, devices that have been central to historical fiction and its use by South African novelists such as Nadine Gordimer (see Clingman 1986:187-88). Rural families living on the reserves are made into what Raymond Williams calls a "knowable community," shaped by a novelist "in such a way as to give it identity, presence, ways of reusable articulation" (Williams 1990:165-82).

Ngcobo's insistence on a cumulative plot movement toward an act of violent retaliation against sexual violence suggests the role played by gender awareness in black South African women's writing, and its relationship to State violence and the aftermath of colonialism (see Head 1977; Mvula 1988; Qakisa 1988; Tlali 1989). The conclusion of the novel, while evoking solidarity between Jezile and Siyalo, also draws the limits of the body as metaphor.[10] The body, writes Jean Comaroff, is "a tangible frame of selfhood" which "mediates all action upon the world and simultaneously constitutes both the self and the universe of social and natural relations of which it is a part" (1985:6-7). The South African legacy is still immured in forms of violent control and aggression inflicted on women (Hansson 1991). The tragic "vortex" that concludes the novel is an index to the semi-occlusion of rural African predicaments in the mass migrations to the cities, under apartheid, and in the emergence of an educated, urban African elite.

The story Ngcobo tells is also the story of African women's labour: "the country women are the backbone of the South African superstructure" (Bush 1984:8). They maintain homes for absent husbands, supplement meagre wages, produce and raise the next generation of workers (Bush 1984:8). The labour of serfs generally, as J.M. Coetzee has pointed out, was elided in the late-nineteenth-century South African pastoral. The rural labour of African women has been doubly elided in white South African fiction, except for occasional glimpses, such as the one we get in Gordimer's *July's People* (1981), which is in a displaced futuristic setting. Ngcobo makes visible what Njabulo Ndebele calls "the unacknowledged presence of Black labour and the legitimacy of the political claims based upon that labour" (1994:4). The differentiated process of labour incorporation for men and women, and the different costs, are detailed within a family setting which is repeatedly shattered by punitive state interventions.

Ndebele has pointed out that the role of literature in the crisis of transition is not an easy one: "It throws up a problematic of its own within the broad cultural crisis" (1994:9). Ngcobo's novel, written within that crisis, looks backward and forward, finding an avenue "in the history of the survival culture of the people" (Ndebele 1994:8). Though *And They Didn't Die*, as Eva Hunter has argued, works within a broad framework of historical and social referentiality (Hunter 1994:120), subjectivity is shown as constructed within what Benita Parry calls "antagonistic forces and heterogeneous signifying practices, solicited and situated by conflicting ideological addresses" (Parry 1994:22). These ideological addresses include radical PAC politics, racialized gender violence, anti-apartheid activism and a critique of customary African law. Ngcobo's novel is a form of anti-pastoral that looks backward over fifty years to Sol Plaatje's noble Barolong couple, Mhudi and Ra-Thaga, embedded in visionary pastoral romance. The insistent narrative focus on Jezile and her shifting subjectivity "affirm cultural identity as a new and insurgent subjectivity that has been fought for and reconstructed in the process of struggle" (Parry 1994:22). The story Ngcobo tells in *And They Didn't Die* is the story of what cannot afford to be forgotten in the construction of a democratic future for South Africa. Ngcobo is in accord with Fanon's pan-African vision when she writes of the relationship between South Africa and the rest of Africa: "Where the white government sees state barriers, we see gates, not to enter and pillage or encroach on other people's territories but to enter in good will, and together with fellow Africans we shall create a new impregnable African Continent" (Ngcobo 1991:199).

Notes

1 Mridula Udayagiri writes that "development has been a problematic concept, because it perpetuates unequal relations in the global economy, and ignores perceptions of progress that may be very different from those of policy-makers" (1995:160). She also suggests that theories of development and underdevelopment "remain firmly anchored in emancipatory paradigms that emerged in the Age of Enlightenment" (1995:160).

2 Biographical details are taken from the interview by Robert Bush (1984:5-8).

3 Zoe Wicomb says ambivalent social attitudes towards women are rather like those that characterize writing itself: "the consecration of women as virgins or mothers or other fetishization of Woman which at the same time allows women as human beings to be treated with contempt" (1994:574).

4 Margaret Daymond writes in her introduction to *South African Feminisms* that the essays in the collection "begin to uncover a history of complicity

between apartheid ideology and the patriarchalism of nineteenth-century Calvinism, tracing an overlap between the institutionalisation of racial 'apartness' and masculinist epistemology" (1996:x-xi).

5 Carol Boyce Davies describes African feminism as "a hybrid of sorts"; there is "a struggle against women's own internalised oppression" (Boyce Davies and Graves 1986:241). For Ngcobo this struggle clearly took place over time in her increasing confidence in representing rural women's lives in fiction.

6 Brian Worsfold gives an excellent account of the political context for the novel in his article on Ngcobo in *Altered State: Writing and South Africa* (1994).

7 Ngcobo had been pressured by her first publisher, Longmans, to add an optimistic epilogue to *Cross of Gold* (Bush 1984:7).

8 Jackie Cock (1987) discusses the South African domestic worker as one instance of the "trapped worker."

9 Customary law offered forms of protection but at the cost of the woman's loss of autonomy in communally identified functions within marriage and childbearing (see Nhlapo 1991). Independence, migration and incorporation into urban wage labour brought a new set of problems, economic insecurity and often a neo-colonial repackaging of patriarchy (see Jochelson 1995; also Cheater and Gaidzwana 1996).

10 Grant Farred cites the inscriptions on the body of forms of male power, and discusses different sites of oppression and resistance in his article on *And They Didn't Die* (1993).

References

Baker, Houston A., Jr.

  1984 "To Move without Moving: Creativity and Commerce in Ralph Ellison's Trueblood Episode." In Henry Louis Gates, Jr., ed., *Black Literature and Literary Theory*, 221-48. New York: Methuen.

Bazilli, Susan, ed.

  1991 *Putting Women on the Agenda.* Johannesburg: Ravan Press.

Beinart, William, and Colin Bundy

  1987 *Hidden Struggles in Rural South Africa.* London: James Currey.

Boehmer, Elleke, Laura Chrisman and Kenneth Parker, eds.

  1994 *Altered State? Writing and South Africa.* Mundelstrup: Dangaroo Press.

Boyce Davies, Carole, and Anne Adams Graves

  1986 *Ngambika: Studies of Women in African Literature.* Trenton, NJ: Africa World Press.

Bozzoli, Belinda, with Mmantho Nkotsoe

  1991 *Women of Phokeng: Consciousness, Life Strategy and Migrancy in South Africa, 1900-1983.* Portsmouth: Heinemann.

Bryce, Jane

  1994 "Writing as Power in the Narratives of African Women." In Anna Rutherford, Lars Jensen and Shirley Chew, eds., *Into the Nineties: Post-Colonial Women's Writing*, 618-25. Mundelstrup: Dangaroo Press.

Bush, Robert
1984 "Do Books Alter Lives?" *Wasafiri* 1, 1:5-8.
Cheater, A.P., and R.B. Gaidzwana
1996 "Citizenship in Neo-Patrilineal States: Gender and Mobility in Southern Africa." *Journal of Southern African Studies* 22, 2:189-200.
Clingman, Stephen
1986 *The Novels of Nadine Gordimer: History from the Inside.* Johannesburg: Ravan Press.
Cock, Jacklyn
1987 "Trapped Workers: Constraints and Contradictions Experienced by Black Women in Contemporary South Africa." *Women's Studies International Forum* 10, 2:133-40.
Coetzee, J.M.
1988 *White Writing: On the Culture of Letters in South Africa.* New Haven: Yale University Press.
Comaroff, Jean
1985 *Body of Power, Spirit of Resistance.* Chicago: University of Chicago Press.
Davis, Geoffrey
1994 "I Speak as a Woman Person: Geoffrey Davis Interviews Emma Mashinini." In Anna Rutherford, Lars Jensen and Shirley Chew, eds., *Into the Nineties: Post-Colonial Women's Writing,* 579-97. Mundelstrup: Dangaroo Press.
Daymond, M.J., ed.
1996 *South African Feminisms: Writing, Theory and Criticism 1990-1994.* New York and London: Garland.
1992 "Some Thoughts on South Africa, 1992: Interview with Lauretta Ngcobo." *Current Writing* 4, 1:85-97.
Escobar, A.
1984-85 "Discourse and Power in Development: Michel Foucault and the Relevance of His Work to the Third World." *Alternatives* 10, 3:377-400.
Farred, Grant
1993 "'Not Like Women at All': Black Female Subjectivity in Lauretta Ngcobo's *And They Didn't Die.*" *Genders* 16:94-112.
Fanon, Frantz
1967 *Toward the African Revolution.* Translated by Haakon Chevalier. New York: Grove Press.
Gates, Henry Louis, Jr., ed.
1984 *Black Literature and Literary Theory.* New York: Methuen.
Gordimer, Nadine
1982 *July's People.* London: Penguin, 1982. Originally published in 1981.
Hansson, Desiree
1991 "Working against Violence against Women." In Susan Bazilli, ed., *Putting Women on the Agenda,* 180-93. Johannesburg: Ravan Press.

Head, Bessie
1977   *The Collector of Treasures*. London: Heinemann.
Hunter, Eva
1994   "'We Have to Defend Ourselves': Women, Tradition and Change in Lauretta Ngcobo's *And They Didn't Die*." *Tulsa Studies in Women's Literature* 13, 1 (Spring):113-26.
Hunter, Eva, and Craig Mackenzie, eds.
1993   "Lauretta Ngcobo" (1980 interview). In *Between the Lines II*, 97-116. Interviews with Nadine Gordimer, Menan du Plessis, Zoe Wicomb, Lauretta Ngcobo. Grahamstown: NELM.
Jochelson, Karen
1995   "Women, Migrancy and Morality: A Problem of Perspective." *Journal of Southern African Studies* 21, 2:323-32.
Johnson, Barbara
1984   "Metaphor, Metonymy and Voice in *Their Eyes Were Watching God*." In Henry Louis Gates, Jr., ed., *Black Literature and Literary Theory*, 205-19. New York: Methuen.
Lodge, Tom
1983   *Black Politics in South Africa since 1945*. Harlow: Longman.
Marchand, Marianne H., and Jane L. Parpart, eds.
1995   *Feminism, Postmodernism, Development*. London: Routledge.
Millin, S.G.
1986   *God's Stepchildren*. Johannesburg: Ad. Donker. Originally published in 1914.
Mzamane, Mbulelo
1985   "Sharpeville and Its Aftermath: The Novels of Richard Rive, Peter Abrahams, Alex la Guma and Lauretta Ngcobo." *Ariel* 16, 2:31-44.
Mvula, Kefiloe Tryphina
1988   "The Naked Night." In *Women in South Africa: From the Heart—An Anthology*, 45-51. Johannesburg: seriti sa sechaba.
Ndebele, Njabulo
1994   "Liberation and the Crisis of Culture." In Elleke Boehmer, Laura Chrisman and Kenneth Parker, eds., *Altered State? Writing and South Africa*, 1-9. Mundelstrup: Dangaroo Press.
Ngcobo, Lauretta
1981   *Cross of Gold*. London: Longmans.
1986   "The African Woman Writer" and "My Life and My Writing." In Kirsten Holst Petersen and Anna Rutherford, eds., *A Double Colonization: Colonial and Post-Colonial Women's Writing*, 81-82 and 83-86. Mundelstrup: Dangaroo Press.
1989   Introduction to *Footprints in the Quag: Stories and Dialogues from Soweto*. Cape Town: David Philip.

1991 "A Black South African Woman Writing Long after Schreiner." In Itala Vivan, ed., *The Flawed Diamond: Essays on Olive Schreiner*, 189-99. Mundelstrup: Dangaroo Press.

1991 *And They Didn't Die*. New York: George Braziller.

1994 "Now That We're Free." In Anna Rutherford, Lars Jensen and Shirley Chew, eds., *Into the Nineties: Post-Colonial Women's Writing*, 568-70. Mundelstrup: Dangaroo Press.

Nhlapo, Thandabantu

1991 "Women's Rights and the Family in Traditional and Customary Law." In Susan Bazilli, ed., *Putting Women on the Agenda*, 111-23. Johannesburg: Ravan Press.

Parry, Benita

1994 "Some Provisional Speculations on the Critique of 'Resistance' Literature." In Elleke Boehmer, Laura Chrisman and Kenneth Parker, eds., *Altered State? Writing and South Africa*, 11-24. Mundelstrup: Dangaroo Press.

Paton, Alan

1948 *Cry, the Beloved Country*. New York: Charles Scribner's.

Pechey, Graham

1994 "'Cultural Struggle' and the Narratives of South African Freedom." In Elleke Boehmer, Laura Chrisman and Kenneth Parker, eds., *Altered State? Writing and South Africa*, 25-35. Mundelstrup: Dangaroo Press.

Plaatje, Sol T.

1957 *Mhudi*. Lovedale: Lovedale Press. Originally published in 1930.

Qakisa, Mpine

1988 "Storm on the Minedumps." In *Women in South Africa: From the Heart—An Anthology*, 154-60. Johannesburg: seriti sa sechaba.

Ramphele, Mamphela, with Chris McDowell

1991 *Restoring the Land: Environment and Change in Post-Apartheid South Africa*. London: Panos.

Rutherford, Anna, Lars Jensen and Shirley Chew, eds.

1994 *Into the Nineties: Post-Colonial Women's Writing*. Mundelstrup: Dangaroo Press.

Said, Edward

1993 *Culture and Imperialism*. New York: Knopf.

Schreiner, Olive

1985 *From Man to Man*. London: Virago. Originally published in 1926.

Tlali, Miriam

1989 *Footprints in the Quag: Stories and Dialogues from Soweto*. Cape Town: David Philip.

Udayagiri, Mridula

1995 "Challenging Modernization: Gender and Development, Postmodern Feminism and Activism." In Marianne H. Marchand and Jane L. Parpart, eds., *Feminism, Postmodernism, Development*, 159-77. London: Routledge.

Vivan, Itala, ed.

1989   *The Flawed Diamond: Essays on Olive Schreiner*. Mundelstrup: Dangaroo Press.

Walker, Cherryl

1982   *Women and Resistance in South Africa*. London: Onyx Press.

Wicomb, Zoe

1994   "Why I Write" and "Comment on Return to South Africa." In Anna Rutherford, Lars Jensen and Shirley Chew, eds., *Into the Nineties: Post-Colonial Women's Writing*, 573-76. Mundelstrup: Dangaroo Press.

1992   "Nation, Race and Ethnicity: Beyond the Legacy of Victims." *Current Writing* 4:15-20.

Williams, Raymond

1970   *The English Novel from Dickens to Lawrence*. New York: Oxford University Press.

Willis, Susan

1984   "Eruptions of Funk: Historicizing Toni Morrison." In Henry Louis Gates, Jr., ed., *Black Literature and Literary Theory*, 263-83. New York: Methuen.

Worsfold, Brian

1994   "Black South African Countrywomen in Lauretta Ngcobo's Long Prose Works." In Elleke Boehmer, Laura Chrisman and Kenneth Parker, eds., *Altered State? Writing and South Africa*, 111-19. Mundelstrup: Dangaroo Press.

9

Five Minutes of Silence: Voices of Iranian Feminists in the Postrevolutionary Age

Nima Naghibi

In March of 1979, one month after the anti-imperial revolution in Iran, the country sustained five days of mass feminist demonstrations. Although a large body of outspoken Iranian women had marched against the oppressive practices of the monarchy during the revolutionary period, these same women, now at considerable risk to themselves, marched against the misogynist policies of the Islamic regime to the taunts and insults of the religious right who chanted, "*rusari ya tusari*," which translates as "cover your hair or receive a blow to your head."[1] Within days, the Iranian revolutionary government expelled American feminist Kate Millett from the country. Shortly after Millett's expulsion, seventeen European women and one Egyptian woman from *le Comité international du Droit des Femmes*, an organization presided over by Simone de Beauvoir, went to Iran in a show of support for their "Iranian sisters." This contingent of self-proclaimed "international" feminists travelled to Qom, the religious centre in Iran, and demanded an audience with religious leader Ayatollah Khomeini. Khomeini granted them a five-minute interview during which he was confronted with a barrage of questions regarding the

Notes to chapter 9 are on pp. 141-42.

status of Iranian women. Khomeini responded—in the words of French feminist Katia Kaupp—with "le silence total" (1979:49).

I would like to offer a reading of the ramifications of Khomeini's five minutes of silence and of its echoes within the conflict-ridden arena of Iranian feminist debates. Khomeini's symbolic silence during his interview with a group of Western feminists in Iran represents, at the most obvious level, a stubborn taciturnity regarding his position on Iranian women and an active participation in stifling the voices of these women. But I believe that this silence is also a production of second-wave and prerevolutionary Iranian feminist discourses. I am arguing that this silence evokes a language of (temporary) loss. In this paper, I suggest that a language for an anti-imperialist Iranian feminism was subsumed by the imbrication of three other voices: the voices of Western feminists, the voices of prerevolutionary Iranian feminists (currently living in the Diaspora) and the voices of patriarchal nationalists. More importantly, however, I would like to suggest that this anti-imperialist feminist voice was subsumed only temporarily. It re-emerged into the political sphere at the moment of the presidential elections in May of 1997 when the newly elected (and widely perceived as "moderate") President Mohamad Khatami came to power with 69 percent of the popular vote. This vote was comprised mostly of the support of Iranian women and of Iranian youth. The sudden (and belated) recognition by the West of a collective feminist voice in postrevolutionary Iran speaks to a problem of subaltern representation. Implicit in my paper is a recognition of the irreducible presence of the anti-imperialist feminist subject whose "unreadability" by global feminists resulted in an eighteen-year absence of representation in Western and Iranian diasporic intellectual discourses.

The age-old binary of Western (imperialist) feminism and Iranian (nationalist) tradition is one which has deep historical roots in Iranian intellectual history. One of the most prominent Iranian intellectuals in the 1960s was Jalal Al-e Ahmad whose work was influential in mobilizing the ideas behind the anti-imperial revolution of 1979. In *Gharbzadegi* (1962), which translates as "westomania" or "westoxification," he critiques the 1936 Unveiling Act legislated by Reza Shah by stating that the physical unveiling of women is but a cursory gesture to their status as "equal" citizens. He claims that this putative new-found equality between men and women is a farce because the *gharbzadeh* woman, the woman who has become westoxified, is just a shell of a woman who has lost her true calling which, according to Al-e Ahmad, is the exalted role of motherhood. Although I agree that the forced unveiling of women accomplished little in addressing the inequality between the positions of men and women in Iranian society, his insistence that Iranian women should revert to their roles as guardians of Persian tradition and culture is a stereotype that legitimates the kind of oppressive nationalist discourse which only makes room for a patriarchal anti-imperialist rhetoric and silences all feminist voices in the name of *gharbzadegi*.

Patriarchal nationalist discourses in Iran carry within them the anxiety of emasculation; colonial domination or imperial influences are perceived as a direct challenge to male potency and control. The threat of colonial powers or the infiltration of imperialist influences in a third-world country is seen as inherently feminizing and as a personal affront to the masculinity and the *gheyrat*—the concept of male honour which has deep cultural roots in Iran—of the third-world man. The sexualization of the colonized third worlder feeds into the powerful and oppressive metaphor of the nation as woman who is always vulnerable to penetration and rape. The more powerful the imperialist presence, the weaker the position of the third-world subject, and the more this subject position becomes associated with "effeminate" and "weak" female identities. Al-e Ahmad asserts that the "west-stricken man is a gigolo. He is effeminate. He is always primping; always making sure of his appearance. He has even been known to pluck his eyebrows!" (1982:70). To be colonized or to be susceptible to imperialist cultures, then, is to be weak and female; thus, women's actions and women's bodies must be controlled by indigenous (male) cultures in order to protect the nation from colonization and emasculation and in order to prove the *gheyrat* of the Iranian man.

The concept of *gheyrat* translates into exclusionary Iranian nationalist discourses that continue to elide Iranian women's active participation in the revolution. During the revolutionary period of 1978 Iran, the majority of Iranian peoples from all social classes came together to call for the overthrow of the Pahlavi regime. As a symbolic protest against the imperialist policies of the monarchy, many upper-middle-class, urban-educated women who had never before worn the veil donned the chador voluntarily as they took to the streets in the spirit of revolution. Once the Shah was successfully deposed in February of 1979, urban middle-class women once again removed the chador which they had worn only as a nationalist and anti-imperialist symbol. One month after the revolution, however, Khomeini announced that "[w]omen should not be naked at work in these Islamic ministries. There is nothing wrong with women's employment. But they must be clothed according to religious standards" (Jaynes 1979:A1). Once Khomeini began issuing statements extolling the virtues of the chador, Iranian women began to feel betrayed by the revolution which they had worked hard to support. Refusing to be cowed by the misogynist tone of the new official discourse, women once again filled the streets; this time, however, they were unveiled.

Into this complicated state of political affairs arrived renowned American feminist Kate Millett with the intention of speaking at a rally scheduled for International Women's Day on 8 March. Predictably, the presence of Millett in the midst of Iranian feminist demonstrations against the veil was seen as a potential threat to the success of the movement by anti-imperialist Iranian feminists. The organizers of the women's rally tactfully suggested that Millett defuse the potentially explosive reaction to her American nationality by calling herself an "international feminist" and this if she would be allowed to speak at all since the International Women's Day rally was under attack by government officials as well as by other opposition groups who believed that women's rights were secondary to the greater question of national formation.

Indeed, the Iranian women's movement was forestalled—at that time—in two ways: first, by appropriating the "cause" of Iranian women, Western feminists interfered with an indigenous anti-imperialist feminist movement. By turning Iranian feminist concerns into an international women's concern, Western women elided the particularity and the specificity of an anti-imperialist Iranian feminism. Second, by taking advantage of the Western (imperial) vs. Iranian (nationalist) binary, the conservative clerics successfully defused the radical potential of the Iranian feminist movement. The presence of Kate Millett and European feminists in Iran at this particular historical juncture allowed the ruling elite to argue that feminism was a Western phenomenon and that all feminist activity in Iran would be perceived as "counter-revolutionary" behaviour. Iranian feminist activists were thus forced to choose between the false binary of the West vs. Iran, and they found themselves choosing to support the tenets of the revolution. The choice was, of course, a spurious one, since to opt for what was seen as an "imperialist" feminism was to declare oneself a counter-revolutionary and a threat to the state.

The predicament of anti-imperialist Iranian feminists in 1979 arose out of the historical associations of feminism with "Westernization" as exemplified by the state-controlled Women's Organization of Iran (WOI) which was directed by the Shah's twin sister Ashraf Pahlavi and the Shahbanou (Empress) Farah Diba. The women of the WOI culti-vated a relationship with second-wave American feminists and were thus accused of applying Anglo-American feminist theories to the radi-cally different situations of women in Iran. The claims about the elitism of the WOI, however, are contested by Haleh Esfandiari in *Reconstructed Lives: Women and Iran's Islamic Revolution* (1997). Esfandiari, a former official of the WOI, defends the organization by stating that its mem-bers were attuned to the feminist movement in the West as well as to the needs of traditional Iranian women (1997:33). Esfandiari's insist-ence on the WOI's sensitivity to the creation of an indigenous feminism, one that would speak to the traditional cultural and religious practices of Iranian women, invokes an image that the organization tried to pro-ject in the late 1970s. But this new image of synthesizing "Western" and "Eastern" feminisms came too late in Iranian feminist history, and the resultant revolutionary feminist movement is indicative of the success of the WOI in attending to the demands of Iranian women.

Contemporary Iranian feminists now face the challenge of maintain-ing a forceful and articulate feminist voice in Iran. The expression of strong Iranian feminist voices can only be maintained by moving away from the dubious position of simply laying blame on the shortcomings of the prerevolutionary Iranian feminist project. By the same token, prerevolutionary Iranian feminists need to recognize the diversity of postrevolutionary Iranian feminist voices.[2] Iranian feminist anthologies and panels at academic conferences in the West often comprise women who offer definitive views on the benefits of prerevolutionary Iranian feminism and on the putative all-encompassing oppression of Iranian women in the postrevolutionary era. An example of this kind of work is a recent article, "Émigré Iranian Feminism and the Construction of the Muslim Woman" by Haideh Moghissi (1999), published as part of a collection of papers presented at an "Émigré Feminism" conference held at Trent University in 1996. In this piece, Moghissi launches a vituperative attack on Iranian academics whom she labels as "neo-conservative" feminists, presumably because they refuse to engage in a celebration of the work of secular Iranian feminists at the expense of the work accomplished by their more religious counterparts. After list-ing the numerous mistaken beliefs held by Iranian feminists with whom she vehemently disagrees, she brings the paper to a close with a sage reminder:

For those of us who lived through the memorable experience of the revolution, and who have watched, in horror, the devastating consequences
of the Islamization policies, and felt the clutches of the Islamists on our
personal lives, the infatuation of academic feminists with "Islamic feminism," and their softening tone *vis-à-vis* Islamic fundamentalism, reminds
one, uncomfortably, of the self-negating actions and discourse of the traditional left when it was thrust into the frenzy of "anti-imperialist" pop-
ulism during the post-revolutionary period. . . . In the writings of neo-
conservative, academic feminists one hears again, tragically, an echo of
this same romantic confusion, surrendering, at the same time, their own
vocation (and obligation) to act as critical intellectuals. (1999:201-202)

Moghissi's representation of the work of Iranian diasporic feminists
who attempt to move away from easy dichotomies of enlightened secular feminism and backward Islamic feminism is shockingly ungenerous
and didactic.

Indeed, Moghissi maintains a scolding tone throughout her paper—
and lest Iranian women should forget their indebtedness to prerevolutionary and diasporic Iranian feminists, she emphasizes the following in
her concluding paragraph: "We have reasons to believe that the struggle
of women inside Iran was positively affected by the efforts of Iranian
feminists outside Iran to bring to light the plight of women under fundamentalist rule, as well as by media reports on the subject and by the
reports by U.N. rapporteurs" (1999:203). The kind of oppressive feminist pedagogy embraced by Moghissi, a feminism that claims to instruct
and to enlighten the presumably ignorant masses of Iranian women,
betrays an anxiety about her own position as a diasporic Iranian feminist whose concerns and goals seem incongruous with those of feminists currently living within and fighting against a system maintained
by the religious orthodoxy in Iran. But, more significantly, this kind of
feminist project unwittingly reproduces the moment of silence in 1979
Qom and contributes to the continued absence of Iranian feminist representations in Iranian nationalist and Western and diasporic feminist
discourses. As Iranian feminists working in the diaspora, it is incumbent upon us to recognize the feminist movements in contemporary
Iran. There is little to be gained from an incessant validation of the
indisputably hard work pursued by prerevolutionary Iranian feminists.
Although it is important to acknowledge the work of our feminist "foremothers," I believe that a productive and engaged dialogue between
the various positions of diasporic and of indigenous Iranian feminists
can only be sustained by enabling conflicting feminist voices to emerge
into the currently contained arena of Iranian feminism.

Iranian feminists need to be receptive to alternative models of feminism and we need to recognize the necessity of discarding or at the very least nuancing older models of Iranian feminist thought. Although many feminists have moved away from "second-wave" feminist ideas, prominent prerevolutionary Iranian feminists, such as former Minister of Women's Affairs and Secretary-General of the WOI, Mahnaz Afkhami, maintain that the project of "global sisterhood" remains a viable model for contemporary Iranian feminist work. Presently, Afkhami is the Secretary-General of Sisterhood Is Global Institute and has on a number of occasions collaborated with Robin Morgan, a noted second-wave feminist who continues to uphold the notion of "universal sisterhood" as a working model for feminist activism. The 1970s moment of "global sisterhood" was undoubtedly an exciting, heady period during which many committed feminists believed deeply in the possibility of uniting women around the globe as sisters in the struggle against a homogenous patriarchal system. This was an exciting time for many feminists as the movement paved the way for a number of women in the professional world, but it also enabled the emergence of other feminist voices who criticized the universal sisterhood for its inattention to differences of culture, race and class. Similarly, in Iran, the work of the WOI came under attack by women who believed that the organization pursued concerns that did not address the specific needs of working-class women. Nevertheless, it is important to recognize that prerevolutionary feminists such as Afkhami struggled to bring questions regarding women's legal, political and social status to the fore of the Iranian political scene. In doing so, these feminists faced numerous obstacles and difficulties as they worked within a political system that was only superficially committed to gender equity. It is equally important to recognize, however, that those women who felt excluded from the feminist ideals of prerevolutionary feminists had a legitimate concern; their choice to reject the Pahlavi regime, and the feminism that anti-imperialist feminists believed the regime espoused, was an informed and thoughtful decision.

The participation of Iranian women in the revolution has been consistently represented, by prerevolutionary Iranian feminists, as paradigmatic of their "false consciousness" and as an irreversible mistake for which they are now suffering. The fact that there are now several women's magazines that openly debate feminist issues in postrevolutionary Iran and the fact that there are a number of outspoken Iranian feminists who occupy powerful and visible positions under the current regime have gone—until only very recently—virtually unnoticed by prominent diasporic Iranian feminists who continue to subscribe to the concept of international sisterhood.[3]

In a now famous essay, "Can the Subaltern Speak?" Gayatri Chakravorty Spivak argues that the desire for global feminist alliances is prevalent amongst women of the dominant social classes in third-world countries (1988:288). Thus, women who are placed in a position of economic and social security can afford to celebrate international alliances. The women of what Spivak calls the "urban subproletariat," on the other hand, find themselves in a position complicated by their disadvantaged social position in relation to the elite feminist groups and to the dominant patriarchal power (1988:288). Thus the agential power and the subject position of the anti-imperialist Iranian feminist is elided in the moment of collusion between the two dominant discourses of international feminism and anti-imperialist patriarchy (1988:308). Through the act of representation, then, the dominant classes affirm their own subject constitution by "cathecting" the figure (and the voice) of the subaltern woman. By transforming the subaltern into an object of study and, by extension, into an object of desire, the dominant classes impede the articulation of subaltern voices.

The 1979 moment of the collusion of Western and anti-imperialist Iranian voices foregrounds the problem of the agency of the subaltern Iranian woman. The effacement of the subaltern Iranian feminist voice—in 1979 and in the years that have ensued—speaks to Spivak's concern that the actual fact of utterance is inconsequential; the difficulty arises from the representation of the utterance, since the subaltern woman is "constructed by a certain kind of psychobiography, so that the utterance itself . . . would have to be interpreted in the way in which we historically interpret anything" (1996:291). Indeed, the voices of Iranian women were "uttered" loudly and their demands vociferously and publicly expressed during the anti-veil protests, but the cultural appropriation of Iranian feminism by Western feminists and the cultural attacks against the West by anti-imperialist activists converged to efface the distinctive demands of Iranian women.

Spivak's apt warning against "an unexamined chromatism" since "there is no guarantee that an upwardly mobile woman of colour in the US academy would not participate [in the reproduction of colonialist structures]" is particularly germane to the current predicament of Iranian feminists who still have to contend with the discursive control of Iranian feminist narratives by diasporic Iranian feminists (1986:

237-38). Concomitantly, Iranian feminists face the taxing project of battling the religious orthodoxy for official recognition as feminists and as agential subjects in Iran. The project of social change is one which, as students of postcolonial work, many of us hope to advance. Thus, by contravening the homogenizing tendencies of prerevolutionary Iranian feminist discourses and by critiquing the presence of Western feminists in Iran at that particular historical juncture, I do not intend to reproduce the same binaries that led to the occlusion of anti-imperialist Iranian feminist demands. The elections of May 1997 have demonstrated that there has been a continuance of voice for an articulate agential Iranian feminism throughout the revolutionary period, and my project now is to find a way to theorize that continuance. Beneath the noise of global sisterhood and Khomeini's five minutes of silence, the continuing voices of anti-imperialist Iranian feminists have been speaking. It is incumbent upon us, as variously positioned postcolonial feminists and diasporic Iranian feminists, to begin the difficult process of learning how to hear them.

Acknowledgments

I would like to express my warm gratitude to Nasrin Rahimieh, Stephen Slemon, Cheryl Suzack, Rachel Warburton and Heather Zwicker, who provided insightful comments on earlier versions of this paper, and with whom I engaged in many stimulating discussions on this subject. My thanks also to Gary Boire and Rowland Smith who organized an exciting conference where I had an opportunity to benefit from the critical insights of conference participants. Finally, I would like to acknowledge the assistance of a Social Sciences and Humanities Research Council of Canada Doctoral Fellowship.

Notes

1 Western media coverage of the repercussions of the postrevolutionary feminist demonstrations was extensive. An article worth citing is one entitled "Iran: Five Days in March. Was the Revolution a Beginning of Women of the World United?" This piece, written by Mim Kelber, was published in *Ms. Magazine* in June of 1979: "[W]hen the [Iranian] women tried to gather for planning [feminist] meetings, they were menaced and sometimes stopped by young men with knives—religious extremists who felt that the role of Ayatollah Khomeini as the symbol of the revolution, and the promise of an Islamic republic, meant that women must return to the seclusion of the veil and the status of chattel. 'We have faced the tanks of the Shah,' said one of the brave women, one of many who had worn the *chador*, a head-to-toe

covering, as a symbol of defiance to the Shah. 'Do you think we can be frightened by boys with knives?'" (1979:90). Kelber offers an insightful summary of the historical trajectory of Iranian feminist struggles which makes this piece well worth reading. Although the article plays on Western fears of the threat of a growing "religious fundamentalism," Kelber does manage to convey the strength and commitment of Iranian women in the face of naked violence.

2   In "Feminisms in an Islamic Republic," Afsaneh Najmabadi (1997) advances a strong argument in favour of a greater appreciation for the work of feminists currently active in Iran. She offers a nuanced analysis of the various feminist positions in Iran and stresses the value of feminist work accomplished in the prerevolutionary and in the postrevolutionary era. Najmabadi's call for a mutual respect and understanding between Iranian feminists in the Diaspora and at home is a concern which drives my own position in this paper.

3   For a detailed description of the various feminist magazines currently published in postrevolutionary Iran, see Najmabadi's "Feminisms in an Islamic Republic" (1997).

References

Al-e Ahmad, Jalal
   1982   *Plagued by the West (Gharbzadegi)*. Translated by Paul Sprachman. Biblioteca Persica: Modern Literature Series, 4. Delmar, NY: Caravan. Originally published in 1962.

Esfandiari, Haleh
   1997   *Reconstructed Lives: Women and Iran's Islamic Revolution*. Washington, DC: The Woodrow Wilson Center Press.

Jaynes, Gregory
   1979   "Bazargan Goes to See Khomeini as Iran Rift Grows." *New York Times*, 9 March:A1, A7.

Kaupp, Katia D.
   1979   "Les visiteuses de l'Ayatollah." *Le Nouvel Observateur*, 26 March:49.

Kelber, Mim
   1979   "Iran: Five Days in March. Was the Revolution a Beginning of Women of the World United?" *Ms. Magazine*, June:90-96.

Moghissi, Haideh
   1999   "Emigré Iranian Feminism and the Construction of the Muslim Woman." In Alena Heitlinger, ed., *Emigré Feminism: Transnational Perspectives*, 189-207. Toronto: University of Toronto Press.

Najmabadi, Afsaneh
   1997   "Feminisms in an Islamic Republic." In Joan W. Scott, Cora Kaplan, Debra Keates, eds., *Transitions, Environments, Translations: Feminisms in International Politics*, 390-99. New York: Routledge.

Spivak, Gayatri Chakravorty

1986   "Imperialism and Sexual Difference." *Oxford Literary Review* 8, 1-2: 225-40.

1988   "Can the Subaltern Speak?" In C. Nelson and L. Grossberg, eds., *Marxism and the Interpretation of Culture*, 271-313. Basingstoke: Macmillan Education.

1996   "Subaltern Talk: Interview with the Editors." In Donna Landry and Gerald Maclean, eds., *The Spivak Reader*, 287-308. New York: Routledge.

10

FAS and Cultural Discourse: Who Speaks for Native Women?

Cheryl Suzack

On 6 August 1996, Justice Perry Schulman of the Manitoba Court of Queen's Bench ordered a twenty-two-year-old Native woman from Winnipeg's inner city to enter a drug treatment program for substance addiction. The woman, who was five months pregnant at the time and who had three children in the care of child welfare agencies, was brought to court by the Manitoba Department of Child and Family Services when she refused to enter a treatment program of her own volition. A spokesperson for the department asked, "how many badly damaged children does a person have a right to bring into this world? It seemed to us that this was such an extreme case that we had to do something" (Mitchell 1996:7). In handing down his decision, Justice Schulman enforced an obscure section of penal law known as *parens patriae* which enables a superior court judge to restrict the rights of persons who are in danger of harming themselves (Mitchell 1996:7). Justice Schulman stated that since the woman was incapable of looking after herself, "he was ordering her into a drug treatment centre for her own protection" (Mitchell 1996:7). While Justice Schulman's ruling was overturned on the grounds that the woman was "mentally competent" to stand trial, the court case remains as a problematic reminder of the implications of imperial governance. For inasmuch as it consolidates and constructs

---

Notes to chapter 10 are on pp. 152-53.

the subject of legal discourse, the legal institution represents the ultimate form of subject constitution: as a form of representational discourse that enables a person to be spoken for politically and as a tropological narrative that enables a person to be represented symbolically (Spivak 1988:276). In the interplay between these two forms of subject-constitution, the woman could neither self-represent as the autonomous subject of Western humanism nor self-efface to avoid emerging as the object of imperial law. Forced to inhabit the space of this double displacement of her subjective reality, the woman was effectively silenced by the imposition of imperial law. Justice Schulman's decision to incarcerate the woman thus enacted a form of symbolic violence that enabled the woman to be identified as a pregnant addict through the disavowal of the material conditions that constituted her social subjectivity.[1]

In the immediate aftermath of the trial, media representations focused on the question of the moral and political implications of the Justice's decision. Pro-life advocates argued on behalf of the rights of the fetus, claiming that the ruling highlighted the "absurdity of current Canadian law, which countenances the killing of the unborn but disallows less grievous injury" (*British Columbia Report* 1996:32). Pro-choice activists maintained that the decision threatened the rights of women "to dispose of their unborn children as they see fit" (*British Columbia Report* 1996:32). The President of the Winnipeg-based Prairie Centre for Innovation in Government and Economy argued on behalf of the nation, claiming that responsibility for the woman's behaviour had become the problem of the "modern welfare state" at the expense of the woman's family and community (*Western Report* 1996:20-21). No one thought to protest the representation of the woman as a "glue-sniffing addict." Shuttled between the moral high ground of interest groups and the punitive measures of the legal system, the woman came to occupy the space of the "objectified other," where neither interest groups committed to social change nor government institutions acting on behalf of the rights of citizens could represent the problematics of her social situation.

Insofar as neither interest groups nor government institutions thought to investigate the social realities of the woman's life, the court case exposes the dissimulated interests of both the legal system and family services in disavowing these conditions. To legitimate the intervention of these institutions in the woman's life, the court required a vision of the woman as incompetent that would warrant the infringement of her rights by the penal system and that would explain the behaviour of family services in removing three children from her care. The stereotype of the pregnant addict provides this legitimacy, for it identifies the paradox that Cynthia Daniels describes as "a woman simultaneously engaged in the destruction of life (addiction) and the perpetuation of life (pregnancy)" (Daniels 1993:98). Within the public record, the woman emerged as the "Native Other" to the rational public self, a "career ward of the state" and citizen of Winnipeg's "welfare mecca" whose identity was secured in the image of the "monster woman" (*Western Report* 1996:20-21).

I want to use the problematics of representation in the Winnipeg court case as a point of departure for the following analysis. I want to examine how the subject-constituting effects of cultural discourses function in popular representations of a medical condition known as Fetal Alcohol Syndrome.[2] My paper focuses on media responses to Michael Dorris's groundbreaking memoir *The Broken Cord*, which recounts Dorris's attempts to come to grips with the impact of this disease on Native American communities. In my examination, I want to take up Gayatri Spivak's call in "Can the Subaltern Speak?" (1988) for a program of investigation that renders visible the mechanism through which the "Third World" is made "recognizable" and "assimilable" to a first-world audience. I undertake this form of analysis in a reading of media and medical representations of FAS in order to illustrate how its circulation as a "crisis" narrative has become associated in the public domain with Native American communities. In its circulation as a "crisis" narrative, FAS serves to refurbish the colonial stereotype of the "drunken Indian" and to engender this stereotype as a condition of Native American women, in particular, and Native American communities, in general. I want to examine the implications of this circulation for Native American women who seem to be increasingly at risk within a cultural climate that legitimates social inequities through the mechanism of criminal prosecution.

The juxtaposition of fetal alcohol syndrome with Native American peoples received widespread public attention with the publication of Michael Dorris's hugely successful, semi-autobiographical memoir *The Broken Cord*. Dorris—a Native American scholar from New Hampshire and founder of the Native American Studies program at Dartmouth College—spent seven years researching and writing this narrative which recounts his search to find answers to his adopted son Adam's learning disabilities (Bailey 1993:128). Dorris states that he wrote this book "to get the word out about the toll fetal alcohol syndrome is taking on children, particularly Native American children" (Bailey 1993:130). The publishing record of *The Broken Cord* attests to Dorris's success: the book sold over 90,000 copies in hard cover and approximately 250,000 copies in paperback. It won numerous critical awards[3] and aired as a made-for-TV movie with an estimated viewing audience of thirty million people (Chavkin and Chavkin, 1993:204, 207). Jimmy Smits of *NYPD Blue* fame played the role of Michael Dorris. As Deirdre Donahue noted in *USA Today*, the book has received "staggeringly positive reviews" (1989:1D).

While the overwhelming popularity of Dorris's memoir has succeeded in focusing public attention on the problem of FAS in Native American communities, it has also instituted a politics of blame that locates the cause of FAS solely with the behaviour of Native American women who drink during pregnancy. This narrative of blame arises out of the manner in which Dorris parallels the act of consuming alcohol during pregnancy with an act of child abuse. Dorris writes of Adam's biological mother,

> If she had come after him with a baseball bat after he was born, if she had smashed his skull and caused brain damage, wouldn't she have been constrained from doing it again and again? Was it her prerogative, moral and legal, to deprive him of the means to live a full life? I had no doubt that there were compelling reasons for her weaknesses, for mistakes, but reason didn't equal right. (*The Broken Cord* 1989:165)

By equating the problem of FAS with an act of abuse, Dorris inscribes the issue as a moral and ethical dilemma that society needs to address. To prevent the abuse, the woman must be made to assume responsibility for her behaviour. To be responsible, the woman must be made conscious of the effects of her behaviour. To be made conscious of the effects of her behaviour, the woman's rights must be violated. The logic of Dorris's argument forces him to a conclusion that seems inevitable. As Cynthia Daniels argues in *At Women's Expense: State Power and the Politics of Fetal Rights*, "For Dorris, as for many who support criminal prosecution, the ultimate answer is incarceration, even sterilization, of women who refuse to stop drug or alcohol abuse" (1993:121).

Although critical responses to *The Broken Cord* may be located along a continuum of opinions supporting or contesting the issue of fetal rights versus maternal rights, none of the reviewers challenge the veracity of Dorris's claim that "FAS raises the prospect of an Aldous Huxley society, with a class of gamma people" (Hughes 1990:28).

Indeed, critics support Dorris's narrative of the deterioration of Native American communities, on the one hand, by mobilizing the stereotype of the "drunken Indian" as evidence of the denial of coevalness[4] of Native American communities, and, on the other, by distancing the American public from the realities of Native American social life through a rhetoric of disintegration. Book reviewer Susan Hill of the *Sunday Times* writes that "among reservation Indian tribes (*sic*) . . . alcohol abuse is a way of life" (1990). Gina Kolata of the *New York Times* states that "the devastating effects of alcohol abuse among American Indians are reaching a new generation, striking children whose mothers drink heavily during pregnancy and resulting in a population that is mentally and physically disabled" (1989:D24). Galen Strawson of the *Independent* asserts that "*The Broken Cord* combines the story of Adam with the larger story of the American Indian disaster, and the still larger story of global alcohol damage" (1990:30). The rhetoric of "abuse," "devastation" and "disaster" that engenders a vision of Native American communities on the brink of destruction also consolidates a vision of Native American peoples as existing out of time and beyond recovery.

In its distancing of Native American communities from the American public, this rhetoric does little to enable a critique of the *real* conditions of social and economic disempowerment within which Native American communities exist.[5] Rather, the "widespread" incidence of FAS becomes the grounds for locating the general breakdown of American society. For like the Native American community under attack by the depraved behaviour of Native women, the American nation is under siege from its own undesirables. For example, Carol Van Strum writes in the *Courier-Journal* that "as taboos crumble—under the demoralizing conditions of reservation life, or with the *liberation* of women generally—the number of alcohol impaired children has increased exponentially" (1989:13A; emphasis added). Joan Beck states in the *Chicago Tribune* that while "the very survival of the Indian people may be at stake, the terrible risks aren't just to Indians. FAS and the far more common FAE may be a basic reason why a hard-core part of the underclass elsewhere can't muster the ability and motivation to pull themselves out of poverty; why they can't learn and act in their own best interests" (1989:27). Gina Kolata asserts in the *New York Times* that

Dr. Sokol of Wayne State University has found that different strains of laboratory animals have different susceptibilities to fetal alcohol syndrome and that black (*sic*) women are more than seven times as likely to have affected children as white women who drink the same amount during pregnancy. [Dr. Sokol] stated that Indians had not been studied in this way, but he would not be surprised if a genetic susceptibility made them at least as vulnerable as blacks (*sic*) are to fetal alcohol syndrome. (1989:24D)

This critical vision of the American people afflicted by the "degenerates within" circulates as a narrative in which the social and economic inequalities in American society are explained by the "crisis" of fetal alcohol syndrome. Just as Native women assume responsibility for the destruction of the Native social body, America's unwanted shoulder the blame for the breakdown of American society in general.

Indeed, the "crisis" of American society at risk from its aberrant citizens—the "Indians," the feminists, the working classes and the "blacks"—finds a corresponding crisis scenario in Michael Dorris's memoir when he imagines the predicament of a community of FAS- and FAE-afflicted Native people endlessly reproducing themselves because they lack the capacity for rational thinking and logical analysis. Dorris writes:

If education and counselling were the major thrust of the prevention effort; and *if* FAS and FAE victims were, relative to women of childbearing age as a whole, unmoved by logic; and *if* women who were FAS and FAE victims had more children, started having them earlier and continued having them longer; and *if* those women who could understand the advertising campaign cut back on their drinking during pregnancy and those women who couldn't comprehend the arguments did not, *then* would not the proportion of FAS victims necessarily grow within any given population? Wasn't the increase exponential? Wouldn't the figures double in ever-abbreviated spans? (1989:180)

It is this language of crisis that has been manipulated in public health reports that measure the impact of FAS on Native American communities.[6] In mobilizing a language of crisis, the medical community is authorized to rescue the "Indians" by increasing its intervention, supervision and control within Native American communities. The process through which control will be implemented and normalized is evident in a report from the Aberdeen Area Indian Health Service Program to the U.S. Department of Health. Representatives from Aberdeen's Health Service suggest that "the need to develop a system to institutionalize FAS surveillance is urgent" and that "Intervention will be most effective if implemented early and provided as a continuum from all aspects of society. . . . These aspects include the school system, family planning services, prenatal clinics, church, community, and establishments where alcohol is served" (Duimstra et al. 1993: 225). Although the report seems to be addressed to raising awareness about the health risks involved for Native American women who consume alcohol while pregnant, in fact, the document outlines a program for "detecting," "surveying" and "identifying" the incidence of FAS in Native American communities (Duimstra et al. 1993:225). Moreover, representatives from Aberdeen Health Services suggest that the presence of the U.S. Department of Health in American Indian communities in the Northern Plains will only be "normalized" if "community ownership" of the program takes place (Duimstra et al. 1993:225).

What are the implications of these new measures for surveillance and control of Native American communities? In a 1994 Public Health Report issued by the U.S. Department of Health and Human Services, public health officials identify FAS as the leading cause of mental retardation in the United States with higher rates of FAS found in "black (*sic*), Alaskan Native, Aboriginal Peoples of Canada, and American Indian populations" (Burd and Moffat 1994:688). This study identifies how "ethnic differences" between "Indian and Aboriginal peoples in the United States and Canada" as one group and "whites" in general were taken into consideration when assessing the rates of FAS in society. More importantly, the investigation concludes that a woman's admission of maternal drinking is a crucial step in identifying and surveillancing the development of FAS among Native American people (Burd and Moffat 1994:688). Given that in 1992, the people of the United States brought criminal charges against "167 pregnant women" "for delivering drugs to the fetus through the umbilical cord" (Daniels 1993:2), and in light of the recent court case against the Native woman from Winnipeg, Manitoba, it would seem that Native American women, like other dispossessed groups, are being forced into untenable and disenabling subject positions in society. Faced with a choice between criminal prosecution by the courts and moral outrage by the public, Native American women are being effectively thrust aside in the race for justice and social responsibility. What the future might hold for Native American women in the current climate of criminal prosecution is difficult to say.

Postscript: 12 November 1999

In a remarkable recuperation of the problematics of the Winnipeg court case, the *Globe and Mail* featured a full-page story on Deborah Gregory (a pseudonym to protect her children) celebrating the happily-ever-after turn that her life has taken. Following the Supreme Court's decision that "no law exists justifying incarceration of an expectant mother for protection of a fetus," the article explains how Gregory overcame her addiction and was on the brink of marrying her partner of several years (Bercovici 1997:D2). For a thirty-three-year-old Edmonton woman, the story is not so triumphant. Charged under the Public Health Act with inhaling an intoxicating vapour, she was sentenced on 22 July 1998 to six months in jail for sniffing solvents (Hall and Gold 1998:A1, A6). A few short hours after being arrested, she gave birth to a six-pound baby boy. Apparently, no mention was made during sentencing of incarcerating the woman to protect her unborn child.[7]

Acknowledgments

I would like to thank Mary Elizabeth Leighton, Nima Naghibi, Daphne Read, Stephen Slemon and Jo-Ann Wallace for their thoughtful and generous readings of earlier versions of this paper. I am also grateful to Gary Boire and Rowland Smith for the opportunity to present this research at the CACLALS Triennial "Commonwealth in Canada" Conference. Research for this paper has been generously supported by a doctoral fellowship from the Social Sciences and Humanities Research Council of Canada and by the Batchewana First Nations of Ojibways.

Notes

1 For a sustained examination of the relationship between convictions of Aboriginal women for "unfeminine," "abnormal" or "threatening behaviour" and moral regulation through the law, see Joan Sangster's "Criminalizing the Colonized: Ontario Native Women Confront the Criminal Justice System, 1920-60" (1999).

2 I would like to acknowledge my indebtedness to the work of Elizabeth Cook-Lynn, whose compelling review of *The Broken Cord* in the *Wicazo Sa Review* (1989) inspired me to examine the intersections of race and gender in the text, and to Maureen McNeil, whose thoughtful keynote address "Foetal Alcohol Syndrome: A Case Study within Cultural Studies of Science and Technology" at the 1995 Cultural Studies Colloquium held at the University

of Guelph motivated my thinking on the relationship between narrative and material realities.

3 Widespread acclaim for Dorris's memoir is evident in the number of scholarly and non-scholarly distinctions that *The Broken Cord* received. In 1989, Dorris was awarded the National Book Critics Award for distinguished non-fiction and a 1989 Christopher Award. In 1990, Dorris received a $5,000 Heartland Prize from the *Tribune* in the category of non-fiction. Additionally, *The Broken Cord* was named as a notable book for 1989 by the American Library Association, *Booklist* and *Library Journal*.

4 Johannes Fabian identifies the "denial of coevalness" as a strategy ethnographers employ to maintain the scientific "truth" value of their observations by relegating others to temporal spaces that they do not themselves occupy. The implication of such a denial is to remove the people observed from an existence in "our" time (1983:33).

5 See James (1992) for a wide-ranging examination of these conditions.

6 In a report to the U.S. Department of Health and Human Services, public health officials referenced *The Broken Cord* for its "graphic portrayal" of the "toll of FAS on Indian people" (Burd and Moffat 1994:688). They also quoted Dorris's suggestion that "the disorder fetal alcohol effect (FAE) is largely unrecognized" (Burd and Moffat 1994:688). In framing Dorris's memoir as a non-fiction, specialized report, public health officials side-stepped the significant question of Dorris's largely autobiographical, retrospective account of his experiences in living with and researching FAS. Additionally, they overlooked the speculative nature of his narrative. In one of the most disturbing passages in the text, Dorris describes two unknown women as they "stagger" along the highway embankment "propped against each other for support" (1989:169). His remarks in passing them—"Their features were similar. They had the look of mother and daughter"—consolidates one of the underlying assumptions of his text: that FAS is a visible disease inscribed on the body and detectable through surveillance.

7 Many thanks to Nima Naghibi, Stephen Slemon and Jo-Ann Wallace for saving the newspaper clippings for me.

References

Bailey, Rebecca
    1993   "Catharsis after Denial." In A. Chavkin and N.F.C. Chavkin, eds., *Conversations with Louise Erdrich and Michael Dorris*, 128-32. Minneapolis: University of Minnesota Press.

Beck, Joan
    1989   "No Amount of Love Can Undo Alcohol's Damage to a Fetus." *Chicago Tribune*, 29 June 1989, perspective sec.:27C.

Bercovici, Vivian
    1997   "Mother Versus Child." *Globe and Mail*, 1 November:D2.

Blades, John
    1990   "Chronicles of Vietnam and a Disabled Indian Child Win Heartland Prizes." *Chicago Tribune*, 23 August:1C.

British Columbia Report
  1996   "No Protection from Abortionists: Legal Measures to Control a Preg-
         nant Glue-Sniffer Won't Set a Pro-Life Precendent." 19 August:32.
Burd, Larry, and Michael E. Moffat
  1994   "Epidemiology of Fetal Alcohol Syndrome in American Indians,
         Alaskan Natives, and Canadian Aboriginal Peoples." *U.S. Department of
         Health and Human Services Public Health Reports* 109.5:688.
Chavkin, Allan, and Nancy Feyl Chavkin
  1993   "An Interview with Michael Dorris." In A. Chavkin and N.F. Chavkin,
         eds., *Conversations with Louise Erdrich and Michael Dorris*, 184-219.
         Minneapolis: University of Minnesota Press.
Cook-Lynn, Elizabeth
  1989   "The Broken Cord." *Wicazo Sa Review* 5, 2 (Fall):42-45. Reprinted in
         Why I Can't Read Wallace Stegner and Other Essays: A Tribal Voice, 11-17.
         Madison: University of Wisconsin Press, 1996.
Daniels, Cynthia R.
  1993   *At Women's Expense: State Power and the Politics of Fetal Rights*. Cam-
         bridge and London: Harvard University Press.
Donahue, Deirdre
  1989   "Alcohol and the Unborn: An Adoptive Dad Pours Out the Anguish—
         Even Love Can't Undo Early Damage." *USA Today*, 8 August, life sec.:1D.
Dorris, Michael
  1989   *The Broken Cord*. New York: HarperPerrenial.
Duimstra, Cindy, et al.
  1993   "A Fetal Alcohol Syndrome Surveillance Pilot Project in American
         Indian Communities in the Northern Plains." *U.S. Department of Health
         and Human Services Public Health Reports* 108, 2:225.
Fabian, Johannes
  1983   *Time and the Other: How Anthropology Makes Its Object*. New York:
         Columbia University Press.
Guthrie, Patricia
  1989   "Alcohol's Child: A Father Tells His Tale." Review of *The Broken Cord*,
         by Michael Dorris. *New York Times*, 30 July, late ed.:1.
Hall, Vicki, and Marta Gold
  1998   "Police Defend Jailing of Solvent-Abusing Mom." *Edmonton Journal*,
         23 July:A1, A6.
Hill, Susan
  1990   "The Power of Paternal Instinct." *Sunday Times*, 12 August, features
         sec.
Hughes, Colin
  1990   "Bitter Lessons from the Reservation." *The Independent*, 4 August,
         weekend books:28.

James, M. Annette, ed.
  1992 *The State of Native America: Genocide, Colonization and Resistance.*
      Boston: South End Press.
Kolata, Gina
  1989 "Alcohol Abuse by Pregnant Indians Is Crippling a Generation of Chil-
      dren." *New York Times,* 19 July:24D.
Mitchell, Teresa
  1996 "Pre-Natal Protection? (Case of Solvent-Abusing Pregnant Woman in
      Manitoba)." *Law Now* (October/November).
Sangster, Joan
  1999 "Criminalizing the Colonized: Ontario Native Women Confront the
      Criminal Justice System, 1920-60." *Canadian Historical Review* 80
      (March):32-60.
Spivak, Gayatri Chakravorty
  1988 "Can the Subaltern Speak?" In Cary Nelson and Lawrence Grossberg,
      eds., *Marxism and the Interpretation of Culture,* 271-313. Urbana: Uni-
      versity of Illinois Press.
Strawson, Galen
  1990 "Bottle-Fed before Birth: 'The Broken Cord: A Father's Story.'" Review
      of *The Broken Cord,* by Michael Dorris. *Independent,* 5 August:30.
Van Strum, Carol
  1989 "Adam's Tragedy." *Courier-Journal,* 12 August, forum sec.:13A.
Western Report.
  1996 "You Can Kill Me, but You Can't Hurt Me: That's the Bizarre Status
      of the Unborn Child in the Wake of the Manitoba Decision."
      19 August:20-21.

11

Can Rohinton Mistry's Realism Rescue the Novel?

Laura Moss

On the back cover of the American paperback edition of
Rohinton Mistry's recent novel *A Fine Balance*, there is
an excerpt from the *New York Times*: "Those who con-
tinue to harp on the decline of the novel ought to . . . consider Rohinton Mistry. He needs no infusion of magic realism to vivify the real. The
real, through his eyes, is magical."[1] The celebration of Mistry's choice
of "a compassionate" realism (and the implicit denigration of magic
realism) is but one critic's perception of Mistry's prose, yet it is also a
comment on contemporary attitudes to the form of realism. The back
cover, written to appeal to an "average" American consumer, depoliti-
cizes Mistry's novel as it is placed in the company of "masters from
Balzac to Dickens." In this light it can appear as if Mistry's use of the
form rescues the (European) novel from the uncomfortable possibility
of being overtaken—threatened, even—by magic realism, a form that
has been most often associated with Latin American writing and therefore recognized as fundamentally non-European. Furthermore, the use
of realism by a writer of what has recently been called the "far rim"
(whether that be India or Canada) is taken to resuscitate the humanist
traditions of the realist novel.[2] Mistry's novel is accepted as having a
sweeping appeal by the back-cover critic precisely because it does not
resemble what has come to be viewed as a postcolonial novel of

Notes to chapter 11 are on p. 164.

157

resistance—whether that be to caste in India or racism in Canada. The reason for this is simple: Mistry's novel is unequivocally realist and the prevalent view—both popular and academic—is that, for whatever reason, realism and resistance do not converge.

While Mistry's novel *resists* on every page, his resistance comes in the form of realism and is therefore often ignored as a focus of the text. The problematic nature of critical assumptions about postcolonial examples of realism stems, at least partially, from the privileging of the notion of resistance in postcolonial discourse. The concept of "resistance" has been fetishized to the point where it is even often presented without an object. At the same time, there has been a critical elevation of writing perceived to be experimental or writing that plays with non-realistic form. Within postcolonial criticism, these simultaneous developments have converged in the production of a profusion of studies linking, and sometimes suggesting the interdependence of, political or social resistance and non-realist fiction. If a text does not fit the profile of postcolonial resistance, as realist texts seldom do, it is generally considered incapable of subversion.

David Carter, in his article "Tasteless Subjects," notes that postcolonial critics tend to present realism as a monolithic whole that is "complicit with the process of imperialism" and therefore with "universalism, essentialism, positivism, individualism, modernity, historicism, and so on" (1992:296). In spite of many examples of recent politically charged realist texts, the critical expectations about the form often hold that it is a reinforcement of conservative, specifically imperialist, ideology. On one hand, this assumption has led to the co-option of literary realism by conservative critics. On the other, it has led to the virtual dismissal of the realist novel by those critics looking for an apparently radical form to hold disruptive content. As part of the larger body of critics in the Academy, postcolonial critics are prominent in establishing such expectations. Non-realist writing is frequently privileged by the critics because of the assumption that its various forms are inherently conducive to political subversion because of their capacity for presenting multiplicity. I challenge the idea, as it has been developed or assumed by many postcolonial critics, that realism is almost necessarily conservative, and non-realist forms are inherently somehow *more* postcolonial—and therefore subversive. What is at issue in this paper, then, is the limited function of criticism when critics place too tight an ideological hold on realism and are not inclined to recognize the varieties of its possibilities or its capacity for multiplicity. I challenge this critical hegemony, arguing that realism is a viable, perhaps even indispensable, form for political and social engagement in post-colonial contexts. As such, the study is a reaction to the positioning of realism as a foil for other more "accepted" forms of insurgence regard-less of whether such positioning is driven from the left or the right.

Realism, for example, is repeatedly set in opposition to magic real-ism. Because of its Latin American literary origins, magic realism has become privileged as a suitable form for the inclusion of politicized commentary in what Jeanne Delbaere has called the "energy of the margins" and Stephen Slemon has now notoriously labeled "postcolo-nial discourse." Wendy Faris and Lois Parkinson Zamora argue that in magic realist texts "ontological disruption serves the purpose of politi-cal and cultural disruption: magic is often given as a cultural correc-tive, requiring readers to scrutinize accepted realistic conventions" (1995:3). In this formulation, realism has "accepted conventions" to which the politically active magic realist text can react. Magic realism opens up a space for the political to enter the text precisely because it is not realism here, while realism without magic is taken to be less capable of opposition. While I quarrel with the *New York Times* reviewer's depiction of magic realism as infused with a dose of magical rhetoric by an invisible but lurking trickster of the "far rim," it does seem that the increasingly popular form has either been characterized as a catch-all of political action or is emptied of its politics.

Realism has a history of political activity in India, but it does not have the international recognition that magic realism has as a form capable of carrying resistance. Rohinton Mistry's *A Fine Balance* traces the day-to-day lives of fictional characters through non-fictional inci-dents in the 1975 State-of-Emergency. The primary function of the "ordinary" characters in *A Fine Balance* is not to be synecdochic of the "Indian citizen" in the Emergency but rather to represent possible examples of what might happen in such a state. Mistry's characters populate a novel that is critical of the resilience of the caste system, the pervasive nature of corruption, the hiring of political crowds, forced labour camps, sexism, "Family Planning" and Indira Gandhi herself.

The four main characters converge in Dina's apartment. As refugees from constricting caste, gender or social roles, they each inhabit a marginal position in the context of India: Dina as a woman and a Parsi; Maneck as a rural Parsi; and Ishvar and Omprakash as leather workers transgressively transformed into tailors. The apartment is a setting at the interstices of culture, or "the overlap and displacement of difference," to use Homi Bhabha's phrase (1997:3). The four characters resist the social positions to which they are relegated by the community and try to foreground their own individuality. If the apartment is viewed as the secular site of convergence of individuals in a disruptive society, then the collapse of the community in the apartment is inevitable in the Emergency—a fact which the more conservative critics tend to ignore. The point is crucial: the individual can not be extricated from the community in this narrative. Bhabha writes that "political empowerment comes from posing questions of solidarity from the interstitial perspective" (1997:3). However, Mistry disempowers his characters after placing them in the putatively interstitial space of Dina's apartment.

The focus on the individual within the community evokes Bhabha's idea of the proximate, the "minority position," the moderate subject, or the "first-in-third" (Bhabha 1997:434). For Bhabha, this position depends on the interstitial space of identification, on the ambivalent position of being at once one in a community (third person) and an individual in society (first person).[3] The moderate subject is articulated in a movement between third and first persons. It is constituted "as an effect of the ambivalent condition of their borderline proximity—the first-in-the-third/one-in-the-other" (Bhabha 1997:434). However, in the Emergency context of *A Fine Balance*, there is no movement allowed between the first and the third. In this realist example the moderate position cannot exist. Conversely, magic realism *relies* on the possibility of the moderate position: the in-betweenness or the "all-at-onceness" which "encourages resistance to monologic political and cultural substructures" (Parkinson Zamora and Faris 1995:3). In Mistry's novel the point of resistance lies precisely in its representation of the impossibility of the moderate position. Mistry's realist novel concludes with the collapse of the apartment community which, in turn, leads to Dina's loss of independence, Ishvar's loss of his legs, Om's loss of his "manhood" and Manek's loss of life.

Some critics have argued about the applicability of the term realism to Mistry's mode of representation.[4] The argument runs like this: it is degrading to see Mistry's writing as derivative of a European form, where the Indian writer has now "caught up," in the literary evolutionary scheme of things, to the point where British writers were in the nineteenth century. While such criticism can fairly be aimed at those critics who call Mistry "worthy of the nineteenth-century masters,"[5] such a view is not necessarily the impetus for all those who label the text realist. A focus on the limitations of social structures is by no means exclusively a feature of Victorian realism, although such fiction was an integral part of the education system in India. A concentration on the undistinguished lives of the lower classes clearly does not suggest that the text's precursor is necessarily Victorian realism. One only has to turn to such disparate classics of "social realism" in India in English as Mulk Raj Anand's *Untouchable*, Raja Rao's *Kanthapura* or Bhabhani Bhattacharya's *So Many Hungers* to think of critical depictions of a diversity of castes. Still, I agree with John Ball's comment that the realist novel is a precursor to Mistry's text, but I add that works of Indian social realism are also likely to be prominent precursors (1996:87).

As with the social realists, at points Mistry can be accused of being overly romantic in his portrait of poverty. The following tableau of workers trying to unblock an overflowing drain illustrates Mistry's propensity to present a lyrical view of poverty:

> then a boy emerged out of the earth, clinging to the end of a rope. He was covered in the slippery sewer sludge, and when he stood up, he shone and shimmered in the sun with a terrible beauty. His hair, stiffened by muck, flared from his head like a crown of black flames. Behind him, the slum smoke curled towards the sky, and the hellishness of the place was complete. (1997:67)

The "interminable serpents of smoke" of Dickens's description of Coketown in *Hard Times* surface here in the slimy serpentine "s's" where the slippery sewer sludge stood up, shone and shimmered in the sun near the slum where fires smouldered, with smoke smudging the air (1990:28). Such alliteration adds to the self-consciously lyrical and somewhat melodramatic qualities of this depiction of the "underworld" (Mistry's word); yet, sewers *do* have black sewer sludge spilling from drains in a state of civic unrest and governmental corruption. This is a romanticized portrait of poverty and filth, but even such a portrait carries pointed commentary within it. It is important to note that Dina views this scene because her train is blocked by "demonstrations against the government" (1996:67). So the sewer scene for Dina—on the top level of a double-decker bus—is juxtaposed with a view of "banners and slogans [that] accused the Prime Minister of misrule and corruption, calling on her to resign in keeping with the court judgments finding her guilty of election malpractice" (1997:67). Mistry's explication of the Emergency context is not simply to provide a setting for a lyrical alliterative passage. There is an irrefutable link between slime and corruption.

In her review of Mistry's first novel *Such a Long Journey*, Arun Mukherjee argues with the comparison to a Victorian realist novel because such a comparison does not consider how the characters' lives are "negotiated in the context of a social environment" (1992:83). Mistry's narrative form, according to Mukherjee, is not realism but rather a representation of the real, as it "attempts to make sense of actual historical events by narrativising them" (1992:83). The necessity for cultural and historical specificity in realist novels is not fully taken into account in this comment. In Mukherjee's configuration of realism, the form simply provides a background for the action of the novel. The use of realism as background is sharply criticized by Chinua Achebe in his essay on Joseph Conrad's use of Africa in *Heart of Darkness*:

> Africa as setting and backdrop . . . eliminates the African as human factor. Africa as a metaphysical battlefield devoid of all recognizable humanity, into which the wandering European enters at his peril. Can nobody see the preposterous and perverse arrogance in thus reducing Africa to the role of props for the break-up of one petty European mind? (1988:257)

While I agree with Achebe's analysis of *Heart of Darkness*, I do not think that such a criticism should be launched against all examples of realism, as Mukherjee seems to. Mistry's realist novel is a case in point. Like Achebe, Mistry works against the notion of using context as a background for development of the individual in the novel. Mistry's recent novel relies closely and clearly on an understanding of its Indian context set in a specific time and place. *A Fine Balance* is emphatically not a World text in Franco Moretti's terms, where the "geographical frame of reference is no longer the nation-state, but a broader entity— a continent, or the world-system as a whole" (1996:50); nor is it a postnational text with sites as interchangeable as postcards, to use Frank Davey's formulation of postnational settings, nor are the political issues constructed in purely globalized terms. In *A Fine Balance*, although we follow the quotidian lives of fictional characters through non-fictional incidents in Indian history, "History is emphatically not the backdrop. Indeed, Dina is proven wrong when she dismisses the Emergency as background. Early in the narrative she explains the Emergency as "Government problems—games played by people in power. It doesn't affect ordinary people like us" (Mistry 1997:75). However, the remainder of the novel slowly details just how it does affect the "ordinary" character in the destruction of the apartment community.

This is clearly a tragic novel; yet many reviewers seem to rely heavily on the assumed conservative nature of its realist form and focus on the universally applicable elements of the apartment community (the optimism evoked in such a communal gathering), rather than the clear disruption of those elements in the conclusion (the pessimism that leads to the inevitable disruption of the community). This is particularly well illustrated in the comments that adorn the novel paratextually: "*A Fine Balance* creates an enduring panorama of the human spirit in an inhuman state"; and "The four strangers start sharing their stories, then meals, then living space, until over the divides of caste, class, and religion, the ties of human kinship prevail"; and even "in this one shabby little apartment, at least, the human family becomes more than a phrase, more than a metaphor, a piety" (Mojtabai 1996:29). Such responses to the novel are undeniably humanist. My response is repeatedly: yes, but—yes, but the fundamental point of Mistry's text is that the "ties of human kinship" do not prevail in his 1970s India. Things have fallen apart; the universalist paradigm can not hold.

Perhaps the finest example of a conservative—even neoimperialist—co-option of Mistry's realism is presented on the flyleaf of the novel. From the *Literary Review of London*, it reads: "A Work of genius . . . *A Fine Balance* is *the* India novel, the novel readers have been waiting for since E.M. Forster." This comment not only exposes the vision of realism as an orientalist technique; it addresses itself specifically to the readers who would consider realism as such. The thinking behind this comment seems to be that, because *A Fine Balance* is not written in the quick syntax of Raja Rao, or the innovative styles of G.V. Desani, Amitav Ghosh or Salman Rushdie, it must be exemplary of the English tradition and therefore more valuable, more marketable, and ultimately more easily canonized in the Great Tradition. To equate Mistry's novel with *A Passage to India* (and to ignore the products of the intervening seventy-one years) thoroughly negates the context of both novels. I can only think that this is done because the reviewer, like many other critics, blindly accepts the notion of an ideologically conservative realism which is by definition an imperial product. The publicists of the American edition of *A Fine Balance* foreground the universal humanist elements of the novel in the comments found on the physical body of the text in order to decontextualize, dehistoricize and ultimately depoliticize the realism in the novel and thus ostensibly make it more palatable for a general American public. Although I do not particularly believe that the novel needed rescuing, I do think that realism does.

Notes

1 This quotation is taken from A.G. Mojtabai (1996:29).
2 See Rushdie (1996:49) for an explication of the term "far rim."
3 Bhabha claims that through his theorizing of "proximity": "we are in a better position to grasp what [Gilles] Deleuze and [Félix] Guattari cryptically describe in *A Thousand Plateaus* as 'becoming minoritarian': a movement *within* the 'in-between . . . constituting a zone of proximity . . . sweeping up the two distant or contiguous points, carrying one into the proximity of the other'" (1997:439). He also works through Deleuze and Guattari's discussion of Kafka's "minor literature" (1997:440). However, Bhabha only seems to use their term loosely as a launching point for his own criticism of the "minority" writer.
4 See, for example, Arun Mukherjee (1992).
5 A *Time* reviewer, cited in the front matter of *A Fine Balance*.

References

Abbas, Khwaja Ahmad
1975   "Social Realism and Change." In Suresh Kohli, ed., *Aspects of Indian Literature: The Changing Pattern*, 145-54. Delhi: Vikas Publishing.
Achebe, Chinua
1988   "An Image of Africa: Racism in Conrad's *Heart of Darkness*." In Robert Kimbrough, ed., *Heart of Darkness*, 3rd ed., 251-62. New York: W.W. Norton.
Ball, John
1996   "Taking the Measure of India's Emergency." *Toronto Review of Contemporary Writing Abroad* 14, 2:82-87.
Bhabha, Homi K.
1997   "Editor's Introduction: Minority Maneuvers and Unsettled Negotiations." *Critical Inquiry Special Issue: Front Lines/Border Posts* 23:431-59.
1994   *The Location of Culture*. London: Routledge.
Carter, David
1992   "Tasteless Subjects: Postcolonial Literary Criticism, Realism, and the Subject of Taste." *Southern Review* 25:292-303.
Davey, Frank
1993   *Post-National Arguments: The Politics of the Anglophone Canadian Novel since 1967*. Toronto: University of Toronto Press.
Delbaere, Jeanne
1992   "Magic Realism: The Energy in the Margins." In Theo D'Haen, ed., *Postmodernist Fiction in Canada*, 75-104. Amsterdam: Rodopi.
Dickens, Charles
1990   *Hard Times*. Oxford: Oxford University Press. Originally published in 1854.

Dollimore, Jonathan
   1990   "Shakespeare, Cultural Materialism, Feminism and Marxist Human-
         ism." *New Literary History* 21, 3:471-93.
Mistry, Rohinton
   1997   *A Fine Balance*. New York: Random House.
Mojtabai, A.G.
   1996   "An Accidental Family." *New York Times*, 23 June:29.
Moretti, Franco
   1996   *Modern Epic: The World System from Goethe to García Márquez*. Lon-
         don and New York: Verso.
Mukherjee, Arun
   1992   "Narrating India." *Toronto South Asian Review*, 82-91.
Parkinson Zamora, Lois, and Wendy B. Faris, eds.
   1995   *Magical Realism: Theory, History, Community*. Durham: Duke Univer-
         sity Press.
Rushdie, Salman
   1996   "In Defence of the Novel, Yet Again." *The New Yorker*, 24 June.
Slemon, Stephen
   1988   "Magic Realism as Post-Colonial Discourse." *Canadian Literature*
         116:9-24.

12

Dislocations of Culture: Unhousing and the Unhomely in Salman Rushdie's *Shame*

Susan Spearey

> In general we are reminded that the word *heimlich* is not unambiguous, but belongs to two sets of ideas, which without being contradictory are yet very different: on the one hand, it means that which is familiar and congenial, and on the other, that which is concealed and kept out of sight. . . . [E]verything is uncanny [*unheimlich*] that ought to have remained hidden and secret, and yet comes to light.
> — Sigmund Freud, "The Uncanny" (1919, reprinted in Freud 1953)

The effect of mass migrations has been the creation of radically new types of human being: people who root themselves in ideas rather than places, in memories as much as in material things; people who have been obliged to define themselves—because they are so defined by others—by their otherness; people in whose deepest selves strange fusions occur, unprecedented unions between what they were and where they find themselves. The migrant suspects reality: having experi-

---

Notes to chapter 12 are on pp. 178-79.

enced several ways of being, he understands their illusory nature. To see things plainly, you have to cross a
frontier.[1]   — Salman Rushdie, "The Location of Brazil"
(1985, reprinted in Rushdie 1991)

While subjectivity may be located in a desire for home—
a desire to be rooted in or affiliated with a certain
ethos or place, for example, or in a particular gendered, racial, sexual, class or cultural identity—the notion of home
itself is far more difficult to situate. Freud's contention that the concept
of the *heimlich*, which operates both at individual and cultural levels,[2]
accommodates simultaneously what is manifest and what is repressed
in any formulation of "home," does not preclude the notion of an originary state of integration and completeness in which home is ultimately
locatable, if not retrievable. Freud writes,

> There is a humorous saying: "Love is home-sickness"; and whenever a
> man dreams of a place or a country and says to himself, still in the
> dream, "this place is familiar to me, I have been there before," we may
> interpret the place as being his mother's genitals or her body. In this
> case, too, the *unheimlich* is what was once *heimisch*, home-like, familiar;
> the prefix "un" is the token repression. (1953:398-99)

If the mother's body is read as analogous to such concepts as "the
mother country," then Freud's (singular) "imaginary homeland" differs
markedly from those multiple "imaginary homelands" evoked by
Salman Rushdie in his essay of the same title, as well as in his fiction.
In a review of Terry Gilliam's film *Brazil*, Rushdie envisages what Homi
Bhabha has termed "the location of culture" as a project which—for
the migrant particularly, but by no means exclusively—is predicated
upon an *unhousing* of the subject from her or his erstwhile assumed
groundings. What this involves is a radical dislocation of spatio-
temporal, ideological and linguistic co-ordinates, but crucially also
their ongoing strategic realignment as relationships between the subject and the various topographies, histories, cultural traditions and
communities inhabited are traced out and reconfigured. Any resulting
confrontation with the otherness of the self or the unhomeliness of the
home—with that which has been "concealed and kept out of sight" in
order to sustain the illusion of stability, scrutability and familiarity—
forces a recognition not only of the repressions inherent in any
mechanism of identity formation, but also of the provisionality of all
groundings.

As in Freud's concept of the *unheimlich*, unhousings born of geo-graphical and cultural migrations serve to defamiliarize the notion of home, and to destabilize the concept of the self which is largely defined against the home context. However, although Freud's model allows for the interplay of a number of disparate variables as the sub-ject's location is mapped (often in order to be set back "on course"), the acts of unhousing described by Rushdie potentially serve to enable the imagining of less restrictive and overdetermining ways of conceptu-alizing movement, historical process, subjectivity and agency. None of these any longer need *necessarily* be formulated in terms of a fall from a state of pre-Oedipal symbiosis and an ensuing series of attempted returns; or to be charted according to processes attending the develop-ment of the ego; or to be explained by the emergence of repressed desires and impulses deriving from the manner in which the child becomes differentiated from the mother. Rushdie's (plural) "imaginary homelands" speak of the multiple affiliations and identifications that come into play in any formulation of subjectivity, of the manifold repressions implicit in each and of the need for a new and revisionary model of charting their shifting interrelations. In the border crossings and acts of cultural translation precipitated by such unhousings lie the possibilities of *dis*locating culture in its hegemonic sense; of unfixing it from its associations with teleological historical imperatives, with entrenched geographical boundaries, with totalizing drives for coher-ence and homogeneity; and with myths of origination and purity which underpin implicit oppositions between the cultural "self" and its "other(s)." The very process of unsettling such assumed foundations serves less to discredit the concept of culture as an a priori category than to mobilize its dynamic critical function as a vehicle of change and a locus of shared ethical responsibility. Recuperating for culture its dynamic critical function necessarily renders subjectivity mutable and multiplex, thereby disturbing fixed and oppositional categories of iden-tity without dispensing with identity politics, and at the same time necessitating the continuous negotiation of location along a number of intersecting axes.[3]

In a related vein, Rushdie, like Bhabha in *The Location of Culture* or Derrida in *Spectres of Marx*, is fundamentally concerned with prob-lematizing the notion of "the present" as that which is limited to the material conditions of the here-and-now. In the epigraph above, he posits instead a process akin to that which Bhabha has elsewhere termed "presencing," and which, according to Bhabha, "begins because it captures something of the estranging sense of the relocation of the home and the world—the unhomeliness—that is the condition of extra-territorial and cross-cultural initiations" (1994:9). Rushdie's migrant can never simply be located in the present; she or he occupies the estranging space between the idea and the place, between the memory and the material existence, between an assumed selfhood and an imposed otherness, and between contesting versions of reality. Since one home continually recedes into the lost space of the then-and-there, while the other or others are always in the process of construction, the present and the not-present are necessarily inhabited simultaneously, and the location of the migrant, like the location of culture, is never definitively identifiable. Furthermore, Bhabha's signalling of the un-housing and the unhomely brings to light an important dimension of Derrida's project in *Spectres of Marx* which often passes unremarked. When Derrida addresses questions of ethics, he asserts that no justice is possible if we do not recognize our responsibility towards "*others* who are not present, nor presently living, either to us, in us, or outside us" (1994:xix). In his consequent plea that we speak to, of and with our ghosts in order to free ourselves from a history impelled by a cycle of vengeance and retribution, Derrida tropes the spectre as a victim of past injustice who seeks not revenge, but acknowledgment and some reconciliatory gesture of redress. In the example he cites of Hamlet's encounter with his father's ghost, the "not-present" is read principally in terms of the temporal dimension of history;[4] and yet always tacit in Derrida's argument is the notion that the "not-present" is as much a function of the "not-here" as the "not-now." The enterprise of unhing-ing Freud's notion of unhomeliness from its static point of origin neces-sitates the strategic development of a less linear and teleological historiography. To extend one's responsibility for the not-present into a spatial dimension—and particularly into spaces of exclusion—is to offer an enabling corrective to such revisionist projects which at once brings to account, and brings into the account—among others—subjects of the "cross-cultural and extra-territorial initiations" of which Bhabha speaks. Without such an identifiable originary locus, the desire for home engenders what is less a recuperative operation of an ideal-ized state than an ongoing ethical negotiation with the many repres-sions that inevitably attend any configuration of homeliness.

The connection between the unhomely haunting and the unhousing of the migrant subject is given play on a number of levels in Rushdie's novel *Shame* (1983), which takes as its focus a nation of migrants and which teems with repressed histories, bodies, narratives, communities and *topoi*. Indeed, Rushdie addresses the unspeakable monsters and the silenced spectres that overspill the borders of Pakistan and its post-Independence history by reconfiguring not only official historical accounts, but also a number of classic Western Gothic texts. The latter include *Frankenstein*, *The Strange Case of Dr. Jekyll and Mr. Hyde*, the fairy tale *Beauty and the Beast* and *Jane Eyre*, each of which stages a return of the repressed in order to level political and ideological critiques of very particular conceptions of home and domesticity. Two related conventions of Gothic which are evidenced in all of these texts lend themselves effectively to an exploration of issues pertaining to culture and location. First, the trope of monstrosity typically serves as an indicator of all that is deemed taboo or unthinkable within a given cultural context, thereby providing a convenient yardstick against which the sanctioned, the permissible and the articulable can be measured. Of course, the monster is ironically almost invariably produced directly *by* the culture in question and speaks very explicitly of what, in Freud's words, "ought to have remained hidden and secret, and yet comes to light" (1953:376). *Shame*'s most pronounced haunting is enacted upon and through the body of Sufiya Zinobia, the idiot child of Raza and Bilquìs Hyder, who, as "shame incarnate" becomes the repository of all the nation's shame and shamelessness.[5] Because Sufiya Zinobia, as the first surviving child, is not the culturally valorized son her parents so long for, she becomes a being made monstrous, but, crucially, also one who undergoes, and later enacts, transformations. "Humiliate people for long enough and a wildness bursts out of them," the narrator explains (1983:117). When the burden of her shame becomes unbearable, uncontainable, she unleashes her anger, exacting her vengeance randomly—but as public spectacle—on the perceived perpetrators of her suffering. She decapitates both humans and animals and enacts violent sexual assaults on young and unsuspecting men, becoming the female equivalent of a mass murderer or serial rapist—an unthinkable monstrosity in what, after all, claims to be the Land of the Pure. In her story, Rushdie enlists Gothic conventions of monstrosity in order to expose the repressive conditions inherent in Pakistan's project of national self-fashioning, while at the same time registering the limitations of the outcomes that are made possible through conventional Gothic forms and the originary myths and oppositional frameworks upon which they are based. The second and related Gothic convention concerns the home (be it a castle, a monastery, an inherited country estate or a London townhouse, to cite but several examples frequently evidenced in eighteenth- and nineteenth-century Gothic novels), which is figured as the locus of specific social, political and ideological values that are in many cases being exposed as outmoded or problematic. Like many Gothic fictions, *Shame* opens with the description of an imposing but crumbling edifice, in the darkest corners of which can be found the memorabilia of the history of a particular region or institution, and the traces of the successive regimes that have governed it. In this case, the labyrinthine halls of Nishapur are cluttered with relics from time immemorial up to the period of the British Raj—vestigal traces of the entire history preceding the inauguration of Pakistan's nationhood. Although the novel continually shifts from one locale to another, it retains its focus on the domestic spaces of its several protagonists. The notion of home thus also retains its conventional significance insofar as *Shame*'s exploration of the unconscious impulses and energies which ultimately work to direct the course of public affairs is focused largely on the interface between the public and the private. Bhabha has noted that "the recesses of the domestic space become sites for history's most intricate invasions. In that displacement, the borders between home and world become confused; and, uncannily, the private and the public become a part of each other, forcing upon us a vision that is as divided as it is disorienting" (1994:9). Rushdie's narrator makes explicit his claim that shame and shamelessness are the twin but similarly repressive forces which have come to impel political action and to define the national ethos of Pakistan; and, indeed, the borders between the public and private in the affairs of the principal players are repeatedly transgressed. Such figuring of home is ideally suited to Rushdie's exploration of the whole concept of homelands—imaginary or otherwise—and particularly to the processes attendant upon the founding of postcolonial nations. *Shame* enlists and reinscribes both conventions not only to critique the process of othering that is implicit in the foundation of any homeland, but also to mobilize this critique as the basis for a more multiplex and nuanced model of social responsibility.

Shame's postmodernist revisions of more traditional Gothic conventions are evidenced in its structure of fragments and variations, and in its resistance to centring its focus on any one character or plot or narrative. The fantastic tale of the Hyders and the Harappas—thinly disguised portraits of the Zias and Bhuttos, respectively—is framed by a number of variations on the theme of shame and shamelessness which serve simultaneously to contextualize, to interpellate, to echo, to de-centre, and to haunt the Gothic tale of Pakistan's history by registering its *multiple* extensions and exclusions. The novel thus offers two distinctive narrative trajectories: first, the horror story which allegorizes Pakistan's official history as a nation, and, second, the narrator's asides and cross-references which serve to disturb the allegory. It is through these asides that a revisionary historiography and politics of location are tentatively mapped out, as the limits of the conventional gothic narrative are examined and exposed.[6] *Shame,* moreover, raises the question as to how, ethically, we can collectively deal with historical legacies which may be rooted only in an idea, but which have far-reaching consequences in the "real" world, both within and beyond the polity or "homeland" in question. To this end, the narrator continually invokes the casualties of the history he is recounting, and gestures ironically or otherwise towards what his narrative cannot or does not relate, towards what it finds unspeakable or indecipherable.

The novel's treatment of such questions of responsibility and the locations from which it can be assumed is usefully approached through an examination of the *Frankenstein* intertext. *Shame*'s emphasis on retracing the trajectory of a utopian vision which has somehow gone awry and has come to be propelled forward by an almost uncontainable momentum finds its parallel in the Frankenstein myth, which Rushdie explicitly references. In Mary Shelley's novel, of course, questions of responsibility are of paramount importance, but in spite of the critiques it levels at all that a masculist Romantic idealism excludes and represses, it nonetheless posits models of historiography and subjectivity which do not substantially revise those which the novel seeks to replace. As Donna Haraway points out in her "Manifesto for Cyborgs," Frankenstein's monster expects "its father to save it through a restoration of the garden, that is, through the fabrication of a heterosexual mate, through its completion in a finished whole, a city and cosmos" (1990:192). Gothic at this juncture, in other words, shares in postmodernism's latter-day interest in interrogating the limits of intelligibility and possibility suggested by Enlightenment and humanist discourses, and yet, like Freud in "The Uncanny," still operates within teleological historical paradigms which posit the beginning and end of history as moments of integration and completeness, the concept of home as something locatable, and the vision of unity and integrity as a desirable end. Rushdie in *Shame* reworks this convention as it is evidenced in *Frankenstein* by wrenching historical narratives from overdetermining teleological structures. For instance, Omar Khayyam Shakil, the peripheral hero with whose birth the novel opens, is not only a man whose marginality renders him a spectator in his own fate, a man who never even becomes the hero of his own life; he is also the son of three possible mothers and an unknown, but allegedly British, father. His origins, in other words, are indeterminate and multifarious, so that his eventual return to "the Mother Country" near the end of the novel can in no way be construed as a prelude to a regained state of pre-Oedipal symbiosis, or of any other form of integration. On the contrary, the portents of this return are, if anything, apocalyptic. The crumbling of this Gothic edifice and the unhousing of its long-sequestered occupants at the end of the novel are perhaps suggestive of an unhousing of all that Pakistan's history has secreted away from public scrutiny. Other moments of origination, such as the foundation of the Islamic state of Pakistan in 1947, are depicted quite clearly as acts of fabrication, as monstrous creations which refuse to admit to their piecemeal construction.

Shame, then, advances a project of unhousing the subject from the geographical, political and cultural centres of focus upon which identity politics has customarily grounded itself. The novel's structure of fragments and variations explicitly foregrounds its own sutures while repeatedly gesturing towards its own inevitable repressions and exclusions. In the "monstrous" figure of Sufiya Zinobia, Rushdie at once makes manifest the horrifying repressions of Pakistan's history, and also explores the limits of the grounded and teleological structures implicit in conceptions of the *unheimlich* as it is formulated by Freud. In her person, Rushdie collapses the angel/fiend dichotomy; she is simultaneously Beauty *and* the Beast, she is Hyder and, once married, Shakil, an Eastern and inverted version of the Jekyll/Hyde figure, and she embodies the worst excesses of both masculine power and feminine unruliness. She is the monstrous woman who fails in her wifely duties, who breaks the bounds of the domestic sphere, and she is the monstrous man whose violence and sexual aggression threaten public security. At the same time, she is neither man nor woman; she is an idiot child—who, on the one hand, elicits sympathy for the humiliations she has endured, and, on the other, more troublingly, cannot assume responsibility for the consequences of the atrocities she has enacted. Rushdie's insistence on the corporeal nature of her humiliations and deeds of vengeance is significant in the light of the fact that he is dealing with a society in which the law quite literally inscribes itself on the body through the punishments it exacts upon convicted criminals and transgressors of Koranic law. But, more importantly, he registers the impasse engendered by the binary logic which informs Pakistan's social codes as well as the conventions of nineteenth-century Gothic and of the *unheimlich*. These paradigms render her character a victim of these extreme oppositions, menacingly present in material terms but disturbingly absent discursively, and, because unspeakable, difficult to define as culpable. The final image of Sufiya Zinobia with which we are left is that of a monster unhoused: "an empty attic. Broken chains, cracked beams. There was a hole in the bricked-up window. It had a head, arms, legs" (1983:239). This evidence or trace of her unhousing poses a horrifying threat to those left behind to play out the narrative of official history.

Through Rushdie's strategic collapsing of opposites into one another, Hegelian dialectics become irrational and retrogressive instead of rational and progressive, and questions of responsibility are elided. As historical and historiographic processes are put under scrutiny in *Shame*, the notion of dialectics becomes a salient focus of concern. Rushdie calls into question the rationalistic Hegelian tenet that *progress* is effected through the confrontation of opposing forces. Pitting shame against shamelessness, or man against woman, or puritanism against epicurianism, he suggests, serves only to escalate the tensions between two increasingly polarized terms until they begin to collapse into each other, and yet somehow a third term—perhaps honour or mutual recognition or responsibility, in this instance—disappears entirely from the equation. Moreover, the polarization of the oppositions creates *excess*, and instead of a rational and progressivist history, we witness the unfolding of an encounter between irrational forces, which propels its combatants into the *nightmare* of history, a spectacle which stages the most feared and horrifying potentialities of either term that attends the emergence of its *unheimlich*. Such an irrational trajectory can only give rise to a history impelled by vengeance and retribution, as evidenced by Raza's overthrow and execution of Isky, and the three sisters' revenge on Raza. The possible conclusion of such a history is figured in the now seemingly prescient vision of a mushroom cloud "in the shape of a giant, grey and headless man, a figure of dreams, a phantom with one arm lifted in a gesture of farewell" with which the novel closes (1983:286). Rushdie shows us not only the horrifying consequences of enforcing rigid binary oppositions, but emphasizes also the effacement of the unthinkable of the opposition—that which never gets produced in history, but which nonetheless haunts the historical narrative, and which has consequences in the real world. It is crucially important that the ghosts of Sufiya Zinobia—and particularly those of the Pakistani immigrants in London whose tragedies the narrator relates in a series of asides—live out the consequences of the history that she literally embodies. If the excess of Sufiya Zinobia is produced *by* history, but is extrinsic to its official record, the ghosts which haunt her story exist at an even further remove. Yet simply to redraw the boundaries of inclusion will inevitably create further repressions, the novel suggests; hence the need to abandon the enterprise of redefining home in lieu of the project of summoning the unhomely.

Herein lies the logic for Rushdie's revisions of conventional Gothic treatments of the home. Even as the various domestic spaces of the protagonists are inscribed in the text, they are simultaneously pitted against recurring images of unhousing. In spite of the narrator's assertion that "Roots, I sometimes think, are a conservative myth, designed to keep us in our places," Rushdie does not simply set up an opposition between rootedness and rootlessness in which the latter is imbued with positive value (1983:86). That Pakistan is from its moment of inception a nation of migrants does not in itself light the way for the innovative acts of cultural translation envisaged by Bhabha. The literal unhousing of Hindus and Muslims in the post-Partition border crossings of 1947 not only gives rise to violent material effects which are graphically evoked in the novel, but is also coterminous with an *imperative* rehousing of the nation in the idea of Islam. This idea is rendered increasingly monolithic and repressive as each of Pakistan's successive despotic rulers finds ways of co-opting its most conservative tenets for the advancement of his own ends. The nation, which was conceived as "the Land of the Pure," enacts both in its acronymic name—"P for the Punjabis, A for the Afghans, K for the Kashmiris, S for Sind and the 'tan,' they say, for Baluchistan"—and its moment of inauguration, a gathering up of the subcontinental Muslim diaspora, and thus begins with rooting people in the idea *rather* than in the place (1983:87). The suturing together of these disparate ethnic groups—which mirrors the piecing together of Victor Frankenstein's monster and indeed of Rushdie's novel—in this instance subsumes the lived reality of cultural diversity in the ideal of theological unity, thereby repressing difference in order to foreground integrity and coherence. Crucially also, because the unhousings and dislocations attendant upon the foundation of nationhood lead only to the reinscription of another static and unitary idea of home, they allow for no further realignment, for "no strange fusions between what [the migrants] were and where they find themselves," and certainly for no dialogue with the dispossessed. Throughout *Shame*, and particularly through the narrator's interjections, it is precisely at the points of interface between the "present" and the "not-present," and between the manifest and the repressed that Rushdie locates the possibilities for escaping paradigms of subjectivity and of historiography which simply question or invert inherited models and the existing power structures within which they operate. Rather than valorizing a rehousing of the subject, *Shame* repeatedly enacts further unhousings, which are metonymically figured in Sufiya Zinobia's continual attempts to redefine and ultimately to transgress the boundaries of the domestic, whether by endlessly shifting and rearranging the furniture, by escaping from behind the screen or by casting off the strictures of an identity determined almost exclusively by a gendered body. All of these endeavours stand in marked contrast to the compelling desire—albeit unrealized—of Frankenstein's monster to accede to the domestic, to situate himself securely within the bounds of social structures and relationships, to move from the banishment of the wilderness into the stability and comfort of the home. Where Shelley works perhaps towards a homogenizing gesture of taming the monster, of drawing it into the fold by redefining the boundaries of home, Rushdie insists upon heterogeneity, and recognizes the inevitability of proliferating acts of repression.

Rushdie, moreover, makes it clear that the repressions he seeks to redress are not only historical; that they profoundly impact upon the present as well, whether in the streets of London or the zenanas of Karachi or Quetta or Mohenjo Daro, or in the living rooms of "Defence" in which government informers are casually planted, or in the many prisons to which critics of the government are confined indefinitely. The question of responsibility for such a history, and the positions from which it can be assumed, comes to light as the narrator anticipates the criticisms to which his story will inevitably give rise:

> *Outsider! Trespasser! You have no right to this subject!* . . . I know: nobody ever arrested me. Nor are they ever likely to. *Poacher! Pirate! We reject your authority. We know you, with your foreign language wrapped around you like a flag: speaking about us in your forked tongue, what can you tell but lies?* I reply with more questions: is history to be considered the property of the participants solely? In what courts are such claims staked, what boundary commissions map out the territories? (1983:28)

The trope of territorial boundaries is significant, because *Shame* demonstrates repeatedly that history *profoundly* impacts on its non-participants—those beyond the various boundaries of its posited "homelands"—whether they be the women who are for the most part excluded from the sphere of public life and kept behind the screen; or the poets, who, like the narrator's friend, are tortured and imprisoned, and are thereby prevented from telling the story; or the emigrants, for whom the legacy of a culture of shame and shamelessness continues to figure as an ominous spectre. As Rushdie's narrator reminds us, "All stories are haunted by the ghosts of stories they might have been." It is precisely in these invocations of ghosts—from spaces of otherness—that the possibilities for dislocation and realignment can be found. In *Shame*, then, Rushdie works tentatively towards developing a new structure through which to address the location of culture: one that self-consciously examines its own limits and textual parameters, one that is fragmented, loosely associated and fundamentally disjoined and one that seeks dialogues with the unhoused ghosts of any given "present." Each of these dislocations sets in dialogue the present with the not-present, and each affords a potential means of recognizing and taking responsibility for the then-and-there, without being utterly determined by it. The effect of Rushdie's revisionism, ultimately, is to register the traces of the many homes or groundings to which one never entirely belongs in spite of the inevitable endeavour to make each of them habitable.

Notes

1 Rushdie's claim that mass migrations have created "radically new types of human being" might seem simply to define the migrant as either extraneous to a normative and grounded identity politics, or as exemplary of a universalized and inevitable condition of uprootedness and disconnection; however, the transformative process towards which he gestures here offers far more interesting possibilities than either of these convenient homologies would allow. This point is borne out by Rushdie's novelistic experiments with migrant subjectivity, in which he refuses either to reinscribe a binary structure of identity politics which situates the migrant as "other" to the indigenous "self," or to reduce the migrant to the status of a "floating subject" who remains potentially excluded from and unimplicated in communal ties and their attendant benefits and social responsibilities.

2 Freud argues that the *unheimlich* experience "occurs either when [an individual's] repressed infantile complexes have been revived by some impression, or when the primitive beliefs we have [collectively] surmounted seem once more to be confirmed" (1953:403).

3 It is important to note that Rushdie retains the distinction between the imaginary realm where such experimental revisionism can be played out, and the realm of lived political realities, wherein it is in the interests of the empowered to deny the efficacy of any such revisionary model. See note 6 below.

4 On p. 4 of *Spectres of Marx* (1994), Derrida quotes Hamlet's lines from Act I, Scene v, "The *time* is out of joint; Oh cursed spight/ That ever I was borne to set it right" (italics mine).

5 Rushdie's narrator depicts this character very explicitly as the *unheimlich* of Pakistan's national ethos when he observes: "This was the danger of Sufiya Zinobia: that she came to pass not in any wilderness of basilisks and fields, but in the heart of the respectable world. And as a result that world made a huge effort of the will to ignore the reality of her, to avoid bringing matters to the point at which she, disorder's avatar, would have to be dealt with, expelled—because her expulsion would have laid bare what-on-no-account-must-be-known, namely, the impossible verity that barbarism could grow in cultured soil, that savagery could be concealed beneath decency's well-pressed shirt. That she was, as her mother had said, the incarnation of their shame. To comprehend Sufiya Zinobia would be to shatter, as if it were a crystal, these people's sense of themselves" (1983:200).

6 In "The Location of Brazil" (1985, reprinted in Rushdie 1991), Rushdie offers a scheme which seems to suggest the rationale underlying his own opposition of the "real" and "dystopian" history of Pakistan as presented in his Gothic allegory and the imaginative and revisionary possibilities implicit in the narrator's interjections. He writes: "Other elements in the film also suggest a vision more complex than the bleak simplicities of *Nineteen Eighty-Four*. . . . In *Brazil*, flight represents the imagining spirit; so it turns out that we are being told something very strange about the world of the imagination—that it is, in fact, at *war* with the 'real' world, the world in which things inevitably get worse and in which centres cannot hold. Angelic Sam and devilish Mr. Tuttle represent the power of dream-worlds to oppose this dark reality. In an age in which it seems impossible to create happy endings; in which we seem to make Dystopias in the way earlier ages made Utopias; in which we appear to have lost confidence in our abilities to improve the world, Gilliam brings heartening news. As N.F. Simpson revealed in *One Way Pendulum*, the world of the imagination is a place into which the long arm of the law is unable to reach.

   "This idea—the opposition of the imagination to reality, which is also of course the opposition of art to politics—is of great importance, because it reminds us that we are not helpless, that to dream is to have power. And I suggest that the true location of Brazil is the other great tradition in art, the one in which techniques of comedy, metaphor, heightened imagery, fantasy and so on are used to break down our conventional habit-dulled certainties about what the world is and has to be. Unreality is the only weapon with which reality can be smashed, so that it may subsequently be reconstructed" (1991:22).

References

Bhabha, Homi
  1994   *The Location of Culture*. London and New York: Routledge.
Derrida, Jacques
  1994   *Spectres of Marx: The State of the Debt, the Work of Mourning & the New International*. Translated by Peggy Kamuf. London and New York: Routledge.
Freud, Sigmund
  1953   *Collected Papers*. Vol. 4, *Papers on Metapsychology/Papers on Applied Psychoanalysis*. Edited by Ernest Jones, M.D. Translated by Joan Riviere. 8th impression. London: The Hogarth Press and the Institute of Psychoanalysis.
Haraway, Donna
  1990   "A Manifesto for Cyborgs: Science, Technology and Socialist Feminism in the 1980s." In Linda J. Nicholson, ed., *Feminism/Postmodernism*, 190-233. London and New York: Routledge.
Rushdie, Salman
  1983   *Shame*. London: Picador.
  1991   *Imaginary Homelands*. London: Granta.

13

A Vision of Unity: Brathwaite, Ngugi, Rushdie and the Quest for Authenticity

---

Mac Fenwick

This paper addresses three questions. First, how are writers and intellectuals creating, maintaining or giving voice to authentic, local cultural traditions in the face of rapid globalization? Second, is there a global voice or tradition growing up around us that can authentically claim to encompass these local voices? And third, what is the relationship between local and global forms? As I hope that the form of these questions makes clear, I believe that an understanding of the relationship between local and global can be approached through an exploration of the notion of authenticity itself.

I would like to begin these notes with three rather lengthy quotations on the nature of the relationship between authenticity and the processes of cross-cultural exchange and encounter. The first two concern the search for forms that authentically represent local traditions, and the third speaks to the creation of an authentically global perspective. The first is from Edward Kamau Brathwaite's *The Development of Creole Society in Jamaica 1770-1820*:

> The single most important factor in the development of Jamaican society was . . . a cultural action—material, psychological and spiritual—based upon the stimulus response of individuals within the society to their environment and—as white/black, culturally discrete groups—to each

other. The scope and quality of this response and interaction were dictated by the circumstances of the society's foundation and composition—a "new" construct, made up of newcomers to the landscape and cultural strangers each to the other; one group dominant, the other legally and subordinately slaves. This cultural action or social process has been defined within the context of this work as creolisation. (1971:296)

This next paragraph is from Ngugi wa Thiong'o's *Decolonising the Mind*:

What they [European-language-speaking members of the comprador neo-colonial class] have produced despite any claims to the contrary, is not African literature. . . . What we have created is another hybrid tradition, a tradition in transition, a minority tradition that can only be termed as Afro-European literature; that is, the literature written by Africans in European languages. (1986:26)

Finally, Salman Rushdie in *Imaginary Homelands*:

The effect of mass migrations has been the creation of radically new types of human being: people who root themselves in ideas rather than places, in memories as much as in material things. . . . [P]eople in whose deepest selves strange fusions occur, unprecedented unions between what they were and where they find themselves. The migrant suspects reality: having experienced several ways of being, he understands their illusory nature. To see things plainly, you have to cross a frontier. (1991:124)

For Brathwaite, creolization is the "cultural action or social process" that has given rise to the authentic creole culture of Jamaica. He argues that this culture has existed from the earliest colonization of the West Indies, but that it has been suppressed by the dominant (white) society's continued mimicry of European metropolitan culture. Brathwaite goes out of his way to state that this creole culture is not "fixed and monolithic" and that "there are infinite possibilities within these distinctions and many ways of asserting identity. A common colonial and creole experience is shared among the various divisions, even if that experience is variously interpreted" (1971:310). The authentic culture of the West Indies is, according to this argument, an expression of the "infinite possibilities" and "various interpretations" embodied within the process of creolization. What is authentically West Indian, according to Brathwaite, is the process of becoming creole. Authenticity is thus grounded not in iconoclastic truth, but in a plurality that rejects all absolute positions.

It is this process of becoming creole that Ngugi's stance would seem to reject. His argument that what the Afro-European writer has produced is "not African literature" begs the question "What is?" Ngugi's apparently iconoclastic answer is quite clear: only a literature that is written in an African language can be authentically African. This difference is not the result of an essential split between the two over the nature of cultural authenticity; rather, their disagreement is the result of their different strategic concerns.

According to Brathwaite, if West Indian writers are to authentically express West Indian experience, they must use what he calls the West Indian "nation language." This nation language, as a product of creolization, is a hybrid blend of "the African aspect of experience in the Caribbean" and an English "which is like a howl, or a shout. . . . And sometimes," he concludes, "it is English and African at the same time" (1984:13). West Indian writers cannot return to the African languages that have been denied to them by slavery; nor can they unproblematically take up the languages of mimicry used by the white cultures. Nation language is the authentic language of the West Indies not only because it is the product of creolization, but because it is the only option currently available to them.

African novelists, on the other hand, have never lost their African languages. These languages may have been ridiculed and denigrated by the imperial rulers, but as Ngugi points out they were never erased from daily use. A return to an authentically African language is thus possible, and, to Ngugi, desirable. The authenticity of African literature would thus seem to reside in an iconoclastic refusal to use any language other than an African one. But this refusal is only a first strategic step in the creation of an authentically African literature; it is one that Ngugi takes because he is able to. The rejection of a creole language like that used by Brathwaite is not a rejection of the processes of cross-cultural exchange: for while Ngugi rejects outright any possibility that English can authentically convey African experience, he at the same time affirms the novel's ability to do so.

Ngugi argues that "the social or even national basis of the origins of an important discovery or any invention is not necessarily a determinant of the use to which it can be put by its inheritors" (1986:68). In Ngugi's project of anti-imperial cultural struggle, cross-cultural exchange and hybrid combinations occur, but at a different level. Instead of a process of linguistic blending, Ngugi looks to the hybridization of genres that allows the African artist to create an authentically African novel by writing a novel in an African language. The novel, Ngugi claims, has antecedents in African folk tale and is itself the outgrowth of classical epic. The novel is thus neither a specifically European nor an iconoclastic and absolute form; it is instead a genre that, like nation language, is an ever-shifting and ever-adapting framework with infinite possibilities. The authenticity that Ngugi appeals to, like Brathwaite's description of creolization, is predicated upon hybridity and cross-cultural exchange. The novel can be authentically African insofar as it is the result of the cross-cultural processes of transmission and reformulation of genre that have translated it from ancient Greece to Europe to Africa.

Just as Brathwaite writes from within an authentically West Indian nation language, Ngugi writes from within an authentically African novel genre, both of which are the result of a cross-cultural process that rejects iconoclastic notions of cultural purity in favour of a vision of cultural forms as inherently partial, relational and processional. The claim of authenticity in both cases is predicated upon the existence of cultural hybridity. Authenticity can thus be defined in these cases as the raising to consciousness of the processes of cross-cultural exchange.

The most profoundly significant similarity between Brathwaite and Ngugi is that they are each interested in raising to consciousness authentically local forms. And so, in uncovering what they have in common despite their apparent differences, we have answered our first question: Brathwaite and Ngugi create authentic local forms by rejecting the iconoclasm of absolute terms and raising to consciousness the very processes of cross-cultural exchange that are the genesis of local tradition. In this answer we now begin to approach our second question: Is there an authentic global voice or tradition that can encompass these local voices? In other words, can we enter into an apprehension of cross-cultural exchange from any perspective other than the local?

The genesis of an answer to this question can be approached through Salman Rushdie's formulation of migrancy. Rushdie, like Brathwaite and Ngugi, privileges hybridity and plurality as the source of an authentic speaking voice. To return to the passage I quoted above: "The migrant suspects reality: having experienced several ways of being, he understands their illusory nature. To see things plainly, you have to cross a frontier." In one of his earliest defences of *The Satanic Verses* Rushdie explains that his novel is "a migrant's-eye view of the world" and that "it rejoices in mongrelisation and fears the absolutism of the Pure. *Mélange*, hotchpotch, a bit of this and a bit of that is *how newness enters the world*" (1991:394). The process of creolization, for Brathwaite, is the hybrid source of an authentic West Indian nation language. The novel's inherent hybridity is, for Ngugi, what allows for the creation of an authentically African novel. The act of migrancy, of uprooting and translation, is, for Rushdie, the source of an authentic perspective from which to view the globe as a whole. Insofar as these three writers make similiar appeals to the processes of cross-cultural negotiation as the source of authenticity, they make the same argument. Where Rushdie significantly differs from Brathwaite and Ngugi is in making his argument a specifically global one. Nation language and the African novel are authentic local forms; Rushdie claims to have achieved an authentic global one. This claim needs to be examined.

The basis of this claim is made on three points. The first, like Brathwaite's, is based on the argument that English is not the sole preserve of the Imperial centre, and that it can, through hybridization and reverse appropriation, be made to speak for and of everyone (" 'Commonwealth Literature' Does Not Exist"). The second claim, like Ngugi's, is his argument that the novel is a form that belongs absolutely to no one culture or tradition ("Is Nothing Sacred?"). Language and genre are both the products and bearers of an impure and hybrid process, and can thus be used to authentically represent any reality.

The third argument that Rushdie makes for the migrant's perspective is its universality: "Migration," Rushdie claims, "offers us one of the richest metaphors of our age. . . . Migrants—borne-across humans— are metaphorical beings in their very essence; and migration, seen as a metaphor, is everywhere around us. We all cross frontiers; in that sense, we are all migrant peoples" (1991:278-79). By saying that the migrant's perspective is universal because everyone is, "in a sense," a migrant, Rushdie empties the word of meaning. Brathwaite and Ngugi, a black worker leaving Soweto for Cape Town or a young Canadian going off to university are not migrants in the sense that the highly educated, financially secure Rushdie is. To equate these cases is to either eliminate difference or, what is far worse, to suspend difference. What Rushdie's argument fails to realize is that the migrant perspective is as much a local and strategic form as Brathwaite's nation language and Ngugi's African novel. That the migrant's perspective is rooted more in a way-of-being rather than in any one socio-geography is irrelevant. To try and claim that the educated class of literate displaced persons is representative of everyone in the world is as impossible to maintain as a claim that we are all West Indian creoles.

Rushdie is conflating the process that creates the migrant with the migrant him- or herself. All along I have been trying to stress that what

Brathwaite, Ngugi and Rushdie have in common is not their strategic, local interests, but a common view that authenticity is based upon a raising to consciousness of the cross-cultural processes of hybridization. To say that we participate in the processes that underlie creolization, the transmission of cultural forms or migrancy is not to say that we are all creoles, cross-cultural artists or migrants. It is, however, to say that everyone who is creole, a cross-cultural artist or an intellectual migrant participates in the same process of cross-cultural exchange. Having said this, we can expand it even further: anyone who participates in the search for or creation of an authentic local tradition—and who amongst us does not?—is part of the same global process of hybridization, cross-cultural exchange and cultural impurity of which individual cultural traditions are the local manifestations.

To answer our second question, then: Is there a global voice that can authentically claim to encompass these local voices? No. There is, however, a global process from which many different local traditions would seem to be drawing their authentic existence. The real usefulness of Rushdie's formulation of migrancy lies not in its supposed universality, but in the emphasis that it places upon perspective. We have already said that migrancy is a local form, strategically adopted and created by an international and educated elite. As such, it does not authentically describe everyone in the world. It does, however, like creolization, raise to consciousness the global processes of hybridity, exchange, partial relationships and impurity that underlie all local traditions—and it does so by emphasizing its view of the world as perspectival. Migrancy, as well as creolization and the African novel, can therefore be regarded as different perspectives onto a global process of cross-cultural exchange and dialogue.

We come, then, to the last of my three questions: What is the relationship between local and global forms? I have already shown how the migrant's claim to an authentically global voice is false, and that migrancy is simply the local form of an educated elite. I have also suggested that this does not necessarily entail the dissolution of the global into an infinite number of locals, insofar as all local forms are authentic perspectives onto the global processes of cross-cultural exchange that they raise to consciousness. This perspectival approach to the creation of authenticity brings with it certain consequences to our understanding of the relation between many local forms and one global process. To claim that there are different perspectives of a single process necessitates the existence of three unities: the unity of world, the unity of humanity and the unity of discourse. It is with these three unities that I wish to end.

First, for there to be different perspectives rather than different truths there must be only one object variously viewed and not many. If it is true that local forms are the strategic manifestations of a global process, then relativism is overcome by the admission that we all share the same horizons of existence. We all find our being in the same world. Second, to talk of perspective implies the same viewing subject. Two wholly dissimiliar people looking at the same thing will have two wholly dissimilar impressions of it, not just varying perspectives. To say that local forms are perspectival gateways into a global process implies that the human person inhabiting each of the local forms embodies the same subjectivity.

Finally, for these different perspectives to exist as perspectives and not as incommensurable impressions, they must be communicable to one another. The stereoscopic vision of the human eye depends upon the brain's ability to combine two images into a single apprehended form. Perspectives are made meaningful only when they are combined. To say that local forms are perspectival is to say that they can be communicated one to the other through a unified human discourse.

To sum up where my search for authenticity has brought me. The authenticating process that Brathwaite, Ngugi and Rushdie pursue is an essentially perspectival one: their works are authentically West Indian, African or migrant only insofar as they raise to consciousness their participation within a global process of exchange—a process that, while capable of an infinite variety of local forms, is prevented from falling into relativism and incommensurability by the three unities of world, humanity and discourse upon which the very concept of perspective depends. The task that this analysis leads to, then, does not end with the elucidation or evaluation of the truths that inhere to various local traditions, but to a never-ending exploration of the global process from which individual cultures derive their perspectival meaning.

References

Brathwaite, Edward Karnau
1971   *The Development of Creole Society in Jamaica 1770-1820*. Oxford: Clarendon.

1984 *History of the Voice*. London: Beacon.
Ngugi wa Thiong'o
1986 *Decolonising the Mind: The Politics of Language in African Literature*.
     London: Currey.
Rushdie, Salman
1991 *Imaginary Homelands*. London: Granta.

14

Cowboy Songs, Indian Speeches and the Language of Poetry

J. Edward Chamberlin

Cowboys are not particularly popular these days, at least among postcolonial academics. Indians are. In both cases, the reasons are not entirely plausible, though plausibility has never interfered with fashion. So I thought it might be interesting to look a little more closely at cowboys and Indians. They come to most of us through our imaginations, rather than through our experiences. Up until quite recently, Indians were best known from the speeches of their leaders, chiefs like Joseph and Tecumseh and Seattle; and more recently, from the writings of their poets and novelists. With cowboys, it has been their songs that hold us, not so much the current ones about cheating hearts and honky-tonk angels but those nine-teenth- and early-twentieth-century songs like "Home on the Range," "Red River Valley" and "Goodbye, Old Paint." One of the first attempts to collect them was also one of the first collections of folk songs in the Americas: John Lomax's 1910 *Cowboy Songs and Other Frontier Ballads*.

The texts of Indian speeches were usually written down at the time they were delivered, and although this process was complicated—and to a considerable degree compromised—by translation and the change from speech to writing, they have become set pieces of poetic power and political rhetoric. They are quoted time and again in defence of

---

Notes to chapter 14 are on p. 206.

Native American rights; and, from the 1800s, encyclopedia definitions of poetry in Great Britain and Europe as well as in Canada and the United States would almost always quote an Indian speech as an example of the purest form of language.

I grew up with these speeches. I knew all about Chief Seattle saying,

> when the last red man shall have perished, and the memory of my tribe shall have become a myth among the white man, these shores will swarm with the invisible dead of my tribe, and when your children's children think themselves alone in the field, the store, the shop, upon the highway, or in the silence of the pathless woods, they will not be alone. . . . The dead are not powerless. Dead—I say? There is no death. Only a change of worlds. (Vanderwerth 1971:121-22)

Or Sitting Bull asking,

> what treaty that the whites have kept has the red man broken? Not one. What treaty that the whites ever made with us red men have they kept? Not one. When I was a boy the Sioux owned the world. The sun rose and set in their lands. They sent 10,000 horsemen to battle. Where are the warriors today? Who slew them? Where are our lands? Who owns them? What white man can say that I ever stole his lands or a penny of his money? Yet they say I am a thief. (Moquin and Van Doren 1973:262)

But it was cowboy songs that held me first as a young child in Calgary in the 1940s, listening to Stu Davis on the radio and trying to yodel like Jimmie Rodgers, and then later in the dry valleys and benchlands of the interior of British Columbia where I lived for part of each year. I had some cowboys in the family too. My grandfather had run the Cochrane ranch around the turn of the century—though in the language of the day that made him a cow*man* rather than a cowboy— ranging cattle from north of Calgary all the way down to the American border. His life on the southern Alberta prairies bound him to those uneasy borderlands between the Blackfoot confederacy and the new bureaucracy of Royal Northwest Mounted Police and Indian agents; and because I grew up with his stories (mostly told me by my mother) I seemed strangely bound to this world as well. It was a time when hunters were being replaced by herders, wooded coulees were becoming cattle wallows, cowboys and Indians were being fenced in, the Métis leader Louis Riel was hanged for treason and the Nez Perce, just across the border, were trying to protect themselves against the brutal encroachments of settlers and the bloody enterprise of soldiers.

Given the traditions of the Nez Perce, it is not surprising that horses were at the centre of this great scene. In one of the most famous moments in the long and sordid history of Indian/white relations on this continent, the Nez Perce Chief Joseph surrendered to the United States General Miles in his camp in the Bear Paw Mountains of Montana, less than thirty miles from Canada and freedom. In doing so, he turned himself and his people over to the mercy of the United States government and its agents. "From where the sun now stands I will fight no more forever," he said. I suspect that if a person knows only one line of an Indian speech, it will be this one. But Chief Joseph said more than this, framing his surrender with the loyalties and treacheries that he had come to appreciate as part of these negotiations. "I believe General Miles would have kept his word if he could have done so," he said later. "I do not blame him for what we have suffered since the surrender. I do not know who is to blame." Then he added, "we gave up all our horses—over eleven hundred—and all our saddles—over one hundred—and we have not heard from them since. Someone has got our horses" (Vanderwerth, 1971:279-80). I want to say something about those horses.

In the late 1920s, wracked with something like guilt for the destitute condition of Indian people in the United States, the Department of the Interior commissioned a report from the Institute for Government Research (later known as the Brookings Institute). Directed by Lewis Meriam, it provided an exhaustive catalogue of the relentless dispossession of Indian land, the systematic destruction of Indian tribes and the brutal dislocation of Indian people. It was filled with righteous (and well-researched) indignation about the breaches of trust that had characterized Indian administration. It was harsh in its criticism of the land-allotment policy that had been in place for a half a century, and it recommended the re-establishment of tribal governments with control over land and resources. It was eloquent in its celebration of the values of community and of place, and the interdependence of spiritual and material values in both Native and non-Native society.

It was also incorrigibly utilitarian in the remedies it proposed. And it was interested in worthiness. So when it came to describing the situation of the Navaho, one of the largest and most powerful of the tribes, it forgot about their horses. Actually, it did not quite forget. It dismissed their horses in one paragraph in its nearly 900 pages. The paragraph was titled "Worthless Horses."

Worthless? These were the horses that worked the land, pulled the wagons, carried the men and women and herded the stock. They had hunted the buffalo on the northern plains, and everywhere, from the

Navajo to the Nez Perce, they haunted the imagination. For these were the horses that also grazed wild on the grasslands, defying the immediate demands of subsistence and signifying not just prestige but a kind of sovereignty. A horse was its own reason for being—not a convenience or a commodity but a covenant, linking survival with power. A covenant between fresh air and freedom to breathe. And this completely confounded those who wrote the Meriam Report.

Horses were in the Americas tens of thousands of years ago; and then, some say, they mysteriously died off, or migrated out. Others claim that in the dryland regions of the west, in those sheltered coulees and canyons of the front range, they stayed on, losing a few toes and gaining a lot of teeth, while their spirits—as well as their speed and strength—helped shape the Aboriginal societies that developed in the region.

Certainly some of the early horses did move north across the tundra and overland to the great plains of Asia. They carried on across the steppes to become the dun-coloured tarpins of the ancient forests of Europe, later bred to war and to working the lands. The Vikings rode them, and these horses were the first to pull a plough. They came back to the Americas, cross-tied and cold-blooded, on boats rowed by the northern voyagers.

Others went south in Asia to Africa. The Persians, especially, valued those with spotted coats, and bred this line. So did the Nez Perce, centuries later, establishing the great Appaloosas in their homelands along the banks of the Palouse River. Their breeding skill is one of the enduring achievements of the cultures of the Americas. The Bedouins swept across North Africa on horses, and into the history of the deserts. Muhammad once kept his horses from water for a week; and when he finally opened the gates and they all rushed out towards the well, he sounded the call to battle. Five of the horses wheeled round. They were the beginning of the great Arab line. There are rules for breeding and training horses in the Koran; and for every barleycorn that is given to a horse, Allah will pardon one sin. Muhammad rode to heaven on a horse; and some of those he left behind came with the Moors to Spain, to found the Spanish breeds that went with Columbus on his second voyage, travelling in high-strung style, suspended in slings.

The iconography of horses has often focused on their utility—for war, for travel, for hunting and farming and ranching. To be sure, the idea of horses as useful runs very deep. But it is certainly not the only idea. For millennia, horses have graced the walls of caves and castles, their form and colour and movement providing inspiration rather than income. They have represented ideals of beauty and elegance and independence as well as of discipline and strength and courage. And while the recreation and sports in which they feature—from racing and driving and jumping and dressage to buzkashi and polo and the skill of the rodeo circuit and the acrobatics of circuses—while these celebrate useful skills, they also embody something of what Wallace Stevens used to call "essential gaudiness." This is what Henry David Thoreau was talking about at the end of *Walden*, when—in one of his wonderfully contradictory remarks—he worries that he has not been extravagant enough in his praise of simplicity, and appeals for a commitment to excess, to wandering from the paths of easy meaning and common sense.

> It is a ridiculous demand which England and America make, that you shall speak so that they can understand you. Neither men nor toadstools grow so. . . . As if Nature could support but one order of understandings. . . . I fear chiefly lest my expression may not be *extravagant* enough, may not wander far enough beyond the narrow limits of my daily experience, so as to be adequate to the truth of which I have been convinced. *Extra vagance*. It depends on how you are yarded. The migrating buffalo, who seeks new pastures in another latitude, is not extravagant like the cow which kicks over the pail, leaps the cowyard fence, and runs after her calf, in milking time. . . . Why level downward to our dullest perception always, and praise that as common sense. The commonest sense is the sense of men asleep, which they express by snoring. (Thoreau 1971:324-25)

Thoreau's cow was like those horses, the ones that represent the indispensable extravagance of the imagination pressing back against the debilitating pressures of reality, affirming not the autonomy of human beings—as some folks who are unfriendly to the imagination might say—but the rhythms and reasonings of nature.

For horses are both a part of nature and—in our stories and songs—a part of us. These are the horses that win battles and horses that represent wealth and power and horses that exemplify traditions of skill and strength and grace and beauty, horses that are prized for their colour and conformation as much as for their courage and craft, horses that fly in the air and horses that work the land. Often the very same horses. In the west they might well be of Indian breeding—Navajo or Nez Perce or Blackfoot or Beaver, all of whom have stories about horses that are central to their culture; or they might have cowboy names—like Old Paint or Doney Gal or Chopo or Pattonio or Strawberry Roan or Midnight the Unconquered Outlaw, all of whom have songs written about them. Or much farther west, they might be the horses that were trained by one of the heroes of Western literature, the one who gets the last word in its greatest epic, Homer's *Iliad*. "Thus held they funeral for Hector, tamer of horses" (Lang et al. 1961:452).

I once knew a cowboy named Hector, riding the rodeo circuit in the Kootenay and Columbia river basins. Like his namesake, he got into a nasty fight over someone else's woman; and he loved telling stories, boasting and teasing and taunting and making all sorts of foolishness and coming up with far-fetched figures of speech about his exploits. Like when that brahma bull he rode for all of 2-1/2 seconds caught him from behind and tossed him back up over the chute in Coeur d'Alene, and he said with a crooked grin that he had just gotten his oil checked. Hector the cowboy and clown. Homer the rodeo announcer. I kind of like the connection.

The first cowboys in the Americas, people always seem surprised to learn, were in the Caribbean. In the years immediately following Columbus's second voyage in 1494—when he offloaded twenty-four stallions, ten mares and a significant number of cattle on the island of Hispaniola—the animals thrived, creating in remarkably short order a surplus of wild, ownerless cattle, along with skilled horsemen who adapted Spanish equestrian techniques and equipment to the new environment. As one José de Acosta described the situation later in the sixeenth century in Santo Domingo,

> the cattle have multiplied so greatly [there] and in other islands of the region that they wander by the thousands through the forests and fields, all masterless. The beasts [are hunted] only for their hides; whites and Negroes go out on horseback, equipped with a kind of hooked knife, to chase the cattle, and any animal that falls to their knives is theirs. (Slatta 1990:9)

Soon settlement spread to the mainland, and horses and cattle migrated across the continent. "By the late seventeenth century," writes historian Richard W. Slatta in his marvellous study of the *Cowboys of the Americas*, "the foundations for Western hemisphere equestrian cultures had been laid: horsemen and livestock coexisting in plains environments" (1990:11). Enormous herds of cattle and of wild horses too roamed the South American and Mexican plains, and a class of (mostly) men emerged, roaming with the animals they hunted and (in due course) herded in geographical and culturally marginal areas, remote from and fiercely independent of the urban elites who were beginning to exercise their dominion over the resources of the plains—land, livestock, water and labour. These men became the *gauchos* of Argentina, Uruguay and the Rio Grande do Sul region of Brazil; the *llaneros* of Venezuela and Colombia; the *vaqueros* of northern Brazil, northern Mexico and the Spanish southwest; the *huasos* of Chile; and the cowboys of the western United States and Canada.

They were more or less self-sufficient, displaying contempt for those who lived in the towns (mixed with envy or nostalgia for the comforts they enjoyed) and disdaining their laws. This last is important, for the legendary freedom of cowboys, especially the wild hunters of Latin America, was often dependent on their evading the legal measures put in place to control them. In those early years, the behaviour of cowboys was routinely criminalized by vagrancy and other legislation designed to serve the interests of the landed class. Many of the early cowboys in Argentina and Brazil were slaves in fact, their lives circumscribed by all the conditions of the slave system. But whether a cowboy was enslaved, indentured or free, whatever independence he enjoyed was paradoxically determined by his labour; and the outlaw reputation of cowboys is rooted in their original way of life, both literally and figuratively outside the law—where illegal hunting and smuggling were, if you will pardon the pun, their stock in trade.

And yet the life of a cowboy was ultimately shaped not so much by flaunting the unfriendly laws of the town as by adapting to the uncertain conditions of the country—the plains and rivers and mountains, the climate and the comrades and of course the animals. One observer of the *llanero* at work in Venezuela in the early nineteenth century remarked that, "although usually styled and considered herders, their habits and modes of life were in reality those of hunters; for the cattle, which constituted their sole wealth being perfectly wild, the exertions required to collect a herd and to keep it together in the neighbourhood of a farm-house, were necessarily violent and incessant."[1]

Incessant is the key word here. Unceasing. And always on the move. Throughout these years, and throughout the Americas, cowboys developed a fairly simple set of characteristics which defined their place on the plains: they had no home; they owned no land; and they never would. Period. How is it, then, that their way of life became the envy of so many people in the years following their heyday in the eighteenth and early nineteenth centuries, the very years when settler ideals of home and native land were being fashioned? Part of it, perhaps, was the apparent simplicity of cowboy life, with its closeness to nature and its distance from the artifices of towns and cities; part of it possibly the escape from routine and the freedom from those very same ties to place and community that were being celebrated, the ties that bind.

Whatever else, it is a curious contradiction. For cowboy life certainly was not easy, even though it made for easy listening in the stories and songs that chronicled it. Cowboys had little security, either of life or labour, and few allegiances except to each other and to their horses. They lived apart—apart from the advantages of the new world's economies, apart from its settlement ideologies and its agricultures, apart from the old-world European and African and Asian cultures that overtook the Americas. Their home was on horseback, where they worked for twelve to fourteen hours a day (unless they were riding night herd, when it would be all the time except for breakfast and dinner), seven days a week, months at a time. Like medieval craft guilds, cowboys were more or less racist and sexist, though there were Indians and more than a few Africans among them, and some women too, mostly much later when cowboy skills turn into spectacles on the rodeo circuit.

From the beginning, horses and cowboys were two sides of the same coin. Even so, the relationship was always complicated. Cowboys owned almost nothing, certainly no more than they could wear, attach to their saddle or carry in their saddlebags, and although they occasionally owned their own horses this was discouraged for it was felt that they might not ride them hard enough; and, besides, when an outfit supplied horses it had more of a hold. On a long trail drive, each cowboy would typically be given a string of eight or ten horses, which remained his as long as he was with the outfit, and—here a sort of proprietorship intervened—no one, not even the foreman, would ride them without the cowboy's permission.

There was another interesting contradiction in the relationship between cowboys and horses. Cowboys depended absolutely on horses for their livelihood and for their lives. But the wildness, the untameable essence, of these horses became part of their appeal. Cowboys would boast about ones that "could pitch more ways than a Chinaman could write," and many early cowboy songs celebrated bucking broncos, especially unrideable ones. At a later stage, by contrast, there were lots of affectionate songs about horses like Old Paint or Doney Gal, both of these interesting because they were mares, and cowboys for a long time throughout many parts of the Americas would ride only stallions or geldings.

"A cowboy's life is a weary, dreary life," begins one cowboy song,

> Some say it's free from care,
> Rounding up the cattle from morning till night,
> In the middle of the prairie so bare.
>
> The wolves and the owls with their terrifying howls
> Disturb us in our midnight dream,
> As we lie on our slickers in a cold rainy night,
> Way over on the Pecos stream.
>
> Spring time sets in, double trouble will begin,
> The weather is so fierce and so cold.
> Our clothes are wet and frozen to our necks,
> And the cattle we can scarcely hold. (John Lomax 1938:15)

The rhymes of these songs are typically simple, like the tunes. In many cases, in fact, the melodies were standard issue, picked up from other lands and livelihoods and languages. This one takes over someone else's words too, words originating in New Brunswick in a song called "The Lumberman's Lament." It starts off:

> The lumberman's life is a wearisome life,
> some say it's free from care,
> But we chop down the pine from morning till night
> In the middle of the forest so drear. (Alan Lomax 1960:355)

Lumberman songs were in fact the originals for quite a few old cowboy verses. There were similarities in the working conditions, with indenture defining the life of many lumberjacks and cowboys just as surely as it did that of Caribbean cane workers. "Yes, we will pay good wages and will pay your passage out, / provided you sign papers that you will stay the route" was a standard song line. One of these songs, the Scots deportation song "Caledon-i-o," became "Canada-i-o," a song composed (or stolen) by some loggers from Maine who spent a winter up at Trois Rivières in Quebec; and this ballad in turn provided the tune and many of the words for "Trail of the Buffalo" and "Trail to Mexico," two cowboy favourites.

But despite the similarities of subject, and although stories and songs of the strength and stamina and stubbornness of lumberjacks became legendary in both Canada and the United States, life on the prairie held terrors unknown to the more-or-less settled conditions of the lumbermen. Trying to hold a herd of cattle in a storm, riding to the front of a stampede at breakneck speed to cut them off and turn them—if your horse stumbled or slipped it meant certain death, and not a pretty one. And the songs in which this life was celebrated are not quite as simple as they sometimes seem.

Let's look, for example, at one called "When the Work's All Done This Fall." There's some uncertainty about who wrote it, though it was first published in the *Stock Grower's Journal* in Miles City, Montana, in 1893. It was said to have originated on a stock trail out of Deadwood, Wyoming. Whatever its provenance, it has been a perennial favourite, recorded in the 1990s in versions as different as the country pop style of Michael Martin Murphey and the traditional folk style of Norman and Nancy Blake. The song tells of a cowboy who, after a lifetime of riding the range, announces that at the end of this season he is going back home to Dixie with what is left of his wages—instead of doing what he would usually do, which is spend it all on drinking, dancing and some other unmentionable activities.

The song turns around images of home: his broken-hearted Mother's home, which we know cannot be quite the same place he left long years ago, but to which he plans to return after this last roundup; his home on the range, one that has held him for so long; and his final home, which he refers to (in a familiar figure of speech) as the "new range" to which he will soon be called by his Master.

The wanderer dreaming of home. It is an old, old theme. In the Americas it takes forms as different as the great old French-Canadian folk song that begins "Un Canadien errant, banni de ses foyers" (A wandering Canadian, banished from his home) and the question posed by the Barbadian Kamau Brathwaite, reflecting in a poem on the rootlessness of West Indian blacks. "Where then is the nigger's home," he asks, "in Paris, Brixton, Kingston, Rome? Here, or in heaven?" (Brathwaite 1973:77).

Home, sweet home. It is where we hang our hat. It is where our heart is. Maybe the same place. Maybe not. It may be the place we came from, five or fifty or five hundred years ago, or the place we are going to when our time is done. When Bob Marley was asked whether his home was *really* in Ethiopia, as the Rastafarian story has it, and whether he *really* hoped to go and live there some day, he replied, "I doan hope. We going" (Marley 1995). The "reallys" are realities in Rastafari. Rastas are going home, like many others. Over Jordan, as it were—which is both a real river, with its wide water and wicked politics, and a place of imagined crossings. A few years ago, during a celebration of the emancipation of slaves in the British colonies in 1838, there was a meeting between the Rastafarians of Jamaica and President

Jerry John Rawlings of Ghana, the region from which many of the slaves originally came. Rawlings recited the reasons why Africa was not such a good place to return to right now, clearly not fancying emigration by new-world idealists to challenge his old-world realities. But each time he paused for breath one of the Rasta leaders would stand up, resplendent in pan-African regalia, and say—with the patience of someone speaking to a person who is a little slow—"but we waan go home."

"There's no place like home," as the old saying has it. It is a very curious saying, for the phrase "no place" is deeply ambiguous. Taking that "like" away—taking that metaphorical foot out of the door—home is no place. Nowhere. It is also somewhere special, unique and utopian—but then, just as we are beginning to have a warm and cozy feeling about it, we realize that utopia *means* "no place." In Herman Melville's novel *Moby Dick*, Ishmael tells us that the strange harpooner Queequeg with whom he is sharing a bed at the Spouter Inn was born on the island of Kokovoko. Then he adds, "it is not down in any map; true places never are" (Melville 1967:56).

"When the Work's All Done This Fall," however slight its ambitions (and we do not want to presume too much on that count just yet), belongs in a tradition of stories and songs about home. It also turns around another notion, one that is not stated in so many words but rather in so few rhymes. Let me try to explain. The chorus of the song goes like this:

> After the round-ups are over and after the shipping is done,
> I am going right straight home, boys, ere all my money is gone.
> I have changed my ways, boys, no more will I fall;
> And I am going home, boys, when the work's all done this fall.

The night after he announces this, the cowboy is out riding herd when a storm comes up. The cattle stampede; he tries to head them off, but his horse stumbles in the dark, falls on him, and he is fatally injured. The final verse of the song tells the words that are carved on the wooden board that marks his grave.

> Charlie died at daybreak, he died from a fall
> And he'll not see his mother when the work's all done this fall.

Now one of the things that I remember thinking first about this song was that the fellow who wrote it must have been pretty short on rhymes. Both in the chorus and in the final verse he rhymes "fall" and "fall"—a sure thing, I know, but embarrassingly simple. Just what you would expect out on the Spotted Wood Trail.

Yet there's method in this monotony, for he makes us immediately aware of the several meanings of "fall" that he is using. In the chorus, "fall" refers both to the season—a season of harvest, of the roundup and shipping of cattle—*and* to the sinner who leads a life of low living. (As the first verse has it, "I am an old cow-puncher and here I'm dressed in rags. / I used to be a tough one and go on great big jags.") The final verse presents another pair: his fall from the horse and the season again, but this time it is a season of death, of another kind of roundup. And, as a result, the song resonates with the various meanings of "fall"—figurative and literal, literary and local, secular and sacred, ripeness and regret. William Wordsworth once said that we are fostered alike by beauty and by fear. Fall figures in both.

And so it did in the cowboy's life which, like that of their horses, was hard and dangerous. Cowboys accepted its crippling and sometimes deadly uncertainties with a fatalism that was tragic and comic by turns, generating a tradition of tall tales and humour that is one of our great legacies of story and song. Anyone who has heard a good rodeo announcer will recognize its latest version. Cowboys celebrated the awesome beauty and fearsome power of the land, and the grim trials and lonely wonders of their livelihood. They dreaded much in their wandering world; and, as we have seen, even as they despised those who settled down they often dreamed of the home they left behind, or the one they might build someday. And so, songs like "Bury Me Not on the Lone Prairie," adapted from an early-nineteenth-century sea-burial tune, were refashioned for the prairies, this one reportedly sung so often during the last decades of the nineteenth century that it used to be said that the horses nickered it and the coyotes howled it. At the same time, cowboys cherished their vagabondage, and the myth remains intact in songs like "Goodbye, Old Paint," traditionally the last waltz at a cowboy dance.

Nowhere is this contradiction caught better than in "Home on the Range," perhaps the best-known cowboy song of all (at least to all of us non-cowboys). Its opening rhyme is all we need: "O give me a home, where the buffalo roam" (Cannon 1988:54). *Home* and *roam*: bound together by their similar sounds, their senses pull in completely contradictory directions. Wandering and settling down. It is hard to imagine a more fundamental human opposition—or a more fundamental condition in the Americas. And we underestimate ourselves if we do not accept that our imaginations take this in every time we sing this song. We do not remember these lines because they tell *one* truth about ourselves, but because they tell two contradictory ones. Or, in the words of a much more recent song—the cautionary "Mothers, Don't Let Your Babies Grow Up to Be Cowboys"—cowboys are "always alone, even with someone they love." I can give this a high-culture turn if you want. "Moi sans moi," the nineteenth-century French poet Stéphane Mallarmé used to say about his poems.

But back to cowboys. I believe that they hold—or perhaps I should say held—our imaginations because of the way they embodied these contradictions in their lives, known to most of us through the art written or played or painted about them. And I also believe, contrary to much postcolonial cleverness, that those of us who wanted to be cowboys when we grew up did not simply want to be part of colonial expansion or frontier violence. We might have, but then again we might not. We wanted something else, something much more deeply engrained not in the history of the West but in the imaginations of children. We wanted lives that were both determined and free, both defined by necessities and defiant of them. We wanted to be both inmates (with our fellow cowboys) and outcasts. We wanted to "bewilder the bourgeois" in ourselves, to be both ourselves and not ourselves. We wanted to be "bound to go," to use that common blues phrase, one that catches the contradiction better than almost any other. We wanted to be hitchhikers and hobos on the roads and the rails. We wanted to be free to wander in straight lines, hunters and gatherers on trains and highways, paradoxically our most powerful symbols of agricultural settlement. And when a phrase like "freedom's just another word for nothing left to lose"—from Kris Kristofferson's song "Me and Bobby McGee," made famous by Janis Joplin and Gordon Lightfoot—eventually caught our imaginations, it did so because we knew that freedom was *not* just another word for nothing left to lose. Cowboys—or stories and songs about cowboys—taught us that as surely as constitutions ever did.

And so we intuitively admired another contradiction about cowboys. They were gloriously extravagant, routinely spending wages from six months on the trail in as many days in town, and wearing clothes and gear that displayed a love of show—boots, spurs, hats, chaps, shirts, saddles, bits and bridles. And yet they developed skills in riding and roping, in herding and hunting down strays, that were models of economy and efficiency, and sometimes of astonishing grace. Some of these you can see on display in any rodeo or stampede; to understand others you need to know something about the weird makeup of horses and cattle and cowboys.

Cowboys never made the clear distinction between work and play that preoccupies agricultural and industrial societies, and even their singing fell between. Most of them believed that songs, or at least the sound of a human voice, helped settle cattle—a notion that is still current in dairy barns around the world—and at night especially they would sing to the herd. When they ran out of tunes, they would launch into a litany of profanities, often comically contradicted by some religious humming, or they might recite the words on a coffee label or a can of condensed milk. And during the day, they would whoop and yell and hoot and holler to move the herd along. As far as I can tell, nobody ever actually heard a cowboy say yippee-ki-yi-o, as one famous song has it, but they might have. Whatever the case, cowboys worked and played with language as they worked and played with everything else they used, creating a lexicon of technical terms lovingly twisted and translated into cowboy lingo: criollo applied to cattle and horses as much as to people; reata migrating to lariat, vaquero to buckaroo, and dar la vuelta (wrapping the end of a rope around the saddle horn) to dally; a willow was a range mare; a waddie a cowboy riding one (or anything else, for that matter); and a slow elk a cattle beast poached by a waddie out of work.

Cowboys also had much in common with Indians, whom they wove their way among and occasionally clashed with—though not nearly as often as those dime-store novels and B-movies suggest. At the end of the day, cowboys and Indians alike were denounced as barbarians, beyond the pale of the settler society. Indeed, in their apparent acceptance of uncertainty and insecurity, they seemed beyond the pale of civilization. Period. Indians, the great horsemen of the plains, were admired by the cowboys even as they sometimes feared them. But they shared a horse culture that went deep into their souls, and they shared too a hunter's sense and sensibility. Like cowboys, Indians reserved most of their resentment for settlers, or nesters as they were called, and for the soldiers who came to force them off their land or fence them in.

Fences and farmers would ultimately do them both in, or at least severely compromise their ways of life. Fences especially. "Don't fence me in" became a catchy refrain for good reason, something of which we sense in Thoreau's celebration of extravagance. In the words of an Alberta cowboy, barb wire is what ruined this country. At first we could keep it cut pretty well, and use the posts for firewood, but it got so, after a while, they were putting up the damned stuff faster than a guy could cut it down. Every homesteader has his little bit fenced off, and there was that whole stretch between Standoff and Fort Kipp. The Cochrane ranch [probably about the time my grandfather took over!] had three strands running for 25 miles, and fence riders straddling it all day. When I saw that I said to myself, I says, "This country's done for"—and you see now I was right. (Slatta 1990:50)

After fences came along, and for the few decades following, cowboys would ride the range year round, living in bitterly cold dugouts in winter, line-riding the fences and wolf hunting. In spring they "rode bog," freeing animals caught by rains and runoff. But, long before fences, it was the weather that always held special terrors and inspired a special kind of imagining for cowboys on the llanos and the pampas, the plains and the prairies. In the North American southwest and northwest, many cattle outfits did not carry tents, and the men took the storms on their Stetsons. One cowboy recalled a night in a plains hailstorm when he had to strip the saddle off his horse and hide beneath it for several hours to protect himself. Of course, if you believe this—and it is undoubtedly true—then you might believe anything. So the tales got taller. One cowboy told of how a gale took away the camp cookstove—and returned the next day for the lids and the poker. That was on the same day that the wind was so strong from the west that the sun was three hours late going down. There were lots of things almost as strange and as scary, but true. In a summer storm, heat lightning would play across the horns of the herd in an eerie blue glow, beads of static electricity formed on the manes of the horses and rolled down the moustaches of the riders, and balls of fire occasionally knocked a man off his horse. In the fall, blue northers (so-called because of the blue of the threatening sky) would blow up out of nowhere and send the cattle stampeding, while the half-frozen cowboys pursued them through the black stormy night.

And then there were the winters on the *northern* plains. One time it got so cold that the thermometer dropped to 95 degrees below zero. The foreman came out to give the cowboys their orders—but the words froze as they came out of his mouth and they had to break them off one by one so they could tell what he was saying. There *are* more reliable accounts. In *Wolf Willow*, the prairie writer Wallace Stegner describes an all-too-typical Saskatchewan scene.

Ice nights, days when a bitter wind lashed and stung the face with a dry sand of snow, mornings when the crust flared up a glare so blinding that they rode with eyes closed to slits and looked at the world through their eyelashes. There was one afternoon when the whole world was over-whelmed under a white freezing fog, when horses, cattle, clothes, wagon, grew a fur of hoar frost and the herd they had gathered had to be held together in spooky white darkness mainly by ear.

On bright days they were all nearly blind, in spite of painting their cheekbones with charcoal and riding with hats pulled clear down; if they could see to work at all, they worked with tears leaking through swollen and smarting lids. Their faces grew black with sun and glare, their skin and lips cracked as crisp as the skin of a fried fish, and yet they froze. (Stegner 1962:152)

But my favourite cold-weather cowboy story is by the western cow-boy painter Charlie Russell, who used to tell about a friend of his who left a poker game in Great Falls, Montana, and froze to death on the street. When listeners would express sympathy, Charlie would say, "Oh that wasn't so bad. We hung a lantern on his ear and used him for a lamppost all winter."

Russell was himself a legendary figure by the end of the nineteenth century. The Canadian folk singer Ian Tyson has a song about him where he tells of the ways in which "Kid" Russell, as he was called, set down the beauty of the western plains and the burdens of everyday life in those twilight days of the prairie frontier. "God hung the stars over Judith basin," the song begins, and Russell painted them. He painted the great herds of buffalo, the riding of broncos and the roping of cat-tle, the cow camps and roundups and stampedes. And he painted the people of the plains, not only the ranchers and rodeo cowboys but the Peigan and the Sioux and the Crow who had been living in the region for millennia. And the extraordinary sunsets. Especially those sunsets.

And so

When the Lord called Charlie
To his home up yonder,
He says, "Kid Russell,
I got a job for you.
You're in charge of sunsets
Up in old Montana
Quite as good as you.[2]

A cowboy fancy, to be sure. But it also embodies a powerful and perennial conviction that works of art bring things to life; that a por-trait can somehow be more real than a person; that truth is much closer to beauty, and perhaps to goodness, too, than our rational minds might like to admit; that stories and songs and paintings and photographs and drumming and dancing and all our various forms of imaginative expression shape the world and nourish the spirit.

For thousands of years, singers and storytellers have wondered about the relationships between real and imagined worlds, between the actual and the virtual, between life and art. The history of art and literature is a history of a feud—or perhaps I should say a dialogue—between mirroring and making, between the notions that art imitates reality and that it creates it. Religions divide and conquer along these lines, and virtually all of our questions about culture come down to an uncertainty about whether language and literature create or merely communicate thought and feeling.

Nobody caught the drama of all this better than that great juggler of contradictions, Oscar Wilde. In an essay called "The Decay of Lying" he lamented the fact that there were so few good liars around, ones who told lies purely for pleasure rather than for profit (as lawyers and journalists do, he added)—ones who told the stories and sang the songs that we call novels and plays and poems as well as the older ones who painted on rocks and carved stones and wood in elaborate designs. Wilde talked about how we see reality in ways that are determined by our imagination, and especially by the imaginative representations of art. And then, in his characteristically outrageous fashion, he offered proof.

> Where, if not from the Impressionists, do we get those wonderful brown fogs that come creeping down our streets, blurring the gas-lamps and changing the houses into monstrous shadows? . . . The extraordinary change that has taken place in the climate of London during the last ten years is entirely due to a particular school of Art. . . . Things are because we see them, and what we see, and how we see it, depends on the arts that have influenced us. To look at a thing is very different from seeing a thing. One does not see anything until one sees its beauty. Then, and only then, does it come into existence. At present, people see fogs, not because there are fogs, but because poets and painters have taught them the mysterious loveliness of such effects. There may have been fogs for centuries in London. I dare say there were. But no one saw them, and so we do not know anything about them. They did not exist until art had invented them. Now, it must be admitted fogs are carried to excess. They have become the mere mannerism of a clique, and the exaggerated realism of their method gives dull people bronchitis. Where the cultured catch an effect, the uncultured catch cold. (Wilde 1970:61)

With all the wit there is also deep wisdom in this argument and in its most famous aphorism, Wilde. This saying has influenced virtually all discussion about the determining power of visual and verbal representation in the century since Wilde wrote it; and its truth is now apparent to us everywhere in the centuries before, in the sciences as well as the arts, and indeed in all the expressions of what we call culture. And in our engagement with cowboys and Indians.

Notes

1 The comments by José de Acosta about Santo Domingo, by Richard Vowell about the llanero and by the Alberta cowboy on fences are from Slatta (1990:9, 17, 50), as are many other details about cowboy life in this essay. Some of the tall tales can be found in Hoig (1958), though most of them can also be heard at any rodeo or ranch house.

2 The cowboy songs have all been sung for over a century, with the exception of Ian Tyson's ode to Charlie Russell from his compact disc *Cowboyography* (Tyson 1994).

References

Brathwaite, Kamau
    1973   "Postlude/Home." In *Rights of Passage*, book one of a trilogy entitled *The Arrivants*, 77. London: Oxford University Press.
Cannon, Hal, ed.
    1988   "Home on the Range." In *Old-Time Cowboy Songs*, 54. Salt Lake City: Gibbs Smith.
Hoig, Stan
    1958   *Humor of the American Cowboy*. Lincoln: University of Nebraska Press.
Lang, Andrew, Walter Leaf and Ernest Myers, eds.
    1961   *The Iliad of Homer*. London: Macmillan.
Lomax, Alan
    1960   *Folk Songs of North America*. New York: Doubleday.
Lomax, John
    1938   *Cowboy Songs and Other Frontier Ballads*. New York: Macmillan. Originally published in 1910.
Marley, Bob
    1995   *Bob Marley Interviews . . . So Much Things to Say*. Interview by Neville Willoughby. Compact disc. Tuff Gong.
Melville, Herman
    1967   *Moby Dick*. Edited by Harrison Hayford and Hershel Parker. New York: Norton.

Moquin, Wayne, with Charles Van Doren
   1973   *Great Documents in American Indian History*. New York: Praeger.
Slatta, Richard W.
   1990   *Cowboys of the Americas*. New Haven, CT: Yale University Press.
Stegner, Wallace
   1962   *Wolf Willow: A History, a Story and a Memory of the Last Plains Frontier*. Toronto: Macmillan.
Thoreau, Henry David
   1971   *Walden*. Edited by J. Lyndon Shanley. Princeton: Princeton University Press.
Tyson, Ian
   1994   *Cowboyography*. Compact disc. Vanguard.
Vanderwerth, W.C., comp.
   1971   *Indian Oratory*. Norman: University of Oklahoma Press.
Wilde, Oscar
   1970   "The Decay of Lying." In Philip Rieff, ed., *The Soul of Man under Socialiam and Other Essays*, 61. New York: Harper Colophon.

Index